WOMANIZING NIETZSCHE
Philosophy's Relation to the "Feminine"

Womanizing Nietzsche

Philosophy's Relation to the "Feminine"

Kelly Oliver

ROUTLEDGE ■ NEW YORK & LONDON

Published in 1995

ROUTLEDGE
29 West 35th Street
New York, NY 10001

Published in Great Britain by

ROUTLEDGE
11 New Fetter Lane
London EC4P 4EE

LIBRARY OF CONGRESS CATALOGING-IN-PUBLICATION DATA

Oliver, Kelly, 1959-
        Womanizing Nietzsche : philosophy's relation to the feminine /
    Kelly Oliver.
            p.   cm.
    Includes bibliographical references and index.
    ISBN 0-415-90681-4   ISBN 1-415-90682-2 (pbk.)
    1. Derrida, Jacques—Contributions in philosophy of woman.   2. Nietzsche,
    Friedrich Wilhelm, 1844-1900—Contributions in philosophy of woman.   3.
    Woman (Philosophy)—History.   4. Feminist theory.   I. Title.
    B2430.D484O55   1995
    305.42'01—dc20   94-25602
                                                               CIP

for Virginia, my mother

CONTENTS

PREFACE

Many contemporary debates over Nietzsche and Derrida focus on the politics, or the impossibility of politics, spawned by their theories. Various critics continue to argue that Nietzsche and/or Derrida make it impossible to talk about any positive politics or strategies for change. Some of these critics have claimed that Nietzsche and/or Derrida leave us with a radical relativism that makes it impossible to choose one strategy, method, or politics over another. Some of these critics also worry that Nietzsche and Derrida have challenged not only the object of our choice, but also the subject who chooses; the deconstruction of the subject makes it impossible to talk about political or ethical agency. While I think that the possibility of agency is an important issue, in *Womanizing Nietzsche* I will not enter the debate from this angle. I do not accept the criticisms of deconstruction that make it out to be some form of nihilism which abolishes strategy, method, politics, ethics, choice, the subject and truth. Neither Nietzsche nor Derrida, even while "deconstructing" these notions, denies the existence of politics, ethics, the subject and truth. For both Nietzsche and Derrida these concepts need to be constantly reevaluated. Woven throughout the fabric of *Womanizing Nietzsche* are readings of texts in which both Nietzsche and Derrida attempt to articulate the possibility of change for the better.

Some of Derrida's critics have latched onto the phrase "*Il n'y a pas de hors-texte*" ("there is nothing outside of the text") and used it to prove that Derrida is a linguistic fatalist who does not believe in the world (*OG* 158). A careful reading of Derrida, however, makes it difficult to defend this position. As Derrida says in an interview: "[i]t is totally false to suggest that deconstruction is a suspension of reference. Deconstruction is always deeply concerned with the 'other' of language. I never cease to be surprised by critics who see my work as a declaration that there is nothing beyond language, that we are imprisoned in language; it is, in fact, saying the exact opposite"(*RK* 123, see also *P* 64). I read Nietzsche and/or

Derrida neither as nihilists who attempt to destroy rather than create, nor as fatalists who cannot imagine any possibility of change for the better. I read Nietzsche and Derrida as visionaries who glimpse something beyond the traditional subject-centered metaphysics and use nontraditional methods to open traditional philosophy onto this beyond. They try to open the discourse to other voices, multiple voices. As Derrida says, "Deconstruction is not an enclosure in nothingness, but an openness towards the other" (RK 124).

Although I do not accept many of the standard criticisms of Derrida, I am not an apologist for deconstruction. For Derrida, deconstruction is not neutral; it intervenes in the polis (FL 8; P 93). Like all theory, however, it does so at the double risk of consolidating the very values that it attempts to displace on the one hand, and setting up new values within the same hierarchical binary structure of the old values, on the other hand (EM 135). These risks of co-optation and consolidation are risks that Derrida insists must be taken (*P* 69). At the same time every text must be called to account for the ways in which it is complicit with the values that it attempts to overturn. This is the kind of diagnosis that I am attempting in *Womanizing Nietzsche*. I insist on reassessing the implicit values, and effects, of Derrida's texts in spite of the explicit project of those texts.

In the same way, I indicate some of the ways in which Nietzsche's texts are complicit with the values that he attempts to undermine. Nietzsche's attempts to open philosophical discourse onto its other are the most powerful in the history of philosophy. More than any other writer, Nietzsche's revolutionary ideas and words have permeated my thinking about subjectivity, ethics, truth and alterity. Nietzsche's texts open up the possibility of imagining doing philosophy otherwise. In *On the Genealogy of Morals*, for example, he sets out an alternative to the Hegelian lordship/bondage relation in which all value is determined in opposition to a hostile outside world; he suggests a way of valuing that is not hostile to everything different from itself, but is tolerant of difference (*OGM* 36–37). Even while engaging (in) the discourse of philosophy, Nietzsche playfully calls that discourse into question. It is in this Nietzschean spirit, using some Derridean reading strategies, that I continue this task of calling on philosophy to account for its values.

My criticism is not the external criticism that there is no positive politics in the writings of Nietzsche or Derrida. My criticism is the internal criticism that both Nietzsche and Derrida, even while opening philosophy onto other voices, prevent the possibility of a feminine voice. Moreover, I argue that their strategies for opening philosophy onto its other(s) are often dependent on the preclusion of a feminine other. So even their various shifts from a philosophy of the subject to a philosophy of the other are constructed through the sacrifice of the feminine other, especially the feminine mother.

Following Hélène Cixous, Alice Jardine, and others, Rosi Braidotti argues that "certain forms of post-Hegelian philosophy (though not all), victims of an unprecedented crisis of legitimation, resort, as the only way out, to a redefinition of the feminine, or of the 'becoming-woman' " (*PD* 9). I agree with this diagnosis of philosophy's need to try to "become woman" in order to avoid the crisis of the Enlightenment subject, man. I will not only diagnose philosophy's desire to "become woman," but also philosophy's success at opening itself onto the feminine. My analysis centers on Derrida's association of Nietzsche with woman in *Spurs*. By engaging in close readings of texts by Nietzsche, Derrida, Irigaray and others, I attempt to use the case of Nietzsche as a way of diagnosing philosophy's relation to "the feminine." The central thesis of *Womanizing Nietzsche* is that while Nietzsche and Derrida, in particular, attempt to open up philosophy to its others—the body, the unconscious, nonmeaning, even the feminine—they close off philosophy to any specifically feminine other. While their texts open up the possibility of talking about those subjects that traditionally have been excluded from philosophy, they continue to exclude the feminine, especially the "feminine mother." I argue that talk of the death of philosophy is the result of this exclusion. Philosophy cannot kill off its feminine other and survive.

Philosophy's survival depends on the feminine not only to make philosophy "honest" in the sense that it represents human experience and not just masculine experience, but also because the masculine defines itself only through its dialectical relation with some feminine. More than this, contemporary philosophy has reached a crisis of the subject and truth, which seem to self-destruct, and feminists and poststructuralists, often in very different ways, are turning to a feminine philosophy or philosophy's "becoming female," to attempt to resuscitate what appears to be a dying discipline.

In the first part of *Womanizing Nietzsche*, "The Ethics of Reading," I diagnose some of the rhetorical strategies that Nietzsche and Derrida employ in order to exclude the feminine and woman. In chapter 1, "Opening and Closing the Possibility of a Feminine Other," I take up the texts of Freud, Nietzsche, and Derrida in order to show that while all three of these theorists attempt to open discourse onto the other, they continue to close off the possibility of a specifically feminine other. In chapter 2,

"Becoming Woman: Autocastration, Emasculation, and Self-Violence as Feminization," I argue that Nietzsche's and Derrida's strategies of self-parody are strategies of self-violence that feminize philosophy by emasculating it and in so doing presume that the feminine is merely the lack of the masculine.

In my first chapter, "Opening and Closing the Possibility of a Feminine Other," I analyze attempts to open a space for the other within Western discourse. Specifically, I take up attempts made by Freud, Nietzsche, and Derrida. My argument is that although all three of these theorists are concerned to open up a space for something other than traditional Enlightenment rationality, and although in various ways and to various degrees they have thereby begun to open up Western intellectual discourse to a specifically feminine other, all three of these theorists at the same time foreclose the possibility of a specifically feminine other. In spite of their attempts to open Western discourse to the unconscious, the body, and the other, at a crucial point all three of them fall back into a phallocentric discursive economy that excludes any active participation by the feminine or woman.

Later, in the third part of the book, "The Ethics of Maternity," I will argue that one of the ways in which Nietzsche and Derrida, in particular, have participated in the exclusion of the feminine and woman is by conflating the two. Within their writing the feminine, the maternal, and woman have been conflated in a way that contributes to the exclusion of all of them. I will try to indicate some important differences between the ways that these three terms—feminine, maternal, woman—operate within Western discourse. One significant attribute that these three terms have in common is that they have all been associated with what must be excluded from philosophy. And in some contemporary discussions (Irigaray's and Derrida's, in particular), they have come to stand (in) for the other excluded by philosophy.

It should become clear, even through my discussion of Freud, Nietzsche, and Derrida in the first chapter, that philosophy's other, or "the other" of philosophy, is made up of different aspects of our experience that have been excluded from, or downgraded within, Western philosophy. The feminine, maternal and woman are constituents of the group of experiences excluded from Western philosophy. What seems telling, however, is that at least three of the discourses—Freud's, Nietzsche's, and Derrida's—that claim to open up the possibility of listening to, or speaking, what has been excluded from philosophy continue to exclude the feminine and woman.

In "Opening and Closing the Possibility of a Feminine Other," I use two different strategies in order to disclose the ways in which Freud, Nietzsche, and Derrida fall back into phallocentric discourse. First I analyze their texts to indicate where and how their theories deny any active feminine subject and/or turn women into mere objects. Second I ask what it means for a woman to read each of these theorists. The answer to this question in each of these cases is extremely telling. For each of these theorists addresses himself to a masculine audience about woman. Within each of these discourses man is the subject and woman is the object. And I will argue that this is not merely an accident of history or rhetoric. These theorists presuppose a feminine object and a masculine subject. There is no room in their discourses for a feminine subject.

In my second chapter, "Becoming Woman: Autocastration, Emasculation, and Self-Violence as Feminization," I argue that the reading and writing strategies proposed by Nietzsche and Derrida to open a space for the other require self-violence. Trying to develop a strategy of doing philosophy that undermines the traditional formulations of that enterprise, Nietzsche uses parody, specifically self-parody. By undercutting himself and his philosophy, Nietzsche attempts to undercut the authority of the philosopher. Derrida takes over Nietzsche's strategy of self-parody but he describes it as a kind of autocastration. Moreover, within Derrida's discourse (and his reading of Nietzsche) this autocastration operates as a way of feminizing philosophy such that it takes the place of its other; it becomes feminine; the philosopher becomes female. The masculine thereby usurps the already marginal position of the feminine by taking over her place as well as his own. I maintain that one effect of Derrida's use of woman in his deconstructive project (in spite of what may be honorable "intentions") is to close off the possibility of doing philosophy otherwise and continue to exclude the feminine other.

In the conclusion of this section, in the spirit of Nietzsche's *On the Genealogy of Morals*, I ask *what does it mean* to proclaim the death of philosophy? Is it the inability to imagine philosophy otherwise? Perhaps even a refusal to imagine philosophy otherwise? With every proclamation of the death of philosophy comes the refusal to admit the other. Some philosophy would rather commit suicide than allow the other to enter its midst. On the model of Freud, Nietzsche, and Derrida, philosophy necessarily requires violence, death, or murder/suicide. The Hegelian dialectical struggle for recognition between the self and the other has been stunted at the stage of the lordship/bondsman relationship. Even there, for Hegel the lord realizes that he cannot kill the bondsman because doing so is in fact a form of suicide; he is dependent on the bondsman for self-recognition. Within this scenario, murder necessarily becomes suicide.

With Freud, Nietzsche, and Derrida, it is possible that philosophy has reached the level of an Unhappy Consciousness which both idealizes the other within itself but at the same time refuses to identify with that other—she must remain outside. At the end of this first section we are left with a philosophy that cannot acknowledge its feminine other without annihilating her. I begin with Freud's case because it provides some very useful diagnostic tools with which to analyze this strange phenomenon in philosophy, this double murder-suicide.

In the second part of this book, "The Ethics of Sexual Difference," I argue that Derrida's attempts to open philosophy to the feminine not only do not succeed but also erase the possibility of sexual difference and reduce all sexuality to the masculine. I read Irigaray's *Marine Lover of Friedrich Nietzsche* as a response to Derrida's *Spurs*. In chapter 3, "The Question of Appropriation," I maintain that Derrida's metaphors of undecidability erase the possibility of any sexual difference and that his metaphors of hymen and invagination merely appropriate the feminine for the masculine. In chapter 4, "The Plaint of Ariadne," I read Irigaray's response to these appropriations and what, in *Marine Lover of Friedrich Nietzsche*, she calls Nietzsche's matricide.

In chapter 3, I criticize Derrida's attempt to open philosophy to a specifically feminine other, particularly in his analysis of Nietzsche in *Spurs*. Through a discussion of Heidegger's reading of Nietzsche and his own reading of a fragment from Nietzsche's notebooks, "I have forgotten my umbrella," Derrida raises the question "What is proper to the text?" His answer is both that this Heideggerian question of propriety may not be a proper question (which, of course, is to continue to ask the question of propriety) and that what is proper to the text is undecidable. In *Spurs*, Derrida develops affirmative deconstruction in order to go beyond a mere negation of the status quo in theory and open onto something new. This something new is some undecidable "concept." In *Spurs*, as in "The Double Session" and elsewhere, the figure of undecidability is the hymen and woman herself. Ultimately for Derrida the opposition between sexual and ontological difference meets this same undecidability; we cannot determine which is primary. In chapter 3, "The Question of Appropriation," I indicate how Derrida's strategies to bring the feminine to philosophy effectively close off the possibility of any philosophy of, or from, the feminine.

Derrida's *Spurs* is a complex essay in which several themes intertwine. In chapter 3, I examine three of *Spurs'* central themes: First, the central question of *Spurs* is "What properly belongs to a text?" Second, one of the central tasks of *Spurs* is to deconstruct the opposition between sexual and ontological difference in Heidegger's philosophy. Third, another central project is to replace the Lacanian logic of castration with what Derrida calls the logic of the hymen.

Derrida's discussion of what properly belongs to the text raises the question once again "where does woman belong in Derrida's texts?" In chapter 3, I argue that woman does not belong in Derrida's discourse, even though (because) he uses the figure of woman throughout that discourse. Derrida's reduction of sexual and ontological difference to an undecidability erases sexual difference. The undecidable erases all difference; if we cannot decide what it is, then how can we maintain that it is different from what it is not? More than this, Derrida identifies the undecidable with woman and the feminine and therefore positions her outside of the discourse of philosophy.

In addition, I argue that Derrida's use of the metaphor of the hymen to figure undecidability reinforces the exclusion of the feminine from the discussion of sexual difference; it renders all sex masculine. The hymen and woman represent the undecidable and thereby fall back into the binary opposition that Derrida is trying to deconstruct. It would be one thing if Derrida's deconstruction of the binaries man/woman or masculine/feminine opened onto an economy of diversity in which we are not trapped by only these two sexualities. If his deconstructive project made possible the multiple sexually marked voices that he imagines in "Choreographies," then it would provide hope for many feminists. But it does not. In spite of his attempts to replace the logic of castration, Derrida's deconstruction remains within the logic of castration, in which everything is defined in terms of the masculine. Within this economy there is only one sex, never even two. Without at least two sexes we cannot imagine more. First, we must get beyond the one.

In chapter 4, "The Plaint of Ariadne," I read Irigaray's *Marine Lover of Friedrich Nietzsche* as a response to Derrida's appropriation of woman in *Spurs*. I argue that although Irigaray never mentions Derrida in *Marine Lover,* he is the implicit addressee of that text. Irigaray criticizes Nietzsche, and implicitly Derrida, because his texts take away from woman without acknowledging the debt they owe to her. I critically compare her analysis of the masculine giving that is always only a taking away with Derrida's analysis of gift giving in *Given Time*. I use some of Irigaray's suggestive remarks about Nietzsche to develop a criticism of Derrida's notion of the impossibility of giving. I diagnose his theory of the gift and its necessary forgetting as another example of forgetting the gift of life that comes from the mother.

In *Marine Lover* Irigaray suggests in her poetic way that Nietzsche's notions of the eternal return and the *Übermensch* are designed to cover over any debt to the maternal. Nietzsche/Zarathustra uses these concepts to give birth to himself without woman. I critically compare several French readings—by Deleuze, Derrida, Pautrat, Kofman—of Nietzsche's eternal return to Irigaray's analysis. I conclude that although Irigaray's analysis is compelling because she identifies a matricide at the heart of Nietzsche's notions of the eternal return and the *Übermensch*, her reading of both notions is strategically one-sided.

In the end of chapter 4, I take up Irigaray's powerful discussion of Nietzsche's gods as notions that, like the eternal return and the *Übermensch*, cover over any debt to the maternal. Out of Irigaray's beautiful poetic philosophy, I present a coherent description of why Dionysus, Apollo and Christ, in various ways, appropriate the maternal. I conclude with some previews of Irigaray's alternative economy of exchange which does not demand sacrifice and death.

In the last part of *Womanizing Nietzsche*, "The Ethics of Maternity," I argue that Nietzsche's critics have overlooked an important distinction in his writings between the figure of woman and the figure of the mother. Then I suggest that, like traditional philosophers, Nietzsche and Derrida associate the figure of the mother with nature. I maintain that ethics is only possible once the mother is seen as a speaking social being and not merely associated with nature. In chapter 5, "Emasculate Conception," I argue that diagnosing the position of the maternal in Nietzsche's writings can give us some insight into his relation to not only the mother but also the feminine and woman. I use Kristeva's theory of abjection in order to identify the mother in Nietzsche's writings as an abject mother who both fascinates and horrifies. I suggest that Nietzsche's work displays a struggle to separate from the mother. It also displays an identification with the mother. In Nietzsche's writings the most desirable mother becomes the masculine mother. The procreative powers of the mother are usurped by the masculine. Nietzsche's critics have tended to either forget about the mother in Nietzsche's texts or reproduce the masculine mother. In particular I analyze David Farrell Krell's *Postponements* and Derrida's *Ear of the Other* to expose the ways in which Krell and Derrida either forget the mother or turn her into a masculine or phallic mother. In the end, I suggest that in Nietzsche's texts and those of these critics there is no woman or feminine apart from the mother and that this mother is an all-powerful phallic mother identified with mother-nature.

In chapter 6, "Save the Mother," I articulate the ways in which Irigaray and Kristeva challenge the traditional psychoanalytic notion of the function of paternity. I play their criticisms of Lacan's paternal metaphor off one another in order to undermine the Lacanian distinction between the paternal metaphor, through which the Name of the Father is substituted for the body of the mother, and the metonymy of desire, through which the demands of language are associated with primary infantile needs. Through my challenge to the metaphor/metonymy distinction, I begin to blur the boundary between needs and desire, between nature and culture. Against the traditional notion of the maternal body, I propose an alternative model which troubles the nature/culture distinction. Using pieces of theories from Kristeva, Irigaray, and Teresa Brennan, I argue that within the maternal body the structure of the social relation is already in place. Therefore the transition from the maternal body into culture is not the abrupt leap prompted by violent threats that Freud and Lacan take it to be.

I suggest that the maternal body and its relation to the fetus and placenta can provide a model for an intersubjective theory of subjectivity as a process of exchanges. Further I maintain that this intersubjective model of subjectivity can provide a model for ethical and social relations that challenges the Hegelian model in which one would-be subject engages in a fight to the death with another would-be subject. I propose that subjectivity itself is ethical in that it is always constituted through a relation with another. I conclude that this maternal model for an ontology of ethics will affect the way in which we talk about our rights and responsibilities and that by acknowledging the importance of the feminine, and the feminine maternal, philosophy may be restored to thinking. Philosophy may no longer have to sound its own death knell.

ACKNOWLEDGMENTS

For helpful comments on various drafts and presentations of parts of this manuscript, I would like to thank Pamela Caughie, Daniel Conway, Andrew Cutrofello, Arleen Dallery, Elizabeth Grosz, Kathleen Higgins, Tamsin Lorraine, Elissa Marder, Noëlle McAfee, Karen Mottola, Henry Ruf, Jana Sawicki, Johanna Seibt, Thomas Seung, Alan Schrift, Byrt Wammack, Roberta Weston, Cynthia Willett, and the students in my graduate seminar at the University of Texas at Austin in the Spring of 1993. Special thanks to Seth Paskin who carefully read the entire manuscript, helped me to clarify my ideas, and kept me calm enough to write them down. For research assistance I thank Carolyn Bottler, Christina Hendricks, and Scott Klarens. Thanks to Pierre LaMarche for preparing the index. For financial support I am grateful to the University of Texas at Austin for a Faculty Research Fellowship for the summer of 1992. Once again I thank Nancy Fraser for her continued support. Thanks to Maureen MacGrogan for her advice and "public relations," which extend well beyond this project. Finally, I could not do anything, and nothing would be worth doing, without the love and encouragement of my friends and family, including Kaos and Wizard, who prefer scratching-posts to books, although books will do in a pinch.

ONE

THE ETHICS OF READING
Reading (at) the End of Philosophy

I call myself the last philosopher, because I am the last man. No one speaks with me but myself, and my voice comes to me like the voice of a dying man! Let me associate for but one hour more with you, dear voice, with you, the last trace of the memory of all human happiness. With you I escape loneliness through self-delusion and lie myself into multiplicity and love. For my heart resists the belief that love is dead. It cannot bear the shudder of the loneliest loneliness, and so it forces me to speak as if I were two. . . And yet, I still hear you, dear voice! Something else dies, something other than me, the last man in this universe. The last sigh, your sigh, dies with me. The drawn-out "alas! alas!" sighed for me, Oedipus, the last miserable man.
       —Friedrich Nietzsche, *Notebooks of the Early 1870s*

INTRODUCTION
Apocalypse Now

Metaphor, then, always carries its death within itself. And this death, surely, is also the death of philosophy. But the genitive is double. It is sometimes the death of philosophy, death of a genre belonging to philosophy which is thought and summarized within it, recognizing and fulfilling itself within philosophy; and sometimes the death of a philosophy which does not see itself die and is no longer to be refound within philosophy.
— Jacques Derrida, *"White Mythology"*

In a lecture entitled "The End of Philosophy and the Task of Thinking" Heidegger asks what it means that philosophy is in its final stage. For him philosophy is metaphysics and with Nietzsche metaphysics has reached its completion; it has come full circle, now biting its own tail as Nietzsche might say. It has thought all that it can think. This leads Heidegger to ask what is the task of thinking at the end of philosophy (Heidegger, EP 55). Which in turn leads him to ask what belongs to thinking. Thinking is not limited to philosophy, especially when philosophy is no longer the "queen" of the sciences but merely their "hand-maiden." Heidegger imagines a thinking that is outside the distinction between rational and irrational, neither metaphysics nor science. He indicates that this possibility is/was in fact the beginning of philosophy. There is an otherwise than metaphysics out of which philosophy is/was born.

Perhaps, then, we need to listen to the voice of this other within philosophy, the voice of the oracle, the *mythos* out of which philosophy is/was born. Behind the Socratic dialectic is the voice of the oracle of Delphi and the power of the multiple voices in Socrates' dreams. Even Aristotle, the scientist, recognizes this need; Heidegger translates from Book IV of Aristotle's *Metaphysics*: "For it is uneducated not to have an eye for when it is necessary to look for a proof, and when this is not necessary" (EP 72). How does that which needs no proof become accessible to thinking? Heidegger answers, "Only the peculiar quality of *that which demands of us above all else to be admitted* can decide about that. But how is this to make the decision possible for us before we have not admitted it? In what circle are we moving here, inevitably?" (EP 72, my emphasis).

Thinking, then, is a kind of a dialogue with an other, that which demands to be admitted, that which has heretofore been excluded. Philosophy should engage in a dialogue with the other within it, the other out of which it was born. To do otherwise is not only to commit a kind of matricide that Irigaray diagnoses as endemic to the history of Western philosophy, but also to commit a kind of suicide or at least bring about a sort of brain death with which philosophy, in Heidegger's terms, stops thinking.

In "White Mythology" Derrida suggests that philosophy, insofar as it is linguistic, is metaphorical: "metaphor seems to involve the usage of philosophical language in its entirety, nothing less than the usage of so-called natural language *in* philosophical discourse, that is, the usage of natural language *as* philosophical language" (WM 209). And metaphor is the death of philosophy (WM 271). Philosophy dies in that a particular "philosophy" is no longer "refound within philosophy," which is to say that it is found elsewhere. Or philosophy dies as a result of the "death of a genre belonging to philosophy which is thought and summarized within it, recognizing and fulfilling itself within philosophy"; which is to say that a type (*genre*) of philosophy reaches its limit and dies. Of course, as Derrida points out, a limit does not mean death. In fact a death does not necessarily mean death, especially in the case of philosophy. Derrida does not believe in the death of philosophy, nor do I (*P* 6). This death is impossible because these proclamations and eulogies are themselves philosophical. Derrida suggests that even if the questions of the life and death of philosophy are not philosophical questions nor philosophy's questions, questions that properly belong to philosophy, that "these should be the only questions today capable of founding the community, within the world, of those who are still called philosophers; and called such in remembrance, at very least, of the fact that these questions must be examined unrelentingly. . . " (VM 79). As Derrida points out, philosophy has a history of predicting about its own death. Our own epoch in this history is punctuated by such predictions, eulogies and prophesies of the death of philosophy.[1] I am concerned to diagnose the meaning of this preoccupation. And precisely what is at stake is the community of philosophers, who is called, or can call *herself*, a philosopher. I am concerned with a certain "death" of genre/gender of philosophy that recognizes and fulfills itself and thereby commits suicide.

This death/suicide is only possible because of a prior murder. The talk of the death of philosophy operates according to a stunted Hegelian model of self-recognition in which self-consciousness is possible only by virtue of the (imaginary) annihilation of the other and the recuperation of the self from its alienation in the recognition of the consciousness of the other. Of course if the self annihilates the other then it loses that which made its self-recognition possible in the first place. On the Hegelian model, the self must both, and at the same time, annihilate the otherness of the other in order to recuperate the self that it has seen reflected in the other, and affirm the otherness of the other so that it does not lose its self in the place of that other. If the self closes off the place of the other or murders the other, then self-recognition cannot take place; without recognizing itself in the other, the self loses any consciousness of itself and thereby loses itself. Yet, on this model, to acknowledge the self's debt to the other is tantamount to suicide; if the other—through and in whom the self recognizes itself—is other, then the self is no longer itself. Self-consciousness is self-alienated; it lives with the other within itself. The lordship/bondsman relation, in which otherness is external, gives rise to Unhappy Consciousness, in which otherness is internal to consciousness. In contemporary philosophy, however, as in the Hegelian model, the self-alienation of self-consciousness has been resolved by sublimating, superseding, repressing, or denying the other within itself.

Within the discourse of Western philosophy, as Derrida would be the first to admit, woman and the feminine have been this excluded other.[2] In fact, Derrida has argued in several places with regard to several figures in the history of philosophy—Plato, Kant, Hegel, Nietzsche, Heidegger—that behind every good man there is a "good woman": He argues that these philosophers set up their theories on a necessary feminine other side; behind the masculine metaphors with which they figure that which they value most is the feminine to which those figures are opposed. Derrida and some of his followers might even see his attempts to unveil this woman behind philosophy as an attempt to make a space for her within philosophy or to open a space within which we can imagine philosophy otherwise—at the end or limit of philosophy we find a new beginning, a new "feminized" philosophy. While it would seem that this Derridian beginning of a feminized philosophy could be the rebirth, rather than the death, of philosophy, I will suggest that the feminized philosophy opened up by Derrida's deconstruction is at most the emasculation of the masculine and at worst the masculine appropriation of the feminine.

Derrida addresses Kant's proclamations of the end/death of philosophy in "Of an Apocalyptic Tone Newly Adopted in Philosophy."

Motivated by persistent questions from his readers, who asked why Derrida's writings are full of the tone of apocalypse, Derrida analyzes Kant's "On a Newly Raised Superior Tone in Philosophy." Adopting his typical position in the margins, both identifying with the text and distancing himself from it, Derrida speaks both of and in the apocalyptic tone: "I shall speak then of/in an apocalyptic tone in philosophy" (ATP 25). Derrida speaks of Kant's attacks on what he calls the "Mystagogues" for speaking in a lordly aristocratic tone because they listen to the voice of the oracle rather than the voice of reason; and the voice of the oracle is prone to all sorts of interpretation whereas the voice of reason has one and only one meaning that is clear to all who listen. Kant maintains that this mystical voice will be the death of philosophy, that it will turn philosophy into poetry. Derrida, sidestepping this debate between true philosophy and poetry, develops some of the general traits of "an apocalyptic type of writing": Apocalyptic writing is full of predictions and it preaches the extreme limits, the ends. (ATP 47) But every apocalypse is given with a promise of light, enlightenment. Apocalyptic writing promises to tell the truth at last. So the apocalypse, the final revelation, is the transcendental structure of all writing (ATP 57). Language is made up of propositions that assert some truth; even if the assertion in question is Nietzsche's "the truth is that there is no truth." Derrida points out that the West has been dominated by a discourse of ends, final revelations, and even the end of ends, the impossibility of revelation; the voice of the philosopher is always the voice of the last man. (ATP 48–49)[3]

Perhaps we should say that the voice of the philosopher is always the last voice since the final revelation of truth is also the final word on the subject; there is nothing more to say. In Derrida's case, however, the apocalypse can also be the revelation that there is no limit to what we can say. He cites his discussion of Nietzsche's "I have forgotten my umbrella," penciled in the margins of Nietzsche's notebook, hanging between quotation marks, in *Spurs*. Writing in/of an apocalyptic tone, Derrida writes ,"*I have forgotten my umbrella* is a statement at once hermetic and totally open, as secret and superficial as the postcard apocalypse it announces and protects against " (ATP 40). With this example Derrida plays the two limits of apocalypse off each other. "I have forgotten my umbrella" either has one simple superficial meaning and there is no more possibility of writing (about it), or it has no one meaning and the possibilities are endless. In the first case we are silenced by the impossibility of saying anything more, and in the second we are silenced by the impossibility of ever saying enough. Somewhere near these limits deconstruction plays with meaning. I will return to *Spurs'* forgotten umbrella and its "postcard apocalypse" in chapter 3.

Derrida reveals that "apocalypse," from the Greek *apokalupsis*, related to the Hebrew *gala*, more originally meant "disclosure, uncovering, unveiling, the veil lifted from about the thing: first of all, if we can say this, man's or woman's sex, but also their eyes or ears" (ATP 27). In his analysis of Kant, Derrida concludes that it is the unveiling of "the body of a veiled Isis, the universal principle of femininity" that threatens philosophy (ATP 46, 41). In the history of Western metaphysics it is the mystics and hermeneutes who seduce the goddess of wisdom using poetry and the "voice of the oracle" rather than the voice of reason. Following Derrida's analysis, we could say that what Kant's mystagogues and the hermeneutes expose is the female body, the female sex, the body that has been inadmissible from the discourse of philosophy, the body that has represented the irrational and poetry. The inadmissible screaming furies threaten to enter philosophy. And these new voices in philosophy emasculate reason. At this point Derrida says that we could add Freud to the protectors of reason: "We could put Freud on the scene as a third robber procuring the key (true or false), sexual theory, namely, that for this stage of reason in which there is only male reason, only a masculine or castrated organ or canon of reason, everything proceeds in this just as for that stage of infantile genital organization in which there is definitely a masculine but no feminine. . . . No sexual difference as opposition, but only the masculine! " (ATP 43). Obviously within the economy of a text such as Kant's (and Nietzsche's) that talks about the *emasculation* of reason, reason is masculine and castration threats come from the feminine. Admitting the feminine into reason, philosophy, and metaphysics emasculates or castrates them. As Derrida points out, within this economy there is only masculine and emasculated; there is no sexual difference. Woman/the feminine threatens to castrate/kill philosophy, even while woman/the feminine is only the absent inverted image of the masculine sex.

Perhaps, then, it is appropriate to philosophy's history to talk about woman ringing the death knell of philosophy, since traditionally, as Derrida points out in *Glas*, woman has been assigned the role of burying the dead. In his analysis of Hegel, Derrida diagnoses "the feminine operation of burial" within which the man entrusts his death to the woman and the woman is responsible for his corpse. In Hegel's view, this is an appropriate task for woman, who is accustomed to the night and the subterranean world of the earth. In addition she is a guardian within the family of an ethics of the singular. Through the burial rituals she protects the singular body of man, his proper individuality, from being eaten by the earth. Paradoxically, the burial ritual, as a symbolic system, separates man from the animals and thereby guarantees that even though his body dies, his spirit does not and that he is thus protected from the cannibalism of the earth; his singularity will not be eaten by worms. On Derrida's analysis, however, the feminine operation of burial "does not oppose itself to the exteriority of a nonconscious matter; it suppresses an unconscious desire. The family wants to prevent the dead one from being 'destroyed' and the burial place violated *by this desire*" (*Glas* 144). And although Hegel does not indicate which unconscious desires are to be guarded against, Derrida does. The dead man is not only subject to the threat of material cannibalism but also imaginary cannibalism: "The two functions of (the) burial (place) relieve the dead man of his death, spare him from being destroyed—eaten—by matter, nature, the spirit's being-outside-self, but also by the probably cannibal violence of the survivor's unconscious desires. That is, essentially, the women's, since they, as guardians of (the) burial (place) and the family, are always in a situation of survival " (*Glas* 146). So at the same time that woman desires to incorporate the dead husband into her memory or into herself, she protects him against her own violent cannibalistic (not to mention necrophiliac) desires. She prevents herself from ingesting, incorporating, his pure singularity, which has already become universal spirit. She prevents him from returning to nature by remaining within nature and tending to his needs from the outside. She is responsible for the details of maintaining the symbolic rituals which maintain the symbolic system but only so long as (and in order that) she remain outside of that system guaranteeing its survival. On this model, when she threatens to move inside, the system seems to collapse and death destroys both the man and his system. Woman, then, provides both the threat and the security against the threat. By threatening to enter philosophy, for example, she threatens its death. But by staying on its outside, acting as its other, she guarantees its survival.

It is interesting that in the middle of his analysis of the feminine operation of burial, Derrida mentions Freud who describes the other side of the burial rite: "the fear of being enclosed in the maternal womb is represented in the agony of being interred alive" (*Glas* 143). And yet in this mention of Freud, Derrida completely passes over the other side of death and its rituals, birth. It is possible to read another set of unconscious desires into "the feminine operation of burial" and Derrida's reading of it. The rituals of death protect man from the cannibalism of nature itself. Rituals are emblematic of culture and return man, as Hegel says, to a community to avoid returning him to the earth out of which he was born (see *Glas* 145). Nature and the feminine/woman provide one and the same threat; they threaten to take man back from culture and return him to his other, nature. The fear of being enclosed in the maternal womb represents not only the agony of being interred alive but also of being part of the feminine/maternal other, the height of emasculation, death by birth itself. Man's claustrophobia within the maternal body is a gynophobia, a fear of being woman; after all within the womb the male is part of a female body. This fear of identification with the maternal body, a fear of birth, is not only cited by Freud but also is manifest in his own writing.

Opening and Closing the Possibility of a Feminine Other

Freud's Femininity: Fear of Birth

Throughout history people have knocked their heads against the riddle of the nature of femininity—Heads in hieroglyphic bonnets, Heads in turbans and black birettas, Heads in wigs and thousand other Wretched, sweating heads of humans. Nor will you have escaped worrying over this problem—those of you who are men; to those of you who are women this will not apply—you are yourselves the problem.
— Sigmund Freud, *"Femininity"*

Many feminists have wondered whose sweating heads have knocked against the riddle of femininity. To whom is Freud speaking? To whom is femininity a mystery? And who can we trust to solve this riddle? This riddle cannot be solved by contemporary science or psychoanalysis (Freud, F 114). Freud tells "us" all he can about femininity, but admits that it is "incomplete and fragmentary." Freud says that we will have to wait for the scientists or turn to the poets to solve the riddle of femininity (F 135). In other words, even if he cannot solve it, there are other men who might be able to. It seems clear that Freud addresses himself to other men about women. Women and femininity are his object but not participants in the discussion.

Sarah Kofman argues in *The Enigma of Woman*, however, that Freud did not want to "speak among men" and exclude women from his discussion of femininity. First, she posits that Freud explicitly addresses himself to a "mixed public": "Ladies and Gentlemen . . ." Second, she asserts that Freud is trying to "establish complicity with the women analysts so as to clear himself of the suspicion of 'antifeminism'" (104). Third, she maintains that Freud cannot be excluding women because that assumes that women are the opposite of men, which is what Freud is arguing against with his bisexuality thesis—Freud claims that all humans, especially women, are innately bisexual, both masculine and feminine.

I disagree. In spite of Freud's ironic "ladies and gentlemen" and his flirtation with the women analysts—I will come back to the bisexuality thesis—it seems undeniable that he makes women the objects of his investigation while men are the subjects: "Nor will *you* have escaped worrying over this problem—those of you who are men; to those of you who are women this will not apply—you are yourselves the problem" (Freud, F 113). Kofman admits that Freud makes women his accomplices in their own objectification, oppression, and silencing (see *EW* 47, 222). And even though she defends Freud as addressing women as subjects, Kofman argues that Freud creates women as the type of object for psychoanalysis that he takes them to be; he/psychoanalysis makes women into hysterics. I maintain that Freud not only makes women into a particular kind of object of psychoanalysis, the hysteric, but also excludes the possibility of women subjects in his discussion of femininity.

One of Kofman's most powerful examples of how Freud turns women into hysterics is her interpretation of Freud's dream of Irma's injection. Freud interprets the dream to be a manifestation of his wish not be responsible for Irma's continued pains. At one point in the dream, as Freud recounts it, Irma refuses to open her mouth and Freud attributes her reluctance to "female recalcitrance." Kofman argues that what Freud's dream tells him is that he has injected his female patients with a dirty solution, psychoanalysis, that makes their sexuality dirty and shameful:

> If Freud has such an urgent need to excuse himself, it is because he knows
> perfectly well that he himself is the criminal. Not only because he has not
> yet cured Irma, but, as another part of the dream indicates, because he
> himself (a transgression attributed in both the dream and the interpretation
> to his friend Otto) has infected her with his symbolic-spermatic
> "solution"—trimethylamin—injected with a dirty syringe. The term
> "trimethylamin" brings to mind the learned solutions he has thrown in his
> patients' faces: if Irma and all indomitable women refuse to open their
> mouths and their genitals, it is because Freud has already transformed each
> of these organs into a "cavity filled with pus," has closed women's mouths
> himself, has made them frigid, by injecting them with a learned, malignant,
> male solution. (*EW* 47)

Kofman suggests that the dream of Irma's injection is another manifestation of Freud's fear of femininity and his fear of listening to women; he is afraid of the terrifying sight of open female genitals or their open mouths.

Many of his feminist critics argue that Freud fears feminine sexuality (for example, Cixous, Irigaray, Gallop).[4] His bisexuality thesis might be further evidence of this fear. In "Female Sexuality" he argues that women are more bisexual than men because they have two erotic zones, one masculine and one feminine; they are hermaphrodites of a sort (FS 228). Freud claims that the women in his audience who are intelligent enough to understand him are more masculine than feminine (F 116-17). But the bisexuality of men goes unanalyzed. What of the feminine in men? Freud protects himself against this radically other sexuality, feminine sexuality, this "Minoan-Mycenean civilization," as he calls it, by always comparing the situation of women to the situation of men, by turning women into men.

There are many ways in which Freud turns women into men, femininity into masculinity. He maintains that for both boys and girls the first love object (with which they identify) is the phallic mother; this makes the mother masculine and it makes infants of both sexes masculine–identified. In addition, Freud claims that there is only one libido, masculine libido. Also, he defines all sexuality, both masculine and feminine, in terms of castration, having or not having the penis.[5] He reduces the clitoris to an inferior penis—never mind that this contradicts his claim that women are already castrated. In "Female Sexuality" he explicitly claims that "it will help our exposition if, as we go along, we compare the state of things in women with that in men" (FS 227).

It will be profitable at this point, in order to analyze Freud's troubled relation to the feminine, to enter a debate between Irigaray and Kofman over Freud's equation of phallus and logos. Luce Irigaray argues that by turning women into men and femininity into masculinity, Freud excludes women and the feminine from culture, from logos (SOW 14). In *The Enigma of Woman* Sarah Kofman, in the name of "intellectual honesty," defends Freud against Irigaray's powerful criticism of "Femininity." She maintains that "nothing in the text ["Femininity"] justifies Luce Irigaray's reading (according to which Freud, like Aristotle, deprives women of the right to the logos and phallus alike). We have seen that things are not that simple. And even supposing that Freud wished to speak among men of the enigma of femininity (which is not the case), that would not suffice to condemn him as a metaphysician" (104). While Kofman is right that Freud's text is fraught with ambiguities, there is plenty in his "Femininity" to justify Irigaray's claim that his theory deprives women of the right to the logos and phallus. And Irigaray does not "condemn Freud as a metaphysician" because he speaks among men about women. Rather, Irigaray condemns Freud as a metaphysician because of the centrality of presence in his account of the evolution of subjectivity and sexual difference: for Freud everything hinges on the sight/presence of the male organ; both masculine and feminine sexuality are defined in terms of its presence.

Irigaray's "condemnation" of Freud as metaphysician, however, is not unambiguous. She maintains that Freud makes a double move in relation to metaphysics:

> Thus Freud would strike at least two blows at the scene of representation. One, as it were, directly, when he destroys a certain conception of the present or presence, when he stresses secondary revision, over-determination, repetition compulsion, the death drive, etc., or when he indicates, in his practice, the impact of so-called unconscious mechanisms on the discourse of the "subject." The other blow, blinder and less direct, occurs when—himself a prisoner of a certain economy of the logos, of a certain logic, notably of "desire," whose link to classical philosophy he fails to see—he defines sexual difference as a function of the a priori of the same, having recourse, to support this demonstration, to the age-old processes: analogy, comparison, symmetry, dichotomic oppositions, and so on. When, as a card-carrying member of an "ideology" that he never questions, he insists that the sexual pleasure known as masculine is the paradigm for all sexual pleasure, to which all representations of pleasure can but defer in reference, support, and submission. (*SOW* 28)

So while in one move Freud exposes a crisis in the metaphysics of presence, with a second move he closes off the possibility of acknowledging the impact of that crisis. The primary processes call into question the metaphysics of a fully present subject, but the identification of those primary processes with the masculine libido closes off all possible discussion of difference. Irigaray argues that Freud leaves us with an economy of representation of the same, a hom(m)o-sexual economy. Kofman, on the other hand, takes issue with Irigaray's claim that Freud invokes science in the name of this masculine economy of the same. She argues that Freud does not invoke science to reassert sameness, as Irigaray claims, but rather to undermine popular opinions and stereotypes with regard to the sexes, especially the notion that the feminine is passive while the masculine is active (*EW*,112, 115).

Yet, if we look at the passage in which Freud most insistently invokes science and denies the connection between femininity and passivity and masculinity and activity, it becomes clear that even while Freud sets out to break down popular prejudice, he reinforces it through his rhetoric. He points out that "the male sex-cell is actively mobile and searches out the female one, and the latter, the ovum, is immobile and waits passively. This behavior of the elementary sexual organisms is indeed a model for the conduct of sexual individuals during intercourse. The male pursues the female for the purpose of sexual union, seizes hold of her and penetrates into her " (F 114). Then he warns that this reduces masculinity to aggressiveness and that in some species the females are stronger than the males; so it is "inadequate . . . to make masculine behavior coincide with activity and feminine with passivity " (F 115). Immediately after claiming that we should not associate masculinity with activity and femininity with passivity, Freud does so anyway. He argues that though mothers exhibit activity, their activity is a sort of active passivity necessary to carry on the species. Next he makes a distinction between passivity and having passive aims. He suggests that even though the female has passive aims, this does not make her passive. He qualifies the later claim by pointing out that we should not underestimate social customs that condition women to have passive aims. But no sooner has he issued this warning than he says, "There is one particularly constant relation between femininity and instinctual life which we do not want to overlook"; this constant is masochism (F 116). So every time that Freud warns us against the prejudices of science in the very next breath he reiterates them.

Although Kofman is right that Freud allows for women to enter society and have the right to the logos and the phallus, women do so only through the masculine. It is only Freud's bisexuality thesis that allows him to admit women into the order of the logos, because for Freud the feminine is antithetical to the logos and the phallus. To feminist ears Freud sounds outrageous when he says: "For the ladies, whenever some comparison seemed to turn out unfavorable to their sex, were able to utter a suspicion that we, the male analysts, had been unable to overcome certain deeply-rooted prejudices against what was feminine, and that this was being paid for in the partiality of our researches. We, on the other hand, standing on the ground of bisexuality, had no difficulty in avoiding impoliteness. We had only to say: 'This doesn't apply to *you*. You're the exception; on this point you're more masculine than feminine' " (F 116–117). Ultimately Kofman explains the ambiguities in Freud's writings on femininity as manifestations of his fear of death. In the following paragraphs, I will explain them as manifestations of Freud's fear of birth.

The riddle of femininity is really the riddle of masculinity. The question that is really at stake for Freud is how is masculinity possible—how can the male, who was once part of the female/mother, be masculine? It is necessary that Freud explain femininity in order to safeguard masculinity. If he can't guarantee that the masculine is not identified with the feminine, one possible safeguard is to make the feminine masculine after all. In this way even if the masculine is identified with the feminine (or the mother), it is not threatened.

I maintain that Freud's solution to this problem is the fetishist's solution. He argues that little girls are in the beginning little men. That is, their sexuality is phallic and they are more masculine than feminine. In fact *this* is the mystery of femininity: how do masculine little girls, little men, become women? For Freud a little girl's erotic zone is masculine and her clitoris is a small penis: "Anatomy has recognized the clitoris within the female pudenda as being an organ that is homologous to the penis; and the physiology of the sexual processes has been able to add that this small penis which does not grow any bigger behaves in fact during childhood like a real and genuine penis " (OSTC 217). The clitoris operates as a penis equivalent. Hers, however, as Freud tells us, is obviously inferior. Why is it inferior if it functions in the same way and brings the same phallic pleasure, and if, as Freud says, "frequent erections of that organ make it possible for girls to form a correct judgment, even without any instruction, of the sexual manifestations of the other sex" (TE 219–20)? As Kofman points out it can only be the size of the girl's "penis" that makes her inferior. Sexual difference, then is not a matter of kind or quality, but a matter of degree or quantity—unless at a small enough size the penis becomes feminine. Perhaps this is Freud's fear. He is afraid that the masculine is really feminine.

This is always the fear of players in what Irigaray calls the "game of castration" (*ML* 80). Within the economy of castration there is no qualitative difference; everything is measured in terms of quantity. Irigaray criticizes the economy of castration because within it there can be no depth: "To simulate depth in the guise of the bigger or the smaller. To bring erection and limpness into the game of castration. And the other into the same: a comparison between the bigger and the smaller, the harder and the softer, etc., until it becomes impossible to evaluate anything except in terms of *less* and *more*" (*ML* 80–81). Playing the game of castration Freud reduces all sexual difference to a question of less and more.

Like the fetishist who cannot bear the mother's castration and substitutes another object for the mother's missing penis in order to protect the mother from castration (and ultimately reassure himself that he is not castrated), Freud substitutes the clitoris for the missing penis. Oddly enough, it is the impossible combination of women's castration and inferior penis that erects masculine sexuality. As Kofman says, "only the Freudian solution, that of granting woman an incomplete sexuality envious of man's penis, makes it possible at once to recognize woman's castration and to overcome one's own castration anxiety" (*EW* 89). "Woman's genital organs arouse an inseparable blend of horror and pleasure; they at once awaken and appease castration anxiety" (*EW* 85).

Like the fetishist, Freud has it both ways. The mother is both castrated and phallic. This ambiguity is necessary for Freud to imagine that masculinity is possible at all. The real problem for Freud is, how is it that the male, once part of the woman's body, becomes masculine? His concern for how the female performs the difficult task of changing both erogenous zones and love objects covers up the prior concern for the male's transition from literal identity with a female maternal body and a psychic identification with the mother to not only a separate body but also a separate sexual identity. One way that Freud explains this transition is to invent the masculine mother, the mother who is either phallic or castrated, but never feminine. So Freud's conflicted theory of femininity and the phallic/castrated mother can be read as symptoms of the fetishist's logic. And these symptoms can be read as manifestations of a fear of birth; man fears his birth out of the body of a woman. For Freud there is nothing more frightening than the thought of being buried alive, which is the fear of internment in the maternal womb.

Freud turns all sexuality and all desire into masculine sexuality and desire. While he opens up the discussion of sexual difference, at the same time he closes off the possibility of sexual difference. In this way, as Irigaray suggests, Freud makes a double move to both challenge and protect a metaphysics of presence that favors the presence of the phallus. He resorts to the fetishist's logic in order to ensure that the phallus is present in both sexes. So while he opens up the discussion of an other to representation—the unconscious, repressed and over-determined—at the same time he closes off the possibility of a specifically feminine other. Freud's psychoanalytic theories invite attempts to represent the other but, like more traditional theories of representation, continue to exclude the feminine from representation.

Nietzsche's Wisdom: A Dagger through the Heart [6]

> *Would a woman be able to captivate us (or, as people say, to "fetter" us) whom we did not credit with knowing how to employ the dagger (any kind of dagger) skillfully against us under certain circumstances? Or against herself; which in a certain case might be the severest revenge (the Chinese revenge).*
> —*Friedrich Nietzsche, Gay Science*

Like Freud, Nietzsche in his way opens up the discussion of representing the other and yet closes off the possibility of representing the feminine other. He opens up the possibility of interpreting otherwise, but he excludes woman from the process of interpretation. As an example, I will read *On the Genealogy of Morals* as a call for a type of reading and writing that engage in active interpretation which is not the product of traditional philosophical rationality. There Nietzsche describes a process of reading and writing otherwise that is sensuous and bodily. Yet for Nietzsche, as for Freud, the body out of which reading and writing surge is always a male body. Like Freud's, Nietzsche's writing denies any place for woman or the feminine except as objects. As we will see, this is evidenced by all (necessarily awkward) attempts to answer the question "As a woman, how can I read Nietzsche's text?"

Nietzsche begins the third essay of *On the Genealogy of Morals* with an aphorism from *Thus Spake Zarathustra*: "Unconcerned, mocking, violent—thus wisdom wants *us*: she is a woman and always loves only a warrior " (*OGM* 97 III 1).[7] What is the relationship between Nietzsche's warrior and the woman, wisdom? Provocatively, Nietzsche suggests that this aphorism is part of a lesson in reading. We cannot learn however, Nietzsche's lesson in reading unless we explore the relationship between the warrior and the woman, wisdom.

In the preface to *On the Genealogy of Morals*, Nietzsche claims that the third essay is an exegesis of Zarathustra's aphorism. The connection between the third essay and the aphorism, however, is far from obvious. In the preface Nietzsche suggests that he is giving us a lesson in "reading as an art." As always, Nietzsche leaves his reader to learn the lesson the hard way, to take up the place of the warrior and do violence to the text, in order to create some connection between this aphorism and the apparent topic of the third essay, the meaning of the ascetic ideal.

The title of the third essay is "What Is the Meaning of Ascetic Ideals?" —a question that Nietzsche asks over and over throughout the essay. He does not repeat the question in order to emphasize some particular characteristic of the ascetic ideal. Rather, he repeats the question in order to emphasize a particular style of reading, genealogy, which diagnoses *the meaning* of various cultural symptoms. The third essay is as much about meaning as it is about ascetic ideals; the meaning of ascetic ideals is a pretext for a performance of reading as interpretation, reading as an art. Not only is Nietzsche artfully reading the meaning of ascetic ideals, he is also reading the meaning of Zarathustra's aphorism—his analysis of the meaning of ascetic ideals poses as an exegesis of Zarathustra's aphorism. More than this, he is reading the meaning of meaning itself: what does it mean to ask about the meaning of the ascetic ideal? What does it mean to do genealogy?

Nietzsche's redoubling of meaning is a *performance* of the dynamics of reading. "What does that *mean*?" asks Nietzsche, "for this fact has to be interpreted: *in itself* it just stands there, stupid to all eternity, like every 'thing-in-itself'" (*OGM* 107 III 7). To answer the question "What does it mean?" we have to interpret. Yet the question "What does it mean?" is the screw upon which the ascetic ideal itself turns; the ascetic ideal requires that life and suffering have a meaning. "What is the meaning?" is the ascetic question par excellence. Nietzsche turns the ascetic ideal back on itself in order to ask "What is the meaning of ascetic ideals?" or "What is the meaning of demanding some meaning?"

In *Nietzsche and the Question of Interpretation*, Alan Schrift suggests that Nietzsche uses meaning "not in the epistemological sense of uncovering the true referent or the accurate representation of a state of affairs, but rather in the psycho-genealogical sense of *deciphering* the significance which these ideals hold as a symptom of the health or disease of the will to power that has posited them as ideal" (173, my emphasis).[8] Because we have to interpret even Nietzsche's theory of meaning, however, Nietzsche's use of "meaning" can be read *both* in the epistemological sense of uncovering the true referent—the rhetorical maneuver that Schrift himself makes when he claims to uncover the true referent of Nietzsche's use of "meaning"—and in the psychogenealogical sense of deciphering the significance of ideals. It depends on how we read. I will link these two types of reading with the two types of morality that Nietzsche describes in *On the Genealogy of Morals*. I will associate uncovering meaning in the epistemological sense with the slave morality and uncovering meaning in the psychogenealogical sense with the master morality.

We could say that just as Nietzsche proposes an active and a reactive morality in *Genealogy*, he proposes an active and a reactive reading. He describes the logic of slave morality as reactive—imaginarily reactive at that—and the logic of the master morality as active (*OGM* 36–37 I 10).[9] Unlike the slave, the master affirms him directly without a hostile external world. He is unconcerned about differences and this is his potency. He is strong enough not to feel threatened by what is outside himself, what is not he: "While every noble morality develops from a triumphant affirmation of itself, slave morality from the outset says No to what is outside, what is different, what is not itself; . . . [the noble valuation] acts and

18 THE ETHICS OF READING

grows spontaneously, it seeks its opposite only so as to affirm itself more gratefully and triumphantly—its negative concept low, common, bad is only subsequently-invented pale, contrasting image in relation to its positive basic concept—filled with life and passion through and through" (OGM 36-37 I 10).

Like the noble morality, the artful reader does not say no to difference in order to affirm only the self same.[10] Like active morality, active reading affirms itself directly and is therefore open to differences. Whereas active reading opens and multiplies the text, reactive reading closes and narrows the text. Just as the slave can only affirm himself in opposition, as a reaction, to a hostile external world, the reactive reader requires an interpretation that puts itself forth against all other interpretations as the only possible truth of the text. This reading is a reaction to what the reader takes to be the transcendent meaning of the text, its true referent. By claiming to have discovered the transcendent meaning of the text, the reactive reader can claim authority for his interpretation alone. Ascetic interpretation is reactive reading at its limit: "The ascetic ideal has a goal—this goal is so universal that all the other interests of human existence seem, when compared with it, petty and narrow; it interprets epochs, nations, and men inexorably with a view to this one goal; it permits no other interpretation, no other goal; it rejects, denies, affirms, and sanctions solely from the point of view of its interpretation . . . . it submits to no power, it believes in its own predominance over every other power—it believes that no power exists on earth that does not first have to receive a meaning, a right to exist" (OGM 146 III 23).

If we apply Nietzsche's analysis of ascetic interpretation to reading texts as well as reading epochs, nations, and men, then we get a description of something like a naive view of reading as an exercise in looking through words to their meanings, what for now I will call "simply reading" as opposed to interpretation. This is uncovering meaning in the epistemological sense of looking for the true referent. But the aphorism is not "understood" when it is simply read in this way; this is reactive or passive reading.

Genealogy is one alternative to reactive reading in that it combines interpretation with diagnosis; this is uncovering meaning in the psych genealogical sense described by Schrift. Genealogy not only interprets the meaning of the "text" (ascetic ideals in this case) but also diagnoses what Jane Gallop calls in another context "the symptomatic effects produced by the presumption that the text is in the very place 'where meaning and knowledge of meaning reside.'"[11] In this sense active reading is distinguished from reactive reading in that it involves a recognition of the investment the reader makes in the text's meaning and diagnoses the symptoms of that investment. Reactive reading, on the other hand, assumes that words are transparent windows onto the text's or the author's meaning. In the preface to *Daybreak* Nietzsche describes the art of reading well as an art that "does not so easily get anything done, it teaches to read *well*, that is to say, to read slowly, deeply, looking cautiously before and aft, with reservations, with doors left open, with delicate eyes and fingers . . ." (D 5).[12] Genealogy is a way of reading that opens on to the other of a text. Yet within Nietzsche's genealogy, that other is not permitted to be feminine.

In Nietzsche's setup in *On the Genealogy of Morals*, however, it is impossible to ask the question of reading without asking the question (Freud's question) "*Was will das Weib?*" "What does woman want?" Nietzsche's lesson in artful reading is an exegesis of the answer to the question "What does woman want?"[13] As Nietzsche sets it out, in order to learn his lesson in reading, we first have to interpret Zarathustra's aphorism, which asks the question "what does woman want?" And answers it, "She wants a warrior." The relationship between the question of reading and the question of woman, however, points to the impossibility of both for Nietzsche. We cannot answer the question of reading— How do we read?—without answering the question "What does woman want?" Yet we cannot answer this question without first reading Nietzsche's aphorism, if not woman's desire itself. Reading, pure and simple, in order to *see through* words to their meaning is not possible. Reading is always necessarily interpretation. We are caught in the hermeneutic circle.

We encounter the impossibility of reading on another level. If wisdom is a woman and therefore wants us to be courageous, unconcerned, mocking, violent, then we *cannot ask* the question "What does woman want?" To ask this question is to be *concerned* with her desire, something a warrior would not do. For once we inquire and show our concern, we are no longer unconcerned and therefore we are no longer desirable readers. As Arthur Danto points out, wisdom does not love those who love he (14). Wisdom does not want a reader, her reader is impossible; she wants (her desire) to be known by heart. This *Weib* wants a carnal knowledge and not a conceptual knowledge. Her love is a sensuous passion far from platonic love. This *Weib* is of doubtful morality. She wants to be had by force. She wants violence [*gewalttätig*]; she wants to be violated [*vergewaltigen*]. She wants a violent, indifferent warrior who cannot reciprocate her love. Wisdom wants a dagger through the heart.

If wisdom is this loose woman, then whom does she love? *How* is it that she wants *us*? Who are *we*? How are we to read the relationship between wisdom and the warrior? Although I will analyze Nietzsche's warrior later, I passionately disagree with Alexander Nehamas, who says that "the conception of the writer as warrior, and not the identification of wisdom with woman, is the crucial feature of this aphorism." Nehamas reads essay III as an application of the aphorism which precedes it. He argues that essay III is a "declaration of war" on the ascetic ideal in which Nietzsche tries to put his own values in the place of ascetic values (115). In his reading, Nietzsche is the warrior waging war against the ascetic ideal (114). Nietzsche is wisdom's beloved. The joint on which this reading turns, however, is the thesis that essay III is waging all-out war against the ascetic ideal. A close reading of essay III reveals that Nietzsche is extremely ambivalent toward the ascetic ideal. Nietzsche is diagnosing the *meaning* of the ascetic ideal in its various modalities rather than condemning it outright.

Most Nietzsche critics and scholars choose to ignore Nietzsche's woman. Like Nehamas, they don't take her seriously. Yet, as I will argue, if we attend to Nietzsche's woman, then our reading of Nietzsche must change drastically. Unlike Nehamas, who engages the warrior but not the woman, I want to investigate the relationship between the two. After all, in Zarathustra's aphorism it seems that the lesson which we are to learn comes from the relationship between the warrior and the woman or the writer/reader and wisdom.

The relationship between the warrior and wisdom can be read, as Michael Newman suggests, as an inversion of the philosopher's love of the Forms in Plato's *Phaedrus*. For Nietzsche, like Plato, love is the means to the noble or aristocratic soul; but Nietzsche inverts the Platonic notions of noble and base.[14] For Nietzsche an elevation to nobility is not an elevation to transcendent Forms which brings with it self-knowledge and a turn away from sensuousness. Rather, for him an elevation to nobility is an elevation to sexual sublimation which brings with it self-mockery and a turn away from ascetic ideals.

Plato's characterization of the ascent to nobility is as bloody and violent as Nietzsche's. In the *Phaedrus* Plato paints a gory picture of the self-violence necessary to overcome baseness in the self and reach the level of nobility in the soul. The black, wanton steed, which represents sensuality in Plato's metaphor, must be violently beaten as if to death so that the soul might overcome its base passions. It is interesting that in Plato's metaphor methods that we might associate with bodily passions and physical violence are associated with the intellect and reason. The Charioteer, reason, uses bodily violence against the black steed, bodily passion. Whereas in Plato's metaphor the methods of physical violence associated with bodily lust are turned against bodily passion, in Nietzsche's genealogy the methods of argument and derision associated with the intellect and reason are turned against reason. In *Genealogy* the white steed receives the whipping.

In addition to the parallel between *Genealogy* and Plato's *Phaedrus*, Nietzschean Eros can be read against Socratic Eros as the latter is articulated in the *Symposium*. In the *Symposium* Socrates claims to have learned from a woman, Diotima, that Eros is the intermediary between ignorance and wisdom and between mortal and immortal or human and divine. In Nietzsche's aphorism, love is the intermediary between wisdom and the warrior, wisdom's love brings them together. Nietzsche not only inverts the sensuous and transcendent in their relationship through Eros, he also inverts the positions of lover and beloved. In both the *Phaedrus* and Socrates' speech in the *Symposium,* the lover uses his wisdom to conquer both his own lust and his reluctant beloved. Nietzsche, on the other hand, puts the warrior in the passive position; wisdom or woman is the lover and the warrior is the conquered beloved. This inversion, however, is unusual in Nietzsche's texts—which is why it seems more promising for a feminine subject. Recall the preface to *Beyond Good and Evil* where Nietzsche asks us to suppose that truth is a woman who is sought after by dogmatic philosophers. Here truth/woman is the beloved hopelessly lost to the impotent lover—what a joke.

The fact that in Zarathustra's aphorism the woman, wisdom, is the active lover and the warrior is the beloved is overlooked by most of the scholars who comment on this passage. As I indicated above, Alexander Nehamas claims that the woman is unimportant in this passage (114) And even Michael Newman, who seems at least interested in the relationship between the warrior and the woman, chooses a course which is "expedient rather than satisfactory" in order to steer clear of the "vexed question of 'Nietzsche and woman'" (279 n. 7). While acknowledging that the warrior is the passive beloved of wisdom, Newman restores a more properly Platonic relationship between lover and beloved, warrior and woman, by asking "who, or what, then does the warrior or noble love?" (264). He restores the warrior to the position of lover. He then positions Zarathustra as the noble warrior/lover; and he answers the question "Who does the warrior love?" by indicating that Zarathustra speaks the warrior's desire when he says that "of all that is written I love only what a man has written with his blood" (264). Newman's warrior is both the writer, Zarathustra (Nietzsche), and the reader who loves only what he himself writes with (his own?) blood. In Newman's reading the warrior loves a reader who does not seek to understand but rather learns by heart—recall that Zarathustra proclaims that "whoever writes in blood and aphorisms does not want to be read but to be learned by heart." Love, after all, is a matter of heart. The beloved reader is necessarily a passive reader who submits to a "branding" with burning aphorisms (cf. Newman 265).

Through the process of reading by heart, the reader is transformed into the noble warrior. By submitting to the text, the reader becomes active. This self-transformation does not take place through Socratic self-knowledge but through "rumination," as Nietzsche says in the preface to *Genealogy*. Newman maintains that *Genealogy*'s "quasi-scientific accounts can also be read as myths for the purpose of the self-education of the reader: indeed for the transformation of the 'knower' into a 'reader' who 'ruminates'" (Newman 267). In this way Nietzsche creates his own reader, who, as we have seen, is necessarily as masochistic and sadistic as his lover, who writes not only with his own blood but also the blood of his readers.

Like Newman, Arthur Danto emphasizes the violence that Nietzsche's texts do to their readers. The aphorism is the best weapon of the philosopher since, like a dagger traveling fast, it lodges itself in its reader. As Danto says, the aphorism is "implanted" in the reader and "metabolized" (15—16). Because Nietzsche's aphorisms are painful, we remember them; like the tortures he describes in book II, they are mnemonic shocks that jolt the memory. On Danto's reading violence is not instrumental but essential to Nietzsche's warrior; this warrior is fighting for the sake of fighting, unconcerned for any cause (Danto 14). In the end, Danto seems to turn Nietzsche into Kant when he claims that to be unconcerned is associated with will and that Nietzsche's goal is to redirect the will—which, of course, prevents Nietzsche from being an unconcerned warrior: "But that is what he would like to have achieved: . . . to replace a morality of means with a morality of principle: to act in such a way as to be consistent with acting that way eternally: to stultify the instinct for significance" (27–28). On Danto's reading, then, the reader and the writer as unconcerned warrior must act in such a way as to "stultify the instinct for significance"; he must engage in the impossible battle, which must be fought for its own sake.

Nietzsche wants a sensuous, violent reading and writing that come from the body.[15] But it seems that this body, for Nietzsche and his commentators, is always only the male body. What happens, however, when unlike Danto, Newman and Nehamas we shift our attention from the warrior to the woman? Remember that Nietzsche's aphorism reads, "Unconcerned, mocking, violent—thus wisdom wants *us*: she is a woman and always loves only a warrior." What happens when woman/wisdom becomes the lover? She becomes the active agent and the warrior becomes the passive beloved, the object of her love. What kind of love belongs to her? Is hers necessarily the violent love? And what does her love teach us about reading and writing? When we read woman/wisdom as the active lover, then what can we learn from Nietzsche's lesson on reading and writing? Furthermore, what happens when Nietzsche's reader is a woman? What happens when a woman takes the place of the warrior seeking favor with wisdom?

It doesn't seem that Nietzsche imagines that wisdom's beloved—this warrior who writes and reads with blood—could be Athena. Certainly Nietzsche's woman reader must laugh or she will feel wounded by his texts. Perhaps, like Irigaray, she can't help but mock Nietzsche for his own fear of the body, of his own body as well as hers. And certainly images of a woman reading and writing with her blood will bring with them very different interpretations of the process of reading and writing.

What would it mean for a woman to write and read with her blood? In *Marine Lover of Friedrich Nietzsche*, Luce Irigaray laments that Nietzsche overlooks woman's blood: "Something red was lacking, a hint of blood and guts to revive the will, and restore its strength" (79).[16] Irigaray suggests that Nietzsche forgets the blood of life, maternal blood, which still makes "a stain, a spot. No one is supposed to notice the opening onto the stage of sameness . . . which is no longer possible without suppressing the whole body" (*ML* 81). Although Nietzsche advocates writing and reading as bloodletting in the manly warrior, he forgets about women's blood that flows into new life without the knife, without self-mutilation or the mutilation of others. Perhaps interpretation can be of the body and fecund without also being violent. The image of a woman reading and writing with her blood promises a creativity that is neither sadistic nor masochistic, that does not require violence toward the reader or self-violence.

As I elaborate later, Irigaray indicates that Nietzsche's texts always promote sameness even when they sing the praises of difference, because Nietzschean difference is always merely difference as defined by the same, or is what she calls "the other of the same" rather than "the other of the other." Another way to say this might be that Nietzsche's notions of active morality and active reading are always merely reactions to the reactive morality and reactive reading. Irigaray claims that Nietzsche denies the fundamental difference of sexual difference. He overlooks woman's difference. In particular, Nietzsche's texts deny the maternal body out of which all human beings are born; and in order to cover over this murder of the maternal body, to wipe away the blood and wash away the stain, he must deny the body altogether. The body always reminds us of that first body, the maternal body, which sustained us; it reminds us of the maternal blood out of which we were born (cf. *ML* 96). For Irigaray to imagine woman's blood is to imagine difference; but Nietzsche cannot imagine woman's blood or what it would mean for a woman to read and write with her blood because the bloodstains on his texts are the result of a murder, matricide—the blood of death and not the blood of life. Woman is not the warrior whom wisdom loves.

So although Nietzsche proposes a way of reading and writing that opens onto its other, a reading and writing from the body, this body is always a masculine body. It becomes clear from attempting to put woman into the subject position as the reader or writer within Nietzsche's discourse that in that place she is out of place. Like Freud, Nietzsche makes woman and the feminine into an object for a masculine subject. Like Freud, while Nietzsche opens philosophy onto the other, the body, he closes off the possibility of a specifically feminine other and there by eliminates the possibility of sexual difference.

Derrida's Feminine Operation: Philosophers in Drag

> *"Would you like me to dress up as a woman?" I murmured.*
> —*Jacques Derrida, Glas 223, 243*

> *I am a woman and beautiful.*
> —*Jacques Derrida, "The Law of Genre"*

In most of his texts Derrida plays with/as woman.[17] In addition, in many of his texts he criticizes his predecessors (Kant, Hegel, Heidegger) for excluding woman. Yet how is a woman to read these texts? Where is she in these texts? Where is her desire? Derrida's texts suffer from the same symptoms as Nietzsche's texts and in some respect Freud's texts as well. It is clear that in his lectures on femininity Freud is speaking to men about women. Women are his objects and the texts give voice to a masculine desire for this feminine object. Although Nietzsche's case is less clear, the awkwardness, if not impossibility, of reading or writing as a woman becomes clear when we examine the metaphors with which Nietzsche describes the processes of reading and writing. In Nietzsche's text the operations of reading and writing can even be interpreted as man doing violence to woman, the violent warrior taking the loose woman. And although Derrida begins his *Spurs* by proclaiming that "it is woman who will be my subject," in that text she is never afforded any subject position; rather she is used to deconstruct a unified subject position (S 37). Like Freud and Nietzsche before him, and so many others, Derrida seems to be speaking to men about women; his case, however, is fraught with ambiguities.

Like both Freud and Nietzsche before him, Derrida is concerned with opening a space for the other. For Freud the other was the unconscious. For Nietzsche the other was the body. For Derrida the other is difference itself. Following Levinas, in order to open philosophy onto difference Derrida shifts from a conception of language as a means of coming to know ourselves, and thereby possessing ourselves, to a conception of language as a means of exposing the other whom we cannot possess. This Levinasian shift is a move from a philosophy of the subject to a philosophy of the other. Derrida is not concerned with the correspondence between philosophical thinking and things in themselves; rather he is concerned with what has been excluded from philosophical thinking.

In an interview Derrida says that his "central question is: from what site or non-site can philosophy as such appear to itself as other than itself, so that it can interrogate and reflect up on itself in an original manner? Such a non-site or alterity would be radically irreducible to philosophy. But the problem is that such a non-site cannot be defined or situated by means of philosophical language" (RK 108). Much of Derrida's writing addresses ways in which traditional philosophical language attempts to conceptualize difference, exteriority and otherness. Operating according to a type of Hegelian logic (without the crucial negation of the negation of difference or particularity) in which the self consolidates itself at the expense of the other, traditional philosophical discourse tries to eliminate all difference, exteriority and otherness. As Derrida claims in "Tympan, " philosophy insists "upon thinking its other: its proper other, the proper of its other, an other proper? In thinking it as such, in recognizing it, one misses it. One reappropriates it for oneself, one disposes of it, one misses it, or rather one misses (the) missing (of) it, which, as concerns the other, always amounts to the same. Between the proper of the other and the other of the proper" (T xi-xii). Ultimately, in much of his writing, Derrida suggests that philosophy closes off the possibility of listening to any other because it always operates within an economy or logic of the proper, making all difference into its own property (T xvi). But how is it possible to relate to any other without making it your own; isn't any object of consciousness an object *for us*? How does Derrida confront this problem? Following the later Heidegger, he makes the problem one of address rather than consciousness.

In "Psyche: Inventions of the Other" Derrida suggests that deconstruction opens a place for the other. As I indicated earlier, he argues that we cannot invent the other or the place of the other because insofar as it is radically other we have no access to it; we do not speak the same language. Yet this other invents us through its call: "For the other is always another origin of the world and we are (always) (still) to be invented" (Psy 61). This is what Derrida calls the paradox of invention. Invention is only possible through the invention of the other, or something other; and yet inventing something other out of the same is impossible. So he formulates the process as originating with the other's call or invitation to "come." This call is a Heideggerian call to thinking. When thinking opens onto the other, then the impossible is possible; invention takes place. Beyond this, however, is the ethical concern that Derrida finds lacking in Heidegger and finds in Levinas. Deconstruction does not open up just the possibility of invention but also the possibility of justice. Derrida says that "to address oneself to the other in the language of the other is, it seems, the condition of all possible justice" (FL 17). Yet, speaking/writing to the other in its own language is as impossible as inventing the other. How can we speak/write in a language that by definition we do not know?

The first step is to expose what makes it possible to speak/write in our language. Speaking, writing, reading are dialogic; they need an other, in the form of another person, meaning, or a text. Only the other makes language possible. Signification brings with it responsibilities, ethical responsibilities: "We are invested with an undeniable responsibility at the moment we begin to signify something (but where does that begin?). This responsibility assigns us our freedom without leaving it with us, if one could put it that way. And we see it coming from the Other. It is assigned to us by the Other, from the Other, before any hope of reappropriation permits us to assume this responsibility in the space of what could be called *autonomy*" (PF 634).

Signification brings with it a responsibility to and from the Other. There is no signification in isolation, no private language. We are born into a system of signification where, although it is not determined and unchanging, meaning is beyond us. Julia Kristeva identifies meaning as the Other within signification. In the shadow of both Heidegger and Levinas, Derrida describes a type of invitation from the Other that both opens up the possibility of communication and obligates us. Following Heidegger, Derrida sees what he calls the "come," the call, from the Other as the very possibility of signification or meaning. We are indebted to this other beyond us because it opens up the possibility of any language, thought or meaning. Language itself and our relationship to it opens up the possibility of our asking both ontic and ontological questions. Following Levinas, Derrida sees the "come" from the Other as an obligation, ultimately an ethical call.

So, following Levinas, Derrida insists on the responsibility to try to speak (to) the other. In the case of inventing the feminine other, however, Derrida is caught in an impossible place, both dressing up as a woman and parodying all attempts to do so. As self-conscious as Derrida's masquerade appears to be, it is still important to diagnose the ways in which his discourse effectively closes off the very space that it attempts to open up. Like Freud and Nietzsche before him, Derrida closes off the possibility of listening to a feminine other even while he is attempting to hear, to speak of/as that other.

When Derrida says that woman will be his subject, he is playing with woman. While she is the subject of his discourse, he also suggests that her position is *his* subject position. Yet Derrida does not identify with the woman in his text. In effect endorsing some of Nietzsche's proclamations about woman, Derrida not only quotes Nietzsche but also reaffirms that woman is "so artistic"; her effect is at a distance; she will not be pinned down and yet one cannot help looking for her (S 47, 55, 71). When a woman reads these passages, where is her position? Is she, like Nietzsche and Derrida, caught looking for the irresistible but elusive woman? Herself? Is her effect a distance from herself? Whose desire is given voice in this text? This is not a woman's desire. When women desire women qua women, they cannot have the kind of distance from themselves that Derrida describes without experiencing a kind of self-alienation to the point of psychosis. Perhaps, then, *Spurs* is merely "the advice of one man to another: a sort of scheme for how to seduce without being seduced" (S 49).

Like Nietzsche's view of reading and writing as the violent warrior's relation to woman, Derrida's view of reading and writing also suggests a violence toward woman. In *Spurs* he proposes that if style is a man, then writing is a woman (S 57). Derrida's spurring operation, which he has identified with the feminine operation, is a violent operation on woman's body itself. Style is the spur that violently penetrates into the material of writing in order to have its way. And woman's body is sacrificed to style. The grand style is a type of violent (self-)mocking warrior. "At this point, where it pierces the veil of truth and the simulacrum of castration in order to impale the woman's body, the question of style must be measured against the larger question of the interpretation of Nietzsche's text, of the interpretation of interpretation—in short against the question of interpretation itself" (Derrida, *S* 171–73, my emphasis).

For Derrida it is the point at which style impales the woman's body that the question of interpretation comes to the fore. In this passage Derrida raises the question of whether this violence *belongs* to the interpretation of Nietzsche's texts and the larger question of whether violence necessarily belongs to interpretation.[18] Does interpretation necessarily impale woman's body? Where does woman belong in interpretation, in reading and writing?

Below I will read Derrida's insistence on self-parody, self-violence, as a violence against the masculine "for the sake of" the feminine. Deconstruction's autocastration emasculates style in order to pose as woman. And as Derrida underlines in both *Spurs* and *Glas*, the operation of posing itself is feminine; posing is the feminine operation (See, *Glas* 246 *S* 69). One possible answer, then, to the question of where woman or the feminine belongs is that each belongs to man; he is feminine so there is no need for woman.

In addition, within Derrida's discourse, affirmation, particularly double affirmation, is another operation of woman. Discussing Blanchot in "The Law of Genre," Derrida maintains that saying "yes, yes," a double affirmation, is "usually" performed by "women," "beautiful women" (not "woman," but women). So perhaps deconstruction's self-referential, self-parodying self-denials are self-affirmations of the double gesture of deconstruction; deconstruction says yes to self-parody by saying yes to parody. It says yes to itself through its parody of itself. Like Nietzsche's ascetic priest whose no to life becomes a series of "tender yeses," deconstruction's self-violence becomes a twisted self-affirmation. Within the logic of his "Law of Genre," deconstruction's self-referentiality—which is always a self-affirmation no matter what else it might be—is itself a feminine operation because it is a double affirmation. But Derrida provides the ground for yet another possible reading of his feminine operation in *Glas* when he asks: What would it mean for a man to want to become a woman? In a detour through Kant in his analysis of Hegel, Derrida answers his question (for Kant?): "What would it mean, for a man, to want to be a woman, seeing that the woman wants to be a man in proportion to her cultivating herself? That would mean then, apart from the semblance of a detour, to want to be a man, to want to be—that is to say, to remain—a man . . . either the man who wants to be only a man wants to be a woman inasmuch as woman wants to be a man; so he wants to be a woman in order to remain what he is. Or else the man who wants to be a woman only wants to be a woman since the woman wants to be man only in order to reach her womanly designs. To wit, the man" (*Glas* 130). All this is to say that "woman wants to be a man, the man never wants to be a woman" (*Glas* 130); and the man who wants to be a woman is suspect. On Derrida's reading of Kant, the man who wants to be a woman is suspected of really only wanting to be, to remain, a man. And sometimes the best way to do that might be through the detour of woman. Taking the place of the other may in fact guarantee that one has a place. Gayatri Spivak calls this double movement—assigning the other the displaced position on the margin and then appropriating that place—which shows up in *Spurs* and *Dissemination*, "double displacement."[19] She argues that the deconstructive philosopher (Derrida) usurps the "place of displacement" and thereby doubly displaces woman. That is, he takes even her already displaced place.

More recently, however, Spivak has suggested a way to reappropriate Derrida's use of "woman," a way to deconstruct Derrida's deconstruction of "woman." She describes a way that we can use deconstruction politically in the project of overcoming oppression. Spivak points out that deconstruction is both a naming and an unnaming. It is misnaming since within its discourse names have no "adequate literal referent."[20] And this is part of Derrida's project to show that there are so many names for her that there is no woman; there is no literal referent to the "woman" of philosophical discourse. While maintaining her suspicions of Derrida's "woman," Spivak suggests that those of us concerned with emancipation from oppressive categories can use this deconstructive naming device politically in order to motivate a continual process of naming the unnamed and thereby unnaming the named (FD 220). Naming, she reminds us, is the effect of particular historical circumstances. If we name "woman" the disenfranchised woman whom we cannot imagine as a literal referent, then in a sense, we have named the unnamable. But, at the same time, as soon as the name conjures some sort of image, the literal referent, always inadequate, begins to fade. The hope of this politicized deconstruction, claims Spivak, is "that the possibility for the name will be finally erased" and its material conditions destroyed (FD 220). In other words, through the use of a deconstruction of names or categories, we can not only give a voice to experiences previously denied a name, but also unname experiences that have been defined only in patriarchal terms. In this way the term "woman" can be used provisionally, subject to continual deconstruction, so that eventually it will no longer refer to the second sex or an oppressed group. What Spivak's analysis suggests is that the continued exclusion of the feminine other and woman is not inherent to the deconstructive methodology.

As Spivak points out, for Derrida "woman" is the name for the double-bind which is at the heart of naming itself. The double bind is the non truth of truth, the fact that all naming is misnaming. If Derrida calls this double bind "woman," then woman must be used against itself. In other words, if the very foundation of deconstruction is this double bind called "woman," then in order to deconstruct "woman" we must use "woman" against "woman." As Sally Robinson argues in another context, "man" is not subject to change.[21] Rather, in a metaphorical sense, "woman" is pitted against "woman" in order to maintain the economy of masculine desire.

For Derrida "woman" becomes the most convenient target in the deconstruction of the subject. Here "woman" is seen as an arbitrary sign which results from relations within a sign system whose phallocentric economy has led to essentialism. "Woman," then, through its ambiguous referent, tentative subject position, and marginal status, becomes a prime exemplar of the status of signs and subjects in general. The predicament of "woman" is the predicament of the subject. In this context, Derrida claims that there is no such thing as a "woman" (*"Il n'y a pas une femme"*), because there is no truth or essence of "woman" (*S*, 100). And, on the other hand, anyone who occupies a tentative position in relation to the phallocratic sign-system, occupies the place of "woman."

Against Derrida I will argue that even if the attempt to do away with "the unified subject" is a desirable goal, it should not begin with the deconstruction of "woman." After all, in some situations it is still necessary for feminists to rally around the identity of "woman." Some of his followers may defend Derrida by arguing that his goal is not just to deconstruct "woman," but also "man" and the woman/man dualism. In fact, Derrida intends (if that word is appropriate for him) to show that hierarchy is inherent in dualism and that we need, therefore, to deconstruct dualism. Yet the target in the deconstruction of the woman/man dualism is woman and not man. The privilege of man's position in this hierarchy is not in itself deconstructed. To aim the deconstructive mechanism at "woman" is a different operation than aiming it at "man." It is much different to disempower the *powerful* than it is to disempower the *powerless*.[22]

The question once again is where is the position of woman in Derrida's text? How does a woman read these texts? How does a woman write? If it is the operation of simulation that makes an operation feminine, then are women to simulate men or women? On my reading it seems that within the economy of deconstruction only men can be women. And women can neither play with the position of woman in the same way as men can nor play within the position of man. In Derrida's reading of Kant, all women want to be men. But if the feminine position, woman's position, is always the position of an object and never the position of a subject, is it necessary for woman to take up the position of man in order to be a subject? Is it true, as Luce Irigaray argues, that any theory of the subject is always appropriated by the masculine?

Derrida reads an answer to this question in Kant: "In fact, even if she truly wanted to, which is not the case, woman could never be a man. The masculine attributes with which she adorns herself are never anything but fake, signifiers without signification, fetishes" (*Glas* 130). While the man's transvestism is not only passable but highly amusing, the woman's transvestism is not passable. She is easily called out. She is called a feminist: "And in truth, they too are men, those women feminists so derided by Nietzsche. Feminism is nothing but the operation of a woman who aspires to be like a man" (Derrida, *S*, 65). Men can perform the feminine operation, an operation that no "real" woman can perform, yet women cannot take up the subject position, traditionally masculine, without being derided as "feminists" just trying to emulate men. This still leaves us with the question "What belongs to woman in Derrida's text and where does woman belong?" I will come back to this question again.

2 Becoming Woman: Autocastration, Emasculation, and Self-Violence as Feminization

As an outline: the last philosopher—modified position of philosophy since Kant. Metaphysics has become impossible— Self-castration. Tragic resignation. The end of philosophy. Only art can save us.
  —Friedrich Nietzsche, *Le Livre du philosophe*[1]

In this chapter I want to take up the question of where woman belongs in Nietzsche's texts and Derrida's texts by examining the *strategies* that they employ in order to open philosophical discourse onto its other. Both Nietzsche and Derrida attempt to undermine traditional philosophical discourse by employing parody and self-parody. Nietzsche attempts to undermine philosophical discourse from within by undermining his own discourse. He maintains that the active and strong writer is one who can laugh, particularly at himself. Derrida takes over Nietzsche's strategy of self-parody and takes it one step further. He suggests that self-parody is necessary for any deconstruction that opens up some other possibilities because without parody we are merely replacing one side of a hierarchical dualism with the other. In some places Derrida characterizes self-parody as a type of autocastration that emasculates philosophy. Through these strategies of autocastration, Derrida suggests that philosophy is feminized. This is, of course, to once again define the feminine in terms of the logic of castration. In fact, on Derrida's reading of Nietzsche, self-parody itself is a feminine operation because, as Nietzsche says, the feminine is what gives itself for what it is not. On Derrida's reading , Nietzsche performs the feminine operation because he engages in self-parody—he gives himself for what he is not. And Derrida himself identifies with woman's marginal position in *Spurs*, because he, too, engages in self-parody. For Derrida self-parody becomes a way to "become woman."

Nietzsche as Ascetic Priest

I suggested earlier that Nietzsche describes a new way of reading and writing that opens onto multiplicity and otherness, what I called an active reading and writing. Given the tradition of philosophical discourse, how does a philosopher engage in this type of reading and writing? Moreover, given that the mechanics of language operate such that any proposition asserts some one truth and seems to close off others, how can we use language to open up the possibility of doing philosophy otherwise?

One strategy that is central to Nietzsche's attempts to use philosophical discourse to undermine philosophical truth is to undermine his own discourse. By using his own philosophy against itself, Nietzsche uses philosophy against itself. He does this in various ways. In *On the Genealogy of Morals*, for example, first, he prefaces the text with remarks that lead the reader in circles through Nietzsche's texts, making it impossible to read them. In addition, he warns his reader that, because he suffers from the very disease which he proposes to diagnose, he is not to be trusted. Further, he maintains that strong readers and writers are those who read and write with their own blood through laughter, laughter at themselves; he claims that only comedy can harm the ascetic ideal. In addition to his strategies for self-undermining (or self-overcoming), he suggests that the active reader and writer create by balancing sensuousness and chastity or body and reason. For Nietzsche, philosophical discourse can be healthy and life-affirming if it comes from the body and blood; but, as we have seen, it turns out that this body and blood are always masculine. I will analyze each of these strategies in the following sections.

The Impossibility of Reading Nietzsche

Nietzsche suggests that "modern men" are not capable of rumination, and, therefore, he says, "it will be some time before my writings are 'readable'" (*OGM* 23 P8). He often anticipates, and writes for, readers of the future. In fact he requires readers of the future, readers who read from the position of the future, retrospective readers; as Nietzsche sets up his writings, they are only readable in retrospect. This is the lesson both of Nietzsche's *description* of reading as art in the preface to *Genealogy* and of his *performance* of reading as art in *Genealogy*. Genealogy, after all, is possible only in retrospect.

Nietzsche frames his reader by indicating that the reader can only read *Genealogy* after reading his "earlier writings" and at the same time positions *Genealogy* as an accessible exegesis of those very writings. Nietzsche says of *Genealogy*, "If this book is incomprehensible to anyone and jars on his ears, the fault, it seems to me, is not necessarily mine. It is clear enough, assuming, as I do assume, that one has first read my earlier writings and has not spared some trouble in doing so: for they are, indeed, not easily accessible [nicht liecht zugänglich]" (OGM 22 P8).[2] Then he mentions the necessarily ambivalent effects (affects) of *Zarathustra* on its reader and cites it as an example of a difficult text. Although Nietzsche says that *Genealogy* is a "sequel" to *Beyond Good and Evil*, he sets up the relationship between *Genealogy* and *Zarathustra* as a trap within which his reader is caught. We cannot read *Genealogy* without first reading *Zarathustra*, but we cannot understand *Zarathustra* without first understanding *Genealogy*. Nietzsche both assumes and denies that his reader can read his past writings.

From the very beginning of *Genealogy*, Nietzsche sets up the impossibility of reading his texts. His lesson in reading Zarathustra's aphorism in essay III becomes an example of the impossibility of reading. It is necessary to have read the earlier text, *Zarathustra*, before reading *Genealogy*, and yet the third essay of *Genealogy* supposedly teaches us how to read *Zarathustra*. We are caught not knowing how to read one without first reading the other. Perhaps this is the circular motion of rumination; in his preface, Nietzsche suggests that his proper reader is a cow and the proper method of reading is rumination.

Nietzsche wants to cultivate a thoughtful, creative reader who actively engages in interpretations, a reader who is willing to work to create an interpretation. Even creative interpretations, however, cannot escape ascribing meaning to the text, just as ascetic priests of all varieties cannot escape ascribing meaning to our suffering. Arthur Danto points out that the conclusion of Nietzsche's analysis of meaning in *On the Genealogy of Morals,* reminiscent of Heidegger's notion of *Dasein*, is that what separates human beings from animals is meaning. Only human beings attribute meaning; only human beings interpret. With self-consciousness comes meaning and with meaning comes bad conscience as we begin to ascribe meaning to our suffering. Danto suggests that "The deep affliction from which he [Nietzsche] seeks to relieve us is what today we think of as hermeneutics: the method of interpretation primarily of suffering. And when he says, in so many places and in so many ways are no facts, only interpretation, he is, I believe, finally addressing the deep, perhaps ineradicable propensity for *ressentiment*. Meaning, *si je puis aphoriser moi-même*, is demeaning" (25).[3]

Nietzsche's Self-Parody
Within its interpretation, active reading acknowledges and diagnoses this ineradicable propensity for interpretation, which, of course, is to admit

that the doctor also suffers from the disease. The doctor, however, teases his patients by reminding them that his disease affects his judgment and thereby undermines his own prescription. In order to counteract the demeaning effects of meaning, he demeans his own quest for meaning; he demeans himself.

For example, *On the Genealogy of Morals* begins with Nietzsche telling us that "we are necessarily strangers to ourselves," himself included (*OGM* P §1, 15). Even more striking is Nietzsche's claim near the end of his apparently self-assured, even cocky, analysis that he, too, is infected with the disease of Western morality and therefore should not be trusted:

> There is reason enough, is there not, for us psychologists nowadays to be able to shake off a certain mistrust of ourselves.
>
> Probably, we too, are still "too good" for our job; probably, we, too, are still victims of and prey to this moralized contemporary task and ill with it, however much we think we despise it—probably it infects even us. (*OGM* III §20, 139)

Part of Nietzsche's reading lesson teaches us to be suspicious, mistrustful readers. As Daniel Conway argues, he teaches us to be suspicious readers by making us mistrust him. Conway argues that Nietzsche's performance of genealogy is made suspicious by the practice of genealogy: "Nietzsche arouses our mistrust of the ascetic ideal by arousing our mistrust of *him*, as a purveyor of the ideal" (80).[4]

Nietzsche also undermines his authorial authority when he defers to his own fictional creations. For example, in the third essay of *On the Genealogy of Morals,* Nietzsche attributes his aphorism to "the work itself," to his fictional creation, Zarathustra. And at the end of the second essay, Nietzsche, mocking himself, claims that only Zarathustra has the right to teach the revaluation of all values; Zarathustra is the rightful teacher, "younger, 'heavier with the future,' and stronger" than Nietzsche himself (*OGM* 96 II 25). Nietzsche inverts the authority of author and text by deferring to the work of art itself, Zarathustra. This deference further complicates the issue of authorship, since nowhere in Nietzsche's writings has the position of Nietzsche's authorship been called into greater question than in *Zarathustra*. Even Nietzsche has no privileged access to Zarathustra's aphorism. Like any artistic reader, he must interpret. He teaches us how to read his texts by displacing his own authority.

Nietzsche does in fact interpret his own writing when, in *On the Genealogy of Morals,* he claims to interpret the aphorism from *Zarathustra* that is affixed to the beginning of the third essay. Recall that this aphorism is part of Zarathustra's lesson "on reading and writing" in

Thus Spake Zarathustra. Nietzsche is teaching us to read his own Zarathustra's lesson on reading. Nietzsche folds reading over onto itself by teaching us to read his lesson on reading. He shows us how to interpret by interpreting himself. In the preface Nietzsche instructs us that "an aphorism, properly stamped and molded, has not been 'deciphered' [*entziffert*] when it has simply been read [*abgelesen ist*]; rather, one has then to begin its exegesis [*Auslegung*], for which is required an art of exegesis" (OGM 23 P8), what he later calls "reading as art" [*Lesen als Kunst*]. Yet in "On Reading and Writing," Zarathustra says that "whoever writes in blood and aphorisms does not want to be read but to be learned by heart" (Z 152 I). What does it mean, then, for Nietzsche to *read* Zarathustra's aphorism? And what does it mean that Nietzsche hasn't learned it by heart? He apparently hasn't, for when he quotes Zarathustra's aphorism in *On the Genealogy of Morals*, he forgets or leaves off the first word, "*mutig*," brave or courageous. "*Mutig, unbekümmert, spöttisch, gewalttätig—so will uns die Weisheit: sie ist ein Weib und liebt immer nur einen Kriegsmann*" (KS II 306).[5] "Courageous, unconcerned, mocking, violent—thus wisdom wants us: she is a woman and always loves only a warrior."

Perhaps by the time of *On the Genealogy of Morals*, Nietzsche has decided that writing and reading have nothing to do with courage; he asks, "Why am I speaking of courage [*Mut*]: only one thing is needed here, the hand, an uninhibited, a very uninhibited hand" (OGM 159 III 26).[6] We don't need *Mut* in order to write and interpret; we need only an uninhibited hand, an unconcerned, mocking, violent hand that wages war through writing.[7]

Laughing at Oneself

Mutig in its origin also means heart, as in "to be learned by heart" or taken to heart. Zarathustra's reading lesson (unlike Nietzsche's?) is about having the heart, the courage to write and read with blood. It is a lesson in reading and writing from the heart, with blood, and yet maintaining the view from the peaks that gives one the ironic distance with which to laugh at all "tragic seriousness," including seriousness in oneself (Z 153 I, "On Reading and Writing"). Zarathustra says, "I am courageous . . . courage wants to laugh." "On Reading and Writing" is about having the courage to laugh at the spirit of gravity. Laughter is the weapon of courageous warriors who write and read with the body and its organs and fluids: "Not by wrath does one kill but by laughter. Come, let us kill the spirit of gravity!" (Z 153). Wisdom loves only the courageous, unconcerned, laughing, warrior.

To laugh, especially at oneself, requires reading and writing with blood. Nietzsche's own wit is incisive and cuts to the quick. If the greatest challenge is to kill the spirit of gravity in oneself, then, once again, aggression must be turned inward—using its own logic, the ascetic ideal must be turned against itself—and one must write with one's own blood. Every artist, says Nietzsche "arrives at the ultimate pinnacle of his greatness only when he comes to see himself and his art *beneath* him—when he knows how to *laugh* at himself" (*OGM* 99 III 3). It is only from the *spöttisch* position on the peak that the artist can see himself and his art beneath him in order to laugh at himself. The reader/writer as artist must be violent and mocking toward himself. Only through parody, especially parody of oneself, can the "crudest form . . . of the antinature of the ascetic ideal" be overcome (*OGM* 99 III 3).[8] In the *Antichrist* Nietzsche suggests that asceticism can become active in "the most spiritual men" whose "joy is self-conquest": "The most spiritual men . . . find their happiness where others would find their destruction: in the labyrinth, in hardness against themselves and others, in experimentation; their joy is self-conquest; asceticism becomes in them nature, need and instinct. Difficult tasks are a privilege to them; to play with burdens which crush others, a recreation" (*AC* 57).[9]

The artist or genealogist is a faker who laughs at himself. Unlike the priest he is not a serious representative of the ascetic ideal. The ascetic priest is the most serious representative of the ascetic ideal because he is a reactive reader. He provides an interpretation of suffering and bad conscience that he takes seriously; he believes in himself and sees only himself everywhere he looks.[10] He promotes his interpretation at the expense of all others without the self-parody that characterizes the artist or the genealogist who sees his interpretation as yet another symptom of the disease.

We could say that laughter, like most Nietzschean notions, has both a reactive and active form. The difference between them is the difference between *laughing at* and *laughing with*. "How many *comedians* of the Christian-moral ideal would have to be exported from Europe today before its air would begin to smell fresh again?" asks Nietzsche (*OGM* 159 III 26). He describes these comedians as espousing sham ideals in heroic trappings. They are charlatans through and through; worse than this they are *transparent* charlatans. And for this reason—that they do not take their ideals seriously even as they take themselves seriously—they are laughable. The seriousness of those comic figures who merely flirt with the ascetic ideal because it is fashionable cannot be taken seriously. They are not courageous. They cannot laugh; rather they are laughed at.

Nietzsche mocks their weakness, their effeminacy, their emasculation: "this lascivious historical eunuchism, this flirting with ascetic ideals, this justice-tartuffery of impotence!" (*OGM* 158 III 26).

Yet in the next section of the third essay, Nietzsche says that only laughter can harm the ascetic ideal: "the ascetic ideal has at present only *one* kind of real enemy capable of *harming* it: the comedians of this ideal—for they arouse mistrust of it" (*OGM* 160 III 27). The comedians of the ascetic ideal who are the real enemy of the ascetic ideal are those who not only do not take their ideals seriously but also do not take themselves seriously. Those comedians of the ascetic ideal who merely flirt with that ideal because it is fashionable make us laugh. We laugh at them. But when the real enemy of the ascetic ideal employs that ideal against itself by employing it against himself, then the comedian becomes a warrior sacrificing himself for a laugh. This comedian's laughing *at* himself is his laughing *with* his readers. The reactive comedian, on the other hand, is a reactive reader who takes the presentation of his sham ideals too seriously. He can't laugh at himself even though he is a joke.[11] These jokers are impotent and therefore cannot be taken to heart, especially by wisdom. She is a woman and loves only a warrior who is "hard" enough to be elevated and laugh at the same time. She loves a warrior who is hard on himself, constantly overcoming himself. Self-overcoming is always both destructive and creative and as such is violent. Writing as self-overcoming is going to be writing as *Streitschrift*, polemic—*Genealogy*'s subtitle is "*Eine Streitschrift*." Only through conflict can something new appear.

Nietzsche employs his philosophy of self-overcoming in his own writing. Through self-parody he engages in a process of self-overcoming that is designed to induce philosophy's self-overcoming. By undercutting his own position of authority, Nietzsche undercuts the authority of the philosopher, and thereby of philosophy. He introduces what he sees as the fertile seeds of self-overcoming so that a new way of doing philosophy might be born. He imagines doing philosophy otherwise. He imagines a philosophy of the body to replace the tradition of downgrading the body and the sensuous.

The Wedding of Sensuousness and Chastity

For Nietzsche various instantiations of the ascetic ideal are self-overcoming insofar as they give birth to something else, something life-affirming. Even bad conscience, within which the ascetic ideal festers, is "an illness as pregnancy is an illness" (*OGM* 88 II 19). Nietzsche suggests that bad conscience gives birth to a great health; and at the end of the second essay he alludes to the *Übermensch* as this offspring, this *Mensch* of the future who will restore values to the earth (to our sensuous, finite existence) and about whom only Zarathustra, "heavier with the future," can teach us. He also talks about the artist as the "womb" out of which the art work grows and about philosophy's "periods of great pregnancy" and its "'maternal' instinct," which "ruthlessly disposes of all other stores and accumulations of energy, of animal vigor, for the benefit of the evolving work" (*OGM* 100, 111, 110). Creative uses of the ascetic ideal can be signs of strength rather than weakness when they don't deny sensuousness but instead give birth to a work of art. These works of art, although born of the discipline of an ascetic ideal, must come from the body and its organs and fluids, heart and blood.

These works of art come from the union of chastity and sensuality: "For there is no necessary antithesis between chastity and sensuality; every good marriage, every genuine love affair, transcends this antithesis" (*OGM* 98 III 2). The tension between chastity and sensuality is "one more stimulus to life. It is precisely such 'contradictions' that seduce one to existence" (*OGM* 99 III 2). The ascetic ideal in women is such a seduction, part divine and part animal. "In the case of women," says Nietzsche, the ascetic ideal is "at best one more seductive charm, a touch of *morbidezza* in fair flesh, the angelic look of a plump pretty animal" (*OGM* 97 III 1). Zarathustra is another such seduction. Both chaste and sensuous, Zarathustra is pregnant with, sire to, the future [*Zukünftigeren*] (*OGM* 96 II 25). He teaches the *Übermensch*, the embodiment of a healthier way of valuing. As such, Nietzsche says that *Zarathustra* provides the first "counterideal" to the ascetic ideal (*EH* 313).[12] Zarathustra is the sensuous high priestess of the cult of the *Übermensch*.

Wisdom is seduced by this contradiction between chastity and sensuousness. She loves the chaste sensuality of a "more severe, harder, healthier" ascetic ideal, a counterideal that is fecund and gives birth to something beyond itself (see *OGM* 137 III 19). Wisdom loves only potency, a robust laughing potency, which wants self-overcoming through procreation. *Is* it this tension between chastity and sensuality that makes for a genuine love affair between wisdom and the warrior?

Wisdom loves those warriors who read and write from the bodily force of their sexual energy, which builds through the tension between sensuality and chastity. The sensuality of writing becomes apparent even in Nietzsche's interpretation of Schopenhauer. Schopenhauer, Nietzsche suggests, characterizes the aesthetic as the result of subduing sex drives. Nietzsche argues against Schopenhauer that with the aesthetic "sensuality is not overcome . . . but only transfigured and no longer enters consciousness as sexual excitement" (*OGM* 111 III 8). Nietzsche opposes

Schopenhauer to Stendhal, who characterizes the aesthetic as the arousal of sex drives: "the sight of the beautiful obviously had upon him the effect of *releasing* the *chief energy* of this nature (the energy of contemplation and penetration), so that this *exploded* and all at once became the master of his consciousness" [*OGM* 111 III 8].[13] Nietzsche's metaphors of releasing and exploding conjure images of masculine sexuality. For Nietzsche writing seems to be one release of masculine sexual energy.[14] And the body that gives birth to the new philosophy is the male body. In *Ecce Homo*, once again using what could be interpreted as masculine metaphors of sexual rhythm, Nietzsche describes his own expression, intention and art, in the uncanny Dionysian polemic *Genealogy,* as a result of a tremendous tension that gradually builds to a fierce tempo until in the end something new is conceived: "Every time a beginning that is *calculated* to mislead: cool, scientific, even ironic, deliberately foreground, deliberately holding off. Gradually more unrest; sporadic lightning; very disagreeable truths are heard grumbling in the distance—until eventually a *tempo feroce* is attained in which everything rushes ahead in a tremendous tension. In the end, in the midst of perfectly gruesome detonations, a new truth becomes visible every time among thick clouds" (*E H* 312).

The difference between the warrior and the priest is that the priest is impotent (OGM 33 I 7). The priest is impotent because he is concerned and serious; moreover, unlike the artist/warrior he denies, rather than sublimates, the bodily force that drives him. For Nietzsche impotence is the real enemy of life; "one is today ashamed of hardness," says Nietzsche. (*OGM* 114 III 9). It is no wonder that he chooses the god of fertility, Dionysus, whose symbols are blood red wine and the tumescent phallus, to represent life's force. Repeatedly, moreover, Nietzsche figures degenerate life in the form of the slave morality and the ascetic ideal in terms of castration, emasculation, effeminacy, and impotence. The most emasculating aspect of degenerating life and the ascetic ideal is its attempt to foreclose interpretative possibilities and insist on one "objective" standard:

> Let us be on guard against the snares of such contradictory concepts as "pure reason," "absolute spirituality," "knowledge in itself": these always demand that we should think of an eye that is completely unthinkable, an eye turned in no particular direction, in which the active and interpreting forces, through which alone seeing becomes seeing something, are supposed to be lacking; these always demand of the eye absurdity and nonsense. . . . But to eliminate the will altogether, to suspend each and every affect, supposing we were capable of this—what would that mean but to castrate the intellect? (OGM 119 III 12)

That which multiples perspectives is potent, healthy, full of life's force, while that which narrows perspectives is impotent, sick, cut off from life's force. Wisdom wants a potency that is an enemy to all that is impotent, emasculated, or castrated.

For Nietzsche, wisdom is coupled with brute sensuousness and animal aggression in the figure of the unconcerned, mocking, violent warrior. The ascetic denial of the body becomes the focusing of bodily energy, the fusion of chastity and sensuousness that gives birth to healthy values and healthy readers and writers. Yet the healthy reader seems to be one who cannot read. And the healthy writer seems to be one who undermines everything that he says. As Nietzsche says in his own self-contradictory way: "An aphorism, properly stamped and molded, has not been 'deciphered' when it has simply been read," and yet, as I have noted, "whoever writes in blood and aphorisms does not want to be read but to be learned by heart." Taking Nietzsche to heart requires that we attempt the impossible and, like the warrior, have our way with the text in order to venture a reading. Here, however, we must take care, because the warrior, like the figures of the ascetic ideal, reading, wisdom, and woman, is ambiguous; Nietzsche suggests that the worst readers "act like plundering soldiers"—what better way to mock without concern than to plunder?[15] Isn't that what Nietzsche does to the ascetic ideal? Like the plundering soldier he steals its armor and wears it mockingly, making fun of his enemy. By doing so, however, he is always also mocking himself. He dresses up as a priest in order to laugh at himself. This laughter is the only thing that sets the faker apart from the real thing.

Within Nietzsche's texts the active reader and writer is strong enough, hard enough, to engage in self-overcoming and self-undermining, which are separated from priestly self-flagellation only by laughter. But even this laughter is a way of undermining the self. It is laughter turned against the self, laughter turned inward. It seems that within this scenario, in order to open up the possibility of doing philosophy otherwise, an author must subject himself to self-violence. He must take a dagger to his own heart in order to read and write with blood from the heart. In Nietzsche this violence is characterized by masculine metaphors of potency and hardness, and the inability to laugh while wounding oneself is taken as a sign of effeminacy and emasculation.

Deconstruction as Autocastration

Femininity is the Truth (of) castration.
—Jacques Derrida, "Le Facteur de la Vérité" in The Post Card

Following Nietzsche, Derrida maintains that philosophical discourse must become self-parodic in order to open itself onto its other. He proposes a deconstruction that is not only negative but also affirmative to perform this function. Using parody, affirmative deconstruction goes further than other types of criticism of the status quo. For Derrida parody enables affirmative deconstruction to challenge not only traditional concepts but also traditional structures and the very conditions of doing philosophy. This parody, however, becomes associated with auto-castration. And in the end, Derrida suggests that autocastration feminizes the text of philosophy. The process of feminization through emasculation has serious consequences for the relation to the other, specifically the feminine other that Derrida takes as his model. As I argue below, the move to feminize philosophy through emasculation still operates within a masculine economy of castration, and effectively forecloses the possibility of a feminine other. Derrida promises, however, that his new form of deconstruction opens onto, and answers the call of, the other and thereby opens onto the possibility of doing philosophy otherwise. I will begin this section with an analysis of the potential of Derrida's affirmative deconstruction to open onto the space of the other, or otherness. My thesis is that Derrida's methodology is not appropriate to his task—that is, opening philosophy onto its other. Specifically my analysis of what Derrida calls *affirmative deconstruction* will suggest that his methodology still operates within the economy or logic of the *propre*, proper—in the sense of property, ownership, one's own proper self, or the self-same. This is the very economy or logic that Derrida suggests he is trying to escape. Moreover, even if Derrida's deconstruction is promising as a way to attend to "the other" of Western metaphysics and opens up possibilities of doing philosophy otherwise, at the same time it closes off the possibility of philosophy speaking to, or from, a specifically feminine other.

In "Of an Apocalyptic Tone" Derrida indicates two elements essential to affirmative deconstruction: It must undermine its own dependence on the discourse that it deconstructs by employing parody and irony and it must posit an alternative to the deconstructed discourse. Derrida argues that the two important differences between deconstruction and "progressive demystification in the style of Enlightenment" (ATP 60) are that deconstruction engages in the discourse that it is deconstructing *ironically* and thereby undermines apocalyptic discourse (by undermining itself) and that deconstruction suggests something other (ATP 60–61). While Enlightenment demystification exposes falsity, tricks and illusions, it does not ask to what end; it does not suggest something other.

According to Derrida, Heidegger's writing shares this same short-coming. Heidegger's *Destruktion* is only negative and not also affirmative. Although Heidegger addresses the call from the other within philosophy and insists that philosophy thrives only by listening to the call from what has been inadmissible to it, Derrida claims that the ethical responsibility to the other is lacking in Heideggerian destruction:

> I do not know whether from this nameless thing called the final solution one can draw something which still deserves the name of a lesson. But if there were a lesson to be drawn, a unique lesson among the singular lessons of murder, from even a single murder, from all the collective exterminations of history (because each individual murder and each collective murder is singular, thus infinite and incommensurable) the lesson that we can draw today—and if we can do so then we must—is that we must think, know, represent for ourselves, formalize, judge the possible complicity between all these discourses and the worst (here the final solution). In my view, this defines a task and a responsibility the theme of which (yes, the theme) I have not been able to read in either Benjaminian "deconstruction" or Heideggerian "Destruktion." It is the thought of difference between these destructions on the one hand and a deconstructive affirmation on the other that has guided me tonight in this reading. (FL 62–63)

In this passage from "Force of Law," an essay on justice, Derrida identifies a responsibility for reading and writing, an ethics of reading and writing. This responsibility takes hold as soon as we begin to signify. We not only have a responsibility to other people but we also have a responsibility to face up to the other within our own texts, the meaning (and non-meaning) that these texts generate. Derrida suggests that deconstruction holds texts responsible for their complicity with the worst, in his example the holocaust. His essay in *The Ear of the Other*, for example, is an attempt to diagnose the complicity of Nietzsche's writing and Fascism. In the passage above Derrida calls on the holocaust, possibly the limit case, to explain the relationship between deconstruction and ethics and politics.[16] He promises a deconstructive affirmation that takes us beyond a Heideggerian destruction and makes possible a responsibility for ourselves and to the other.

Derrida suggests that this responsibility requires an examination of the very structures and conditions of discourse. In order to change the structure and conditions of discourse we need to go beyond a negative decontruction. We need to engage in an affirmative deconstruction that first inverts traditional hierarchies but does not stop there. More than this—and this is what separates deconstruction from Enlightenment demystification—deconstruction unsettles the conditions of its own production; it undermines itself. The affirmative deconstruction is a double-movement that not only undermines traditional concepts but creates spaces for new concepts by engaging in a parody of itself. By undermining itself, deconstruction exposes the ways in which our discourse needs its other. Derrida suggests that it is the double movement of deconstruction that opens on to the other and makes/marks the possibility of difference:

> The deconstruction I am invoking only invents or affirms, lets the other come insofar as, in the performative, it is not only performative but also continues to unsettle the conditions of the performative and of whatever distinguishes it comfortably from the constative. This writing is liable to the other, opened to and by the other, to the work of the other; it is writing working at not letting itself be enclosed or dominated by this economy of the same in its totality. . . . the [classical] economic circle of invention is only a movement for reappropriating exactly what sets it in motion, the difference of the other. (Psy 61)

In order to get beyond classical economies of signification in which invention is merely the reappropriation of difference into the logic of the same, Derrida suggests that we employ a deconstruction that affirms difference; as such it goes beyond the negative strategy that he identifies with Heidegger's *Destruktion* and opens the possibility of the difference of the other. Derrida maintains that in the history of Western philosophy the difference of the other that has been excluded can be, and often is, figured as feminine difference. But it remains to be seen whether or not deconstruction fulfills its promise to open onto feminine difference.

Although he also denies that deconstruction is a formal strategy of reading, in several places Derrida does describe the procedure of what he calls "affirmative" deconstruction. In the interviews in *Positions,* Derrida talks about the double gesture, double mark, or double science of deconstruction. the process seems to include three moves: The first move is to overturn existing hierarchies; the second is to introduce a "concept" that is beyond the opposition; and the third is to mark the interval between the original hierarchical opposition and the new "concept" (*P* 41–43). The first stage is necessary so that we don't too quickly try to jump beyond metaphysical oppositions, which is destined to failure. The second is necessary so that we don't remain stuck on the level of metaphysical oppositions. And the third, dependent on the first two, opens up another economy of meaning beyond a metaphysical economy that turns everything into a question of possession. The first stage of inversion makes way for the second stage of the undecidable concept; and examining the difference between the original hierarchical concepts and the new undecidable concepts opens up the possibility of a new way of valuing. Derrida insists on this third phase, marking an interval between the first two phases, because deconstruction is never a matter of simply introducing new concepts. The "concepts" that occupy the new space opened up by the inversion cannot be posited in the same way as the old oppositional concepts. They must operate within a different economy altogether; they must break out of the economy that reduces everything to the same, the proper, property. Derrida says in *Positions*: "to remain in this phase (the first phase of overturning) is still to operate on the terrain of and from within the deconstructed system. By means of this double, and precisely stratified, dislodged and dislodging, writing, we must also mark the interval between inversion, which brings low what was high, and the irruptive emergence of a new 'concept,' a concept that can no longer be, and never could be, included in the previous regime" (*P* 42).

Derrida cites examples of his new "concepts":

> The *pharmakon* is neither remedy nor poison, neither good nor evil, neither the inside nor the outside, neither speech nor writing; the *supplement* is neither a plus nor a minus, neither an outside nor the complement of an inside, neither accident nor essence, etc.; the *hymen* is neither confusion nor distinction, neither identity nor difference, neither consummation nor virginity, neither the veil nor unveiling, neither the inside not the outside, etc.; the *gram* is neither a signifier nor a signified, neither a sign nor a thing, neither a presence nor an absence, neither a position nor a negation, etc. (*P* 43)

These new "concepts"—pharmakon, supplement, hymen, gram, etc.—operate within an economy of undecidables. In Derrida's view, it is the possibility of this new economy of undecidables that takes his deconstruction beyond Heidegger. Derrida's philosophy does not just negate or deny the traditional economy of truth; rather it opens up a new economy. Between the double movements of deconstruction, "one can operate both an overturning deconstruction and a positively displacing, transgressive, deconstruction" (*P* 66). And this opens up the possibility of determining "*otherwise*, according to a differential system, the *effects* of ideality, of signification, of meaning, and of reference" (*P* 66). Derrida opens up the possibility of difference with the introduction of undecidable "concepts" after the inversion of a hierarchical opposition. He suggests that these concepts can never be contained within the logic of the proper. I will return to Derrida's undecidables in the next chapter when I argue that Derrida's use of inversion to open onto the Other is problematic. For now, I will focus on Derrida's insistence on parody or irony in affirmative deconstruction.

Derrida introduces his notion of affirmative deconstruction in *Spurs*, his reading of (Heidegger's) Nietzsche. He claims that *Spurs* launches "a new phase in the process of deconstructive interpretation, that is to say affirmative"[40] (S 36-37). Later in *Spurs* Derrida takes up Heidegger's discussion of Nietzsche's inversion strategy. In seeming agreement with Heidegger, Derrida indicates that Nietzsche wants more than a mere reversal of values. He does not want to merely affirm an inversion of the original hierarchy. Rather he wants to transform the hierarchical structure. "What must occur then is not merely a suppression of all hierarchy, for an-archy only consolidates just as surely the established order of a metaphysical hierarchy; nor is it a simple change or reversal in the terms of any given hierarchy. Rather, the *Umdrehung* [inversion] must be a transformation of the hierarchical structure itself" (S 81). It is not the values of the terms in the hierarchy that have been re-valued but the very value of hierarchy itself that has been re-valued.

But how does one perform this reversal of values that challenges the very value structure itself? How does one perform the double movement of affirmative deconstruction such that the reversal of values opens onto a way of valuing otherwise? This is the problem that Nietzsche addresses with blood, both the blood of his readers and his own blood. As I have previously argued, for Nietzsche this type of self-overcoming requires violence, particularly self-violence in the form of self-parody. Derrida seems to follow Nietzsche's lead when he claims in *Spurs* that in order to go beyond merely a reaffirmation of a now inverted hierarchy the inversion strategy must be accompanied by parody: "For the reversal, if it is not accompanied by a discrete parody, a strategy of writing, or difference or deviation in quills, if there is no style, no grand style, this is finally but the same thing, nothing more than a clamorous declaration of the antithesis. Hence the heterogeneity of the text" (S 95).

In this passage Derrida is pointing to the heterogeneity of Nietzsche's texts, which he says is the manifestation that Nietzsche "had no illusions" that he would ever know the ontological effects of any of his subject matter (S 95). It is curious, however, that Derrida proposes that his own strategy will not be to take up that heterogeneity which prevents metaphysical delusions and instead will formalize the "principle" of the positions of woman in Nietzsche's texts "in order to mark the essential limit of such a codification and the problem that it entails for reading" (S 95). Derrida's strategy, then, is to set the metaphysical trap in order to make his reader feel its sting. Of course at that point it is too late, we have been caught once again in the metaphysics of presence, and our only alternative is to chew off a limb in order to escape. Like Nietzsche, Derrida does violence to his reader; in places within his discourse this violence becomes figured in terms of castration. In spite of the fact that he suggests that *Spurs* provides an alternative economy to the Lacanian economy of castration (which I will analyze later) within Derrida's scenario there is no way to escape castration. The only defense against castration is autocastration, no defense at all.

Toward the end of *Spurs,* Derrida teases his reader by suggesting that the totality of his text might be a parody, a parody of Nietzsche perhaps, certainly a parody of Heidegger, and necessarily a parody of itself: "Suppose further that in some way the totality which I (so to speak) have presented is also an erratic, even parodying graft" (S 135). Even while talking of parody Derrida makes fun of his own use of "I" "(so to speak)." Even in *Spurs,* a text that launches affirmative deconstruction, a text where he presents a reading of Nietzsche's texts that do not force them to deconstruct themselves, Derrida ends by undermining his own reading project. How are we to read this possible parody? This of course is Derrida's point, that the meaning of his text is as radically undecidable as Nietzsche's "I have forgotten my umbrella." Yet the only way to read this text that cannot decide—that suggests that everything the reader has heretofore taken seriously is a joke—is as self-parody.

If the history of philosophy is the history of violence, effacement and castration, as Derrida claims in "White Mythology," then Derrida's self-parodying deconstruction is just the latest phase in this history of violence. As with Nietzsche's ascetic priest, violence is turned inward and directed against the self. It is as if the only way that Derrida can imagine opening a space for the other is by killing off the self. The only way to prevent murder is by committing suicide. Clearly we are still trapped within the Hegelian master-slave dialectic where one exists only at the expense of another.

Derrida refers to his strategy in *Glas* as a type of autocastration. He talks of castrating oneself in order to avoid castration. Here he calls this process "Medusa'ing oneself" or even "eating" oneself (*Glas* 202). In another self-referential and self-undermining move, couched within his discussion of Genet's *Our Lady of the Flowers,* Derrida claims that if he writes in two columns that he cannot be castrated because he castrates himself:

> If I write two texts at once, you will not be able to castrate me. If I delinearize, I erect. But at the same time I divide my act and my desire. I—mark(s) the division, and always escaping you, I simulate unceasingly and take my pleasure nowhere. I castrate myself—I remain(s) myself thus—and I "play at coming" [*je "joue à jouir"*]. (Glas 65)

Derrida's "playing at coming" is reminiscent of Nietzsche's description of woman as the actress who "gives herself for," "gives herself airs," "even as she gives herself,"—an aphorism from the *Gay Science* that Derrida makes much of in *Spurs* (GS §361; cf. *Spurs* 69). Is this play at coming and auto-castration the "feminine operation" that Derrida associates with Nietzsche in *Spurs* even while operating from a self-proclaimed marginal position that he intimates could be the space of this feminine operation? Derrida claims that Nietzsche performs the feminine operation because his texts undermine themselves; he plays with truth by playing with the truth of his own texts. Derrida identifies Nietzsche with both the castrating and castrated women.[41] Is castration the feminine operation? Is autocastration the operation that feminizes? For Derrida the feminine operation seems to be the operation of autocastration. It is the operation that under-cuts itself and gives itself for something that it is not. It is the masculine operation of identifying with woman and the feminine by emasculating himself. It is this operation that feminizes the masculine text.

Derrida feminizes his text so that he won't have to face a feminine other. Although, unlike Heidegger, Derrida does not ignore Nietzsche's "it [the idea] becomes female," he uses becoming female to fortify philosophy against the suicide that it finally commits through its long history of murdering its other which has been represented by the feminine. While Derrida makes gestures to acknowledge the otherness of the specifically feminine other, at the same time he forecloses any possibility of recognizing any other in the feminine because the masculine has become the feminine. She is what he has made her; and more than this she is what he has made himself. She is nothing in herself. She is neither self nor any longer other. The masculine self therefore has no other through whom to find its self-recognition and dies along with her.

TWO

THE ETHICS OF SEXUAL DIFFERENCE
The Problem of the One and the Many

If within yourself you no longer find the strength to live, might it not be time to listen to the other, rather than tear holes in her body and drain her blood drop by drop? It is voices from beyond the grave who take such food, is it not? Messengers of death who drink such wine?
— Luce Irigaray, *Marine Lover of Friedrich Nietzsche*

INTRODUCTION
Why Sexual Difference?

Traditionally philosophers have avoided or ignored the question of sexual difference. They have formulated theories of neuter subjects and sexually neutral experience. Sex was taken as a secondary or even accidental characteristic. Often the male subject and experience were taken as the norm. But what if the notions of neuter subjects and sexually neutral experience are fictions not only because the characteristics traditionally associated with such subjects and experiences leave out much of human experience, but also because subjects and their experiences are always sexed? What if the onset of subjectivity, the very ability to conceive of oneself as a subject, is simultaneous with the onset of conceiving of oneself as belonging to a particular sex? Of course, this is the revelation of psychoanalysis. Freud links the onset of subjectivity to the onset of sexuality, for him always defined in terms of masculine sexuality. If philosophers take seriously this premise of psychoanalysis, then any theory of the subject is also a theory of sexual difference (or the lack of it).

In *Bodies That Matter* Judith Butler, describes how the subject is always sexed and how a subject's sex is constituted and normalized through cultural institutions and prohibitions. She maintains that "the subject, the speaking 'I,' is formed by virtue of having gone through [such] a process of assuming a sex" *(BM* 3). For Butler, sex is not the biologically given material body on which the cultural associations of gender are overlaid. Rather, sex is a cultural norm that continually shapes bodies. Butler proposes what I will call a dialectic between material bodies and their cultural-linguistic construction. She does not commit to either the belief that (sexed) bodies are purely cultural or linguistic constructions or the belief that (sexed) bodies are precultural or prelinguistic; rather (sexed) bodies are both constructed by culture and language *and* in excess of that construction:

> To posit a materiality outside of language, where that materiality is considered ontologically distinct from language, is to undermine the

possibility that language might be able to indicate or correspond to that domain of radical alterity. Hence, the absolute distinction between language and materiality which was to secure the referential function of language undermines that function radically. This is not to say that, on the one hand, the body is simply linguistic stuff or, on the other, that is has no bearing on language. . . . every effort to refer to materiality takes place through a signifying process which, in its phenomenality, is always already material. (BM 68)

She takes this same line of argument with regard to the subject. The subject is neither purely culturally or linguistically constructed nor is it entirely outside of culture and language; rather the subject is both constructed by and in excess of culture and language: "Subjected to gender, but subjectivated by gender, the 'I' neither precedes nor follows the process of this gendering, but emerges only within and as the matrix of gender relations themselves" (BM 7). We could say that both the material body and the subject or "I" emerge in the intersection "between" nature and culture, the encounter "between" matter and language. This emergence, or "between," serves to problematize, even deconstruct, the oppositions nature/culture, matter/language. As I argue later, the boundaries between nature and culture blur to a point where we have to rethink both categories and their relationship to each other.

On Butler's analysis there is always an "outside" to language and culture, an outside that is constitutive of the norms of language and culture. Following Kristeva, Butler claims that identity is constituted by excluding or "abjecting" certain possibilities in order to define what is against what cannot be (BM 3). We can reconstitute identity by investigating what has been excluded so that our culture and its norms can be (identical to themselves). Butler suggests that within our culture some bodies matter and some bodies do not matter; a body has material, matter, only if it has significance for the culture.

Throughout her writing Irigaray has argued that the feminine body is a body that does not matter; it has been excluded from our culture. She continually argues that there is only one sex, the masculine: "The law that orders our society is the exclusive valorization of men's needs/desires, of exchanges among men. What the anthropologists call the passage from nature to culture thus amounts to the institution of the reign of hom(m)osexuality" (hommo—man, homo) (TS 171). She argues that the "'feminine' is never to be identified except by and for the masculine, the reciprocal proposition not being 'true'" (TS 85). Within Western culture feminine sexuality is the sex which is not one: the feminine is not a sex; it is always merely the flip side of the masculine. And feminine sexuality is not just one sexuality. It is not centered on one place; rather its erogenous zones are multiple.

Irigaray does not propose that we replace the masculine with the feminine. Rather, in her writing she continually calls for two sexes that must engage in reciprocal exchange and communication; she calls for an ethics of sexual difference. Ethics requires obligations between different subjects, and if there is only one masculine subject relating only to himself, then there can be no discussion of obligations to others; there can be no ethics. Irigaray imagines an ethics of sexual difference, an ethics founded on erotic wonder through difference. She calls for an ethics of passion through which each sex rejoices in the wonder of the other to the point of divinity. She says that "a sexual or carnal ethics would demand that both angel and body be found together" (TS 127). The ethics of sexual difference found relationships on the divine in-between represented by the embodied angel. This ethics reconceives of relationships based on an erotic excess that results from an exchange with difference, the other.

Irigaray's concern, however, with the primacy of sexual difference is not only a concern for ethics but also a concern for metaphysics. I read her insistence that sexual difference is primary and that we need two sexes as a return to the ancient metaphysical problem of the one and the many. Some of the ancients, Parmenides for example, proposed that all is One in order to ensure that we can know reality. Yet proponents of this view had a very difficult time explaining change and difference. But if all is not One, then is all change and difference without the possibility of identity? As soon as we allow that change and difference are real, then how can we know anything? This was Plato's problem. Once we allow any change or difference, haven't we stepped onto the slippery slope that leads to Cratylus's position, shaking our fingers? How can we say anything about this ever changing reality? Irigaray proposes that originally we are two, not just one; and these two don't merely engage in finger shaking, but in meaningful and reciprocal dialogue across (because of) difference. Until there are two (different sexes), there cannot be more, the many.

If there are not two (different sexes) not only is the many impossible, but the one is impossible as well. Irigaray maintains that in our culture everything has been defined in terms of the masculine subject relating to himself. This self-relationship, which does not detour through any other, is no relationship at all. Even the masculine subject cannot sustain itself without an other who has not been subsumed into his own identity. In this regard, until there are two, there cannot be one. In a Hegelian move, Irigaray says that "because he fails to leave her a subjective life, and to be on occasion her place and her thing in a subjective dynamic, man remains within a master-slave dialectic" (ESD 10). In this master-slave dialectic, unless each self-consciousness is both master and slave for the other, then there cannot be any self-recognition by either. There is not one self-consciousness until there are two self-consciousnesses. In addition, if we are ever to live together as one couple, one society, one people, we must first be two (and more) (cf. SG 179).

A unifying love requires two: "It takes two to love. To know how to separate and how to come back together. Each to go, both he and she, in quest of self, faithful to the quest, so they may greet one another, come close, make merry, or seal a covenant" (ESD 71). In J'aime à toi, Irigaray proposes an ethics and politics based on love between man and woman. She claims that one of the most pertinent questions of our epoch is that of how to say in other words "I love you" (JH 201). Irigaray explains that in Western culture it is as if men and women speak two different languages and don't realize it, because within our political and social systems all people are supposed to be treated as neuter individuals. Irigaray argues that: "in order to love, it is necessary to be two persons. A person defines itself by a civil identity. But the definition of woman as woman does not exist in the civil Code, neither does that of man insofar as he is man for that matter. Man and woman are not therefore defined as sexed identities in love but as neuter individuals, indeed nonexistent, or as instinctive and reproductive nature" (Jat 205).[1]

For Irigaray sexual difference is primary; until we have sexual difference we cannot have ontological difference. In "Le Féminin and Nihilism," Ellen Mortensen argues that Irigaray's notion of le féminin operates in the same way as Heidegger's notion of Being. She claims that, like Heidegger's Being, le féminin does not appear and yet it is. Because it does not appear—it is not a thing, or a being among beings—we cannot say what it is. We can only say what it is not. Just as for Heidegger describing Being in metaphysical terms turns Being into a being and confuses the ontological and the ontic, for Irigaray describing le féminin in terms of femininity or other characteristics associated with the feminine or woman confuses sexual difference and a patriarchal hom(m)o-sexuality that defines woman and the feminine in terms of the masculine. Mortensen suggests that Irigaray places le féminin and sexual difference in the premetaphysical place of primacy that Heidegger reserves for Being and ontological difference.

For centuries philosophers have been concerned with ontological difference and have forgotten about sexual difference. For Irigaray the problem of sexual difference is the most pressing problem of our age (*ESD* 5). If, as Descartes suggests, wonder is the first passion and therefore the heart of philosophy, then the wonder at sexual difference should be a beginning for philosophy. Few experiences are as wonder-full:

> Thus man and woman, woman and man are always meeting as though
> for the first time because they cannot be substituted one for the other. I
> will never be in a man's place, never will a man be in mine. Whatever
> identifications are possible, one will never exactly occupy the place of the
> other—they are irreducible one to the other. . . . Who or what the other is,
> I never know. But the other who is forever unknowable is the one who
> differs from me sexually. This feeling of surprise, astonishment, and
> wonder in the face of the unknowable ought to be returned to its locus:
> that of sexual difference. (ESD 13)

Irigaray calls for an acknowledgment of sexual difference that gives rise to an experience of wonder and awe that is the source of all thinking. Not only may sexual difference be inseparable from the constitution of the subject, but it may also engender a radical wonder that has been identified with the very possibility of philosophical thought from Plato through Descartes to Husserl. If ontological difference is in any way dependent on sexual difference—either because sexual difference is primary or because sexual difference stands in a dialectical relation to ontological difference—then self-consciousness, ethics, love, and the possibility of philosophical thought are intimately tied to sexual difference. As long as the feminine is excluded from cultural significance and allowed only to subsist, ethics, love and thought are impoverished, starving for an exchange with an other that can provide the breath of life.

In the first part of this book I took up the question "How can a woman read the texts of Freud, Nietzsche, and Derrida?" My thesis is that all three of them try to formulate a theory that opens onto the other of theory—the body, the unconscious, nonmeaning—but at the same time they close off the specifically feminine other. I analyzed the styles used by Nietzsche and Derrida to attempt this opening that also ends up closing. In this part I turn to the question "how can we open philosophy to sexual difference?"

3   The Question of Appropriation

Derrida's *Spurs* raises the question of belonging: What is proper or appro-priate to the text?[1] He uses the texts of Nietzsche as an attempt to decon-struct this question of propriety by bringing the spur, the mark, or the trace from the margins to the center of the text. He bothers us, his read-ers, about where to put these spurs—those thorns in our sides that we would just as soon forget in our readings—that keep pricking us from the margins as we read. Derrida wants to show that what does not seem to belong to the text not only belongs but also anchors the text. Derrida's concern with belonging in *Spurs* comes from Heidegger's claim that Nietzsche's notion of the will to power is a metaphysical notion, that the will to power *belongs* to metaphysics: "In presuming to penetrate to the most intimate reaches of Nietzsche's thinking will, Heidegger concludes that this will, because it aimed to culminate it, still properly *belonged* [*appartenait*] to the history of metaphysics. This might yet be the case—if one persists in the assumption that some single meaning can still be attached to the value of *belonging* [*appartenance*], that this value is not already its own abduction" (*S* 115).

In *Spurs*' second postscript Derrida suggests that by not forgetting Nietzsche's umbrella, we can learn Heidegger's lesson about metaphysics' forgetting of Being. At the end of *Spurs*, Derrida quotes Heidegger: "Thus, in a thousand ways, has the 'forgetting of Being' been represented as if Being (figuratively speaking) were the umbrella that some philoso-phy professor, in his distraction, left somewhere. Forgetting, then, not only attacks the essence of Being inasmuch as it is apparently distinct from it. It belongs to the nature of Being and reigns as the Destiny of its essence" (*S* 143 from *Zur Seinfrage* 17.5.73). What Heidegger forgets, however, and Derrida reminds us, is that the question of belonging may no longer be a proper question.[2]

The most famous and controversial example with which Derrida tries to open up the value of belonging within Nietzsche's texts is the forgot-ten umbrella. While some critics claim that attention given to this umbrella has been the dark cloud in Nietzsche scholarship, Derrida insists that we not forget Nietzsche's umbrella. Nietzsche's umbrella—this fragment in the unpublished notes "I have forgotten my umbrella"—is one of the spurs in his texts that we would just as soon forget, a spur that we might say does not properly belong to the texts of Nietzsche. But how are we to determine what properly belongs? Using Nietzsche's umbrella, can Derrida teach us a lesson so that we might not forget our own—what properly belongs to us and what we ourselves belong to? Or, by remembering the umbrella does Derrida forget the rain without which there would be no need for an umbrella? Is the umbrella just another weapon to fend off the fear of what Irigaray calls "immemorial waters"?

Certainly Nietzsche's texts call into question what it means to belong, to be proper, to own. Nietzsche's texts break with propriety. And by making spurs—those marks in Nietzsche texts that don't seem to belong—central, Derrida calls into question what it means to read and what it means to write. He questions how we determine if a reading belongs to a text and how we determine if a text belongs to the writings of an author. As I have indicated earlier, these questions are always on the surface in Nietzsche's texts, which are full of self-degradation and contradictions. Reminiscent of Nietzsche's reading lesson, Derrida offers a reading of Nietzsche that is also *not* a reading of Nietzsche, or at least also a reading of itself reading.

By using the stray sentence in the margins of Nietzsche's notebooks, "I have forgotten my umbrella," as a prototype text, and by presenting a multitude of possible meanings for this fragment, Derrida suggests that there is no one meaning of a text; in fact there may not be any meaning at all. Ultimately the meaning of this fragment "remain[s] in principle inaccessible" (*S* 125). Derrida uses this mysterious fragment, whose meaning seems perfectly clear in another context, to suggest that all of Nietzsche's writings are undecidable in the same way as the meaning of this fragment. Turning Derrida's thesis back on itself, Derrida's reading of Nietzsche must also be radically undecidable. Because Derrida's text may be a parody, it is impossible to decide on its meaning once and for all. In Nietzsche's case the undecidability of meaning is more extreme because he is dead, while Derrida is at least available for questioning. Not that this questioning, however, can ever be the end of the multiplication of meaning; there is always psychoanalysis.

Unlike much of his other writing, where he engages in a deconstruction of particular texts, Derrida does not deconstruct Nietzsche's texts. Rather, in *Spurs* he presents a reading of those texts. He does decide on a meaning, even if it is a meaning that is designed to self-destruct:

Because it is structurally liberated from any living meaning, it is always possible that it [the fragment] means nothing at all or that it has no decidable meaning. There is no end to its parodying play with meaning, grafted here and there, beyond any contextual body or finite code. It is quite possible that that unpublished piece, precisely because it is readable as a piece of writing, should remain forever secret. But not because it withholds some secret. Its secret is rather the possibility that indeed it might have no secret, that it might only be pretending to be simulating some hidden truth within its folds.

[T]he hypothesis that the totality of Nietzsche's text, in some monstrous way, might well be of the type "I have forgotten my umbrella" cannot be denied. (S 133)

For Derrida the question is still one of authenticity, but unlike the hermeneut, he has given up looking for it. The text might be a parody; its meaning might dissimulate; it may even dissimulate dissimulation; the signature may be a fraud, especially in the case of Nietzsche's writings, given the questionable behavior of his sister, Elisabeth. And more than this "I have forgotten my umbrella" could be a mark that does not belong to Nietzsche's text, a doodle or scribble off to the side of the page. The question, then, is still one of belonging. What is proper to the text?

This was Heidegger's question; and Derrida's re-asking of it may be merely a parody of Heidegger; especially since Derrida suggests that the question of propriety may be an outmoded question. Of course, this suggestion in itself supposes the question of propriety: Is the question of propriety still a proper question? In *Spurs* Derrida argues that the question of propriety operates within Heidegger's texts as a prior question. He makes this argument in order to deconstruct the opposition between sexual and ontological difference. Heidegger makes ontological difference primary: *Dasein* is prior to the ontic categories of sexual differences. And Derrida wants to use Heidegger's texts to invert the hierarchy between ontological and sexual difference in order to eventually perform the affirmative deconstruction that takes us beyond a mere inversion to a displacement of the hierarchy.

Derrida's Riddle: Which Comes First, Sexual or Ontological Difference?

Derrida challenges Heidegger's reading of Nietzsche because Heidegger carefully analyzes every detail in a passage from *Twilight of the Idols*, "How the True World Became a Fable," except for the phrase "*it becomes female.*" Heidegger quotes from Nietzsche: "Progress of the idea: it becomes more subtle, insidious, incomprehensible—*it becomes female. . .*" And as Derrida points out even while respecting Nietzsche's emphasis on "*it becomes female,*" Heidegger treats this phrase as a stray mark that does not properly belong to Nietzsche's text (*S* 85). He ignores it, much as most critics reading Nietzsche's unpublished notebooks have ignored the marginal phrase "I have forgotten my umbrella." Derrida suggests that by "abandoning" the woman in Nietzsche's texts, Heidegger does violence to those texts and violence to woman. Heidegger chooses to ignore sexual difference.

Nietzsche, for his part, on Derrida's reading, inscribes woman, and thereby sexual difference, in his writing; at the same time, however, he erases the very possibility of such an inscription. Derrida maintains that Nietzsche's writings are full of a multitude of different women—some of them castrating, some castrated, and some affirmative—all of whom Nietzsche identifies with even as he dreads them. In the last part of this book, I argue that Derrida's reading of these women in Nietzsche's texts overlooks a crucial difference between the feminine, woman and the maternal. I maintain that Nietzsche identifies with the maternal and dreads or parodies all other forms of femininity.

Derrida concludes that this multitude of women in Nietzsche's writings demonstrates that "there is no such thing as a woman [*Il n'y a pas une femme*], as a truth in itself of woman in itself. That much, at least, Nietzsche has said" (*S* 101). In spite of his claims to undecidability, on this point—woman's nonexistence—Derrida insists on the decidability of the meaning of Nietzsche's text: "That much, at least, Nietzsche has said." The lesson that we are to learn from this reading of Nietzsche, a lesson especially important for Derrida's reading of Heidegger, is that there is no sexual difference in itself. Yet for Derrida ontological difference presupposes this undecidability even while it necessarily conceals it: "Although there is no truth in itself of the sexual difference in itself, of either man or woman in itself, all of ontology nonetheless, with its inspection, appropriation, identification and verification of identity, has resulted in concealing, even as it presupposes it, this undecidability" (*S* 103–5).

Derrida argues that Nietzsche's analysis of sexual difference is based on a process of propriation. He ties this claim to the passage from *Gay Science* where Nietzsche says that woman gives herself for (something that she is not) even while she gives herself. Sexual difference becomes a process of giving and taking; it becomes a matter of property. Derrida maintains that Nietzsche leaves us unable to distinguish between giving and taking, man and woman. "Man and woman change places. They exchange masks *ad infinitum*" (*S* 111). Derrida reads a Hegelian Nietzsche as proposing that woman is woman because she gives, and man is man because he possesses. Yet if woman is a dissimulatress and gives herself for (gives herself airs, fakes it) then she becomes the possessor, the master, and the duped man becomes the possessed—he has been "taken." So the woman and man exchange places. This is woman's masquerade, the feminine operation. The slave becomes the master.

For Derrida, this undecidability between man and woman, the undecidability of sexual difference, undermines all questions of propriety. We can no longer talk about what is proper to woman or what is proper to man. Derrida claims that the operation of propriation itself is a sexual operation; perhaps he makes this claim because the question of what is proper depends on sexual difference—proper for whom? Clearly without the operation of propriation there can be no sexual difference, or ontological difference for that matter. In order to identify something as a being, it is necessary to determine what is proper to it. In other words, to talk about *that* something is, let alone *what* something is, it is necessary to talk about some property of being or particular beings. Derrida uses this type of analysis in order to undermine the distinction between ontological and sexual difference; the question of propriety, the proper, is prior to either.

In several places Derrida attempts to use Heidegger's texts to deconstruct the opposition between sexual and ontological difference. In *Spurs*, "The Law of Genre," the *Geschlecht* essays, *The Ear of the Other*, and the *Question of Spirit*, Derrida takes up Heidegger's insistence on the priority of ontological difference. The question that Derrida hopes to address using Heidegger's texts is, as he says in "Choreographies," an interview in *The Ear of the Other*, "must one think 'difference' 'before' sexual difference or taking off 'from' it?" (*EO* 172). Which comes first, ontological difference or sexual difference? In his reading of Heidegger, Derrida attempts to deconstruct the hierarchy. He uses his strategy of affirmative deconstruction to first invert the hierarchy between ontological and sexual difference and then introduce a new concept that he claims displaces the opposition altogether.

In "*Geschlecht*: Sexual Difference, Ontological Difference" Derrida argues that Heidegger's silence on sex is suspicious. He points out that sexual difference is the only anthropological trait that Heidegger explicitly mentions, in order to neutralize it. Derrida suggests that Heidegger's neutralization of sexual difference could be read as a violent act, a violent operation (perhaps the operation of castration, even the feminine operation?). Through a series of subtle arguments Derrida makes a case for considering ontological difference secondary to sexual difference. He reads Heidegger's *Dasein* as sexual, if not sexually differentiated.[3] Yet difference is at the core of *Dasein*; *Dasein*'s way of being is difference, or at least separation. Through these subtle moves, Derrida begins to ask, "What if sexual difference lies at the heart of ontological difference?" (G[I] 390).

In "Choreographies," Derrida goes further to make the claim that both Heidegger's and Levinas's neutralization of sexual difference in favor of some neutral human being works to reduce sexual difference to one sex, the masculine: "Once again, the classical interpretation gives a masculine sexual marking to what is presented either as a neutral originariness or, at least, as prior and superior to all sexual markings" (*EO* 178). In one of his essays on Levinas's writings, "At This Very Moment in This Work Here I Am," Derrida criticizes Levinas—who signs his text with a masculine "he" indicating sexual difference rather than erasing it—for making the feminine secondary at each turn that he makes sexual difference secondary to human responsibility. Derrida argues that in Levinas's theory "the secondary status of sexual difference signifies the secondary status of the feminine (But why is this so?) and that the initial status of the predifferential is each time marked by this masculinity that should, however, have come only afterwards, like every other sexual mark" (*ATVM* 41). In addition to making the predifferential mark the masculine, Derrida maintains that Levinas makes the masculine the master of femininity (*ATVM* 42). As I will argue later, however, Derrida's own strategy erases sexual difference in favor of the masculine and makes the masculine the master of the feminine.

Derrida does not merely reverse the privilege that Heidegger gives to ontological difference and return it to sexual difference. Nor does he stop by claiming that Heidegger's silence on sexual difference favors the masculine. Rather he explores the possibility of a sexuality that is prior to sexual opposition. He asks, "May one not begin to think a sexual difference (without negativity, let us clarify) not sealed by a two?" (G[I] 401). In "*Geschlecht* II: Heidegger's Hand," Derrida returns to Heidegger's notion that sexual difference was originally not difference as opposition: "The primordial sexual difference is tender, gentle, peaceful; when that difference is struck down by a 'curse' (*Fluch*, a word of Trakl taken up and interpreted by Heidegger), the duality or the duplicity of the two becomes unleashed, indeed bestial, opposition" (G[II] 193). Derrida presents an analysis of this same notion in his text on Hegel, *Glas*. In *Glas* he explains that for Hegel sexual difference is originally sexual diversity; only later does it become sexual opposition (*Glas* 168–69).

Derrida wants to get beyond/before sexual difference as opposition. In "Choreographies," his interview with Christie McDonald, he imagines a "multiplicity of sexually marked voices" that takes us beyond the binary marks of two sexes:

> What if we were to reach, what if we were to approach here . . . the area of a relationship to the other where the code of sexual marks would no longer be discriminating. The relationship would not be a-sexual, far from it, but would be sexual otherwise: beyond the binary difference that governs the decorum of all codes, beyond the opposition feminine/masculine, beyond bisexuality as well, beyond homosexuality and heterosexuality which come to the same thing. As I dream of saving the chance that this question offers I would like to believe in the multiplicity of sexually marked voices. (*EO* 184)

While his goal is admirable, Derrida's choice of metaphors to figure multiplicity is telling. In "*Geschlecht*: Sexual Difference, Ontological Difference," Derrida discusses the preoppositional plurality as an "originary dissemination" (G[I] 393). He opens up a preoppositional space in Heidegger by emphasizing the disseminal structure of *Dasein* and *Dasein*'s "throwness": "This multiplication does not supervene because there is a plurality of objects; actually it is the converse that takes place. It is the originary disseminal structure, the dispersion of *Dasein*, that makes possible this multiplicity" (G[I] 393–94). "Transcendental dispersion is the possibility of every dissociation and parceling out (*Zersplitterung, Zerspaltung*) into factual existence. It is itself 'founded' on that originary character of *Dasein* that Heidegger then called *Geworfenheit*. . . . There is no dissemination that does not suppose such a 'throw'" (G[I] 395).

Using the metaphor that he develops in *Dissemination*, Derrida marks this difference before binary sexual difference as masculine. The dissemination that makes difference possible is the scattering of sperm: "SPERM, the burning lava, milk, spume, froth, or dribble of the seminal liquor" (*DS* 266). "Dissemination affirms the always already divided generation of meaning. Dissemination—spills it in advance" (*DS* 268). The disseminal spilling of difference is characterized as "'nightly emissions' and 'nightly plumes': the solitary quill errs through a semblance of milky ways" (*DS* 274). There is something accidental about dissemination, like the sperm spilled in advance or during a nightly emission. The "seminal spurt" is a throw of the dice (*DS* 285). Who knows which sperm will inseminate or when? There is no mastery involved here. Insemination is without origin: "Germination, dissemination. There is no first insemination. The semen is already swarming. The 'primal' insemination is dissemination" (*Diss* 304).

For Derrida there is no insemination, only dissemination; there is only the scattering of sperm. There is only the masculine element and masculine generation. Writing and language and life itself come to be through dissemination which continuously engenders differences. *Dasein* is thrown in this originary dissemination. *Dasein* is scattered according to a throw of the dice. The relation between the disseminal structure of *Dasein* and the throwness of *Dasein* supposedly makes room for differences without opposition. But if this is the case, it is not because there is a multiplicity of sexual differences, or even the possibility of multiplicity. There is only the masculine element multiplying itself through its disseminal spurts. The orginary structure of *Dasein* along with *Dasein*'s throwness kill off any need for the mother/woman. Insemination never takes place; there is only the dispersion of sperm. *Dasein* is not born but thrown in this dicey masculine game of chance.[5]

Derrida's Undecidability as the Erasure of Sexual Difference

The strategy that Derrida uses in order to open up the possibility of the multiplicity of sexually marked voices is the introduction of undecidable "concepts" after the inversion of hierarchical opposition. In the case of sexual difference, in *Spurs* for example, Derrida inverts the hierarchical opposition man/woman and the hierarchical opposition ontological difference/sexual difference to open onto the undecidable, where we cannot identify what is proper to man as opposed to woman or what is proper to the ontological as opposed to the sexual. It is questionable, however, whether this strategy yields the desired effect and multiplies differences or whether, in fact, it closes off the possibility of difference. I have three criticisms of Derrida's strategy: first, either this strategy leads to the erasure of difference or it operates according to the symptomology of fetishism; second, the binary logic of opposition, or the proper, merely reappears at another level, the level of undecidability versus decidability; and, third, Derrida's undecidables operate within a larger economy of the proper/property, also known as an economy of castration.

Recall that Derrida insists that deconstruction intervenes in the polis, but it runs the double risk of consolidating the very values that it attempts to displace on the one hand, and setting up new values within the same hierarchical binary structure of the old values, on the other hand. One thing that we learn from Derridean deconstruction is that in spite of the author's so-called intentions and the explicit project of the text, we must continually reassess the implicit values, and effects, of the text (FL 63; see also *EO)*. Answering the call from deconstruction, I will diagnose the ways in which Derrida's texts are complicit with some of the values that he attempts to overturn.

Following Nietzsche, Derrida seems to attempt a revaluation of all values by deconstructing the binary oppositions that drive the system of Western values. From within this system of binary opposition he is attempting to change the way that we value. He is attempting to change the way that we value sexual difference, man and woman. If, however, the break down of this hierarchy leaves us with the undecidability between the two terms, then how is sexual difference possible? If we cannot decide between sexes, is there any sexual difference? The goal of deconstruction is to break down hierarchical oppositions in order to make room for differences that are not figured as oppositions. But relying on undecidability to do this might throw the baby out with the bath water: not only is there is no more opposition, but also there is no more difference; we can no longer tell the difference; we cannot decide. Perhaps what we need is not an economy of undecidables, but rather another way of "deciding" or identifying differences that does not necessarily place them within a violent economy of opposition—me or not me, mine or not mine, having or not having.

In spite of Derrida's insistence that the undecidable is an opening onto that which is foreign to the order of the calculable, without sexual difference(s) there can be no multiplicity of sexually marked voices; undecidability makes any mark(s) impossible (See FL 24; EO 184). It seems that Derrida's methodology prevents him from attaining his goal. It may be that to imagine multiplicity first requires an encounter with that which is foreign to the calculable, but undecidability may not be the best strategy for staging that encounter. The risk of erasing all possibility of (sexual) differences may be too great. Moreover, within the history of Western culture, which has been dominated by patriarchies, erasing sexual difference amounts once again to erasing the feminine.[6] The history of Western patriarchy indicates that the erasure of sexual difference could be used once again to give precedence to the masculine over the feminine. In the name of undecidability, every sex becomes masculine. Human beings become mankind. Rendering all difference undecidable is not a way of embracing difference. It is yet another way of rendering everything the sameand we are back within the logic of the proper.

If Derrida's logic of undecidability somehow retains diffences but prevents deciding between then, then it is the logic of fetishism. Not being able to decide is the fetishist's symptom. The fetishist protects himself from castration by both maintaining, and denying, his mother's castration. In fact, he maintains her castration *by* denying it. He sets up substitutes, fetishes, for the missing maternal phallus. In this way he ensures that neither he nor his mother is castratable. The fetish, his refusal to decide, is his protection. The fetishist affirms both castration and its opposite; he affirms both sides of the opposition and refuses to decide between them. In his reading of Hegel in *Glas*, Derrida associates undecidability with fetishism. In fact, in a brief analysis of Freud's theory of fetishism, Derrida characterizes the economy of the undecidable as the economy of fetishism: "In these very subtle cases, then, the structure, the construction (*Aufbau*) of the fetish rests at once on the denial and on the affirmation (*Behauptung*), the assertion or the assumption of castration. This at-once, the in-the-same-stroke, the *du-même-coup* of the two contraries, of the two opposite operations, prohibits cutting through to a decision within the undecidable. This at-once constitutes an economy of the undecidable."(*Glas* 210).

In addition, in his analysis of Genet in *Glas*, Derrida makes a cluster of propositions that can be taken together to conclude that for Derrida the undecidable is the uncastratable, which is the goal of the fetishist. He says,"the undecidable, isn't it the undeniable" (*Glas* 225). And he says , "the undeniable is the uncastratable" (*Glas* 229). So it seems that we can conclude from these two propositions that the undecidable is the uncastratable. In other words, the undecidable protects against castration. Like his use of two columns, or two texts, or his self-undermining text, the text that refuses to decide and insists on the undecidable—affirming each of two opposites—protects against castration by castrating itself (in order to deny its own castration). Recall my analysis of Derrida's strategy of autocastration.

Whereas Freud denies the mother's/his own castration by making the mother masculine and explaining all feminine sexuality in terms of the masculine, Derrida, in addition to making the mother masculine—an argument that I will take up later—turns all sexuality, insofar as it is undecidable, into the feminine. In Derrida's texts, the undecidable is identified with the feminine and metaphors of the female body; and ultimately the feminine undecidable is opposed to, and excluded from, the masculine decidable truth.

My second argument is that by associating the undecidable with his new "concepts," Derrida places the undecidable back into the binary opposition that he attempts to deconstruct. Now we have a binary opposition between the decidable and the undecidable. Although in *Spurs*, for example, Derrida suggests that all texts and concepts are ultimately undecidable, there are philosophical texts and strategies that open themselves up to the undecidable and those that close themselves off and deny their own undecidability. This opposition reenacts the binary hierarchy at another level. As Derrida argues in "White Mythology" traditional philosophy operates on the basis of a double effacement of its own metaphors: "The primitive meaning, the original, and always sensory and material, figure. . . is not exactly a metaphor. . . . It becomes a metaphor when philosophical discourse puts it into circulation. Simultaneously the first meaning and the first displacement are then forgotten. The metaphor is no longer noticed, and it is taken for the proper meaning. A double effacement. Philosophy would be this process of metaphorization which gets carried away in and or itself. Constitutionally, philosohical culture will always have been an obliterating one" (WM 211). Affirmative deconstruction, on the other hand, operates by continually attempting to expose the (second) effacement of metaphor—the denial of the denial of metaphor—and thereby distinguishes itself from traditional philosophy. On this level the opposition becomes one of acknowledging or denying the role of metaphor. Specifically, with regard to sexual difference, by associating the undecidable with woman, Derrida places the undecidable back into the binary opposition that he attempts to deconstruct.

In *Spurs* the question of interpretation and the decidability of the text is always associated with the question of woman. Most of Nietzsche's critics skirt the question of woman; but while Nietzsche's re-marks on woman may seem tangential to the "serious" philosopher, Derrida claims that they are central to analyzing Nietzsche's texts. Because the question of woman in Nietzsche's texts is an undecidable question, it "falls out" [*tombe*] in the same "place" [*position*] as truth: "The question of the woman suspends the decidable opposition of true and non-true and inaugurates the epochal regime of quotation marks which is to be enforced for every concept belonging to the system of philosophical decidability. The hermeneutic project which postulates a true sense of the text is disqualified under this regime. Reading is freed from the horizon of the meaning or truth of being, liberated from the values of the product's production or the present's presence" (S 107).

Just as the concept of woman is undecidable because ultimately there is no woman, so too is truth, and every other philosophical concept, undecidable. Of course, insofar as "woman" doesn't belong in philosophical discourse, she is sexier than traditional philosophical concepts. Derrida uses woman in his texts in order to seduce his reader. He is a womanizer; he plays woman in his texts. Derrida takes great pleasure in unveiling Nietzsche's harem of women and he takes even greater pleasure in doing it for an audience. And it is funny when he says, "it is woman who will be my subject"? (S 37). For in what sense is woman his subject? He plays with the undecidability of woman's subject position so that he can usurp that position and speak from it—woman is *my* subject—in order, in effect, to subject her once again to the discourse of philosophers. Once again this raises the question "Where do women belong within Derrida's discourse?"

Insofar as woman and the feminine are identified with the undecidable, they do not belong within the discourse of philosophy. Philosophy is a discourse of the decidable, and Derrida's undecidable lies beyondof its bounds, threatening it from the outside. At least traditionally, just as philosophy has excluded woman and the feminine, so too has philosophy excluded the undecidable. So what do we gain by identifying woman with undecidability? Now she can be doubly excluded as both woman and the undecidable. Her threat becomes more severe.

If Derrida wants to overcome the binary opposition between man and woman, he cannot do so by identifying woman with the undecidable. He cannot both claim that we cannot decide between man and woman and that this undecidability itself is feminine or figured by woman. To do so is to claim that we have transcended the binary man/woman by reasserting the binary. While it is true that for Derrida the concept of woman is no more undecidable than the concept of man, or the concept of truth or substance for that matter, he uses woman and the feminine as metaphors for the undecidable. By doing so he merely recreates the binary man/woman on another level. Now we have the binary opposition between the decidable and the undecidable. Although Derrida maintains that all texts and concepts are ultimately undecidable, there are philosophical texts and strategies that open themselves up to the undecidable and those that close themselves off and deny their own undecidability.

As did Nietzsche with his two types of reading, active and reactive, Derrida compares two types of reading. Texts either admit or deny their undecidability. This opposition reenacts the binary hierarchy at another level. And in Derrida's analysis, one term of this opposition is figured with metaphors of the feminine and woman. The binary man/woman is also reenacted at this meta(phorical)level.

It is possible to read this problem as a result of Derrida's inversion of man and woman, masculine and feminine. Perhaps he leaves us with the undecidable or woman in the first phase of affirmative deconstruction and not the final phase. Rather than read the undecidable as the telos of deconstruction, perhaps it is merely the inversion itself. In other words, Derrida leaves us with undecidability and identifies that undecidability with woman and the feminine in order to give value and priority to the devalued term of the traditional binary man/woman. Now, instead of having only one sex that is masculine, we have only one sex that is feminine. Even if we accept this tenuous reading of Derrida, there remains the significant problem of maintaining any notion of sexual difference, specifically of feminine difference. If woman or the feminine is valued because it is undecidable, then it is valued for what it is not. Woman is still not valued for what she is; she is not valued for her specificity. She is valued as a metaphor for the impossibility of any specificity.

Derrida criticizes Heidegger's violence against the feminine or woman when he sacrifices sexual difference for the sake of identifying the structure of the existential analytic of *Dasein*, which becomes another way of privileging the masculine. Yet Derrida performs his own violence against the feminine and woman. In *Spurs* he admits that his own procedure is not contrary to Heidegger's violent procedure; just as Heidegger's violence to Nietzsche's text is also a violence to woman—he refuses to see "*it becomes female*"—Derrida's process of reading is the violent operation of impaling woman.[7] He uses woman in his deconstruction. He erases her difference and any possibility of her specificity. He turns her into a metaphor. More than this, with his metaphor, he dismembers woman and appropriates parts of the female body in order to develop his undecidable concepts. One of his primary tropes of undecidability is the hymen. It is a trope that undermines the possibility of the trope, a trope-defying trope; the hymen promotes trope decay.

In the last section of this chapter, "The Logic of Castration: Derrida versus Lacan on having or not having," I will substantiate my third criticism of Derrida's undecidable "concepts," I will demonstrate how, on a larger level, Derrida's own metaphors, his undecidable "concepts" operate within an economy of the proper and property. In spite of their various histories, within post structuralist discourses "pharmakon," "supplement," "hymen," "gram," and "différance" have become Derrida's trademarks. He holds the "copyright" on these terms and their use as metaphors for undecidability. One cannot use them in this way without at least implicitly making reference to Derrida. Moreover, Derrida is not only complicit with his texts circulation within this economy of property, but also he insists on it. His dispute with Lacan is a prime example. I will show that what is at stake in Derrida's dispute with Lacan is the question of property. In the next section, "Derrida's metaphors of undecidability as appropriation of the feminine," I will continue to criticize Derrida's identification of his undecidable concepts with woman, thereby substituting one dualistic opposition (man/woman) for another (decidable/undecidable).

Derrida's Metaphors of Undecidability as Appropriation of the Feminine

Not only is Derrida's hymen a metaphor for the undecidable or in-between, but it also traditionally signifies marriage or union. He introduces the "concept" of the hymen in *The Double Session* where he discusses the hymen (marriage) between Plato and Mallarmé. There he describes the hymen as "a sign of fusion, the consummation of a marriage, the identification of two beings, the confusion between two. Between the two there is no longer difference but identity. Within this fusion, there is no longer any distance between desire (the awaiting of a full presence designed to fulfill it, to carry it out) and the fulfillment of presence, between distance and non-distance; there is no longer any difference between desire and satisfaction. It is not only the difference (between desire and fulfillment) that is abolished, but also the difference between difference and nondifference" (*DS* 209).

The economy of the hymen is one of undecidability and fusion. Two become one, but not merely "one term, a single one of the differends" (*DS* 209). Within the hymeneal economy there is no difference or opposition between two. The hymen is the economy of the between. It is not only the marriage or fusion of two but also the membrane that is between the inside and the outside of woman's body: "The hymen, the consummation of differends, the continuity and confusion of the coitus, merges with what it seems to be derived from: the hymen as protective screen, the jewel box of virginity, the vaginal partition, the fine, invisible veil which, in front of the hystera, stands *between* the inside and the outside of a woman, and consequently between desire and fulfillment" (*DS* 212–13). Hymen, the fusion of two in marriage is itself fused with the membrane from which the term "hymen" is derived. The marriage is consummated by breaking the hymen. The broken hymen is both proof of virginity and proof of the consummation of the marriage.

As Roberta Weston points out in her essay "Free Gift or Forced Figure?," "hymen" is a term that has a long history inscribed by patriarchy. Hymen has been a significant part of marriage rituals within patriarchal cultures for centuries. The hymen has been the means through which the man marks the woman as his property and guarantees that she has not been possessed or spoiled by another. Weston maintains, as she traces the history and etymology of the term, that the hymen plays between the marriage rites and the rights of patriarchy. Weston rightfully criticizes Derrida for *using* the bloodstained history of the hymen even while willfully forgetting that history:

> Jacques Derrida, then, is correct in pointing out that the word hymen has
> no "natural," literal, or purely physical referent: the hymen has no proper

meaning and it means nothing in itself. Derrida, however, uses this acknowledgment to justify a willful forgetting of the history of hymen; that hymen does indeed have a history. As deeply imbricated within patriarchal systems of matrimony as the hymen is, is it possible to use the word as a tool to deconstruct logocentric and phallocentric systems of signification? This is precisely what Derrida attempts to do. His appropriation of the hymen as an antidote to the phallus as transcendental signifier, however, is a symptom of the problem which he aids in perpetuating. Women's properties, including their bodies, their language, and their productive and reproductive rights are appropriated in patriarchal systems but the violence of the operation, both symbolic and otherwise, goes unrecognized as violence because it is rewritten, euphemized, and naturalized through a linguistic operation which allows for and encourages a willful forgetting of the socially figured origins, and the implications of those origins. (iii)

Weston argues that Derrida's appropriation of woman and her reproductive rights is a question of property, the patriarchal question. Derrida can appropriate woman and her body for his writing and then through copyright laws he can ensure that no one else owns his property. Through the laws of copyright, he marks the woman's hymen as his property (Weston vi). Derrida's "hymeneal fable," as Gayatri Spivak calls it, has become one of his trademarks (OG 1xvi).

The way in which Derrida uses the metaphor of the hymen in his discussion of writing raises once again the question, "Where does woman belong?" What belongs to woman? In *The Double Session* he describes writing as "dissemination in the folds of the hymen," dissemination onto the blank white virginal page (*DS* 271; see also 212). Just as the two columns in *Glas* emasculate themselves, the fold in between pages in *The Double Session* feminizes the book. The book is the violent war of sexual difference. Writing, among other things, penetrates the feminine text (*DS* 259; cf. *S* 73). Derrida talks about knives brandished to rupture the virginal folds of the text. He talks about letter openers that "separate the lips of the book" (*DS* 259). He likens this operation to a rape that is perpetual and "has always already taken place and will nevertheless never have been perpetrated" (*DS* 260).

The violent operation of writing is the violence of a mimesis that becomes a mimicry through which the male mimes the feminine, mimes the death of the feminine to the point of his own death. In "White Mythology" Derrida says that mimesis is proper to man—only he imitates properly (*WM* 237). He mimes imitation; he mimes the actress giving herself for even as she gives herself. In *The Double Session* Derrida analyzes the process of mimesis through a story by Mallarmé, "Mimique," in which the protagonist, Pierrot, mimes the murder of his wife, whom he had tickled to death; in the end his pantomime is too much for him and he himself dies. The murder of the feminine and the "writing" of that murder prove too much for the masculine. As Luce Irigaray suggests in *Marine Lover of Friedrich Nietzsche*, in the end, the murder of the other necessitates suicide. I will return to Irigaray's argument in the next chapter.

Woman does not write, she is written on and ripped apart in the process. As Derrida says in *Given Time,* she is always absent from the narrative even if she is "marking its tempo" (*GT* 103). She is not just in the background; she *is* the background. Weston criticizes this positioning of woman; she argues that "the hymen/woman performs like a wallflower fading into the background, her present absence serving as structural support of the writer's mark. The hymeneal surface is variously described by Derrida as a blank piece of paper, a sail, or a veil, but also as various membranes including vellum or parchment, writing surfaces which are made of the skin of dead animals, flayed and stretched taught to receive a writer's marks" (vii). Not only is the hymen stretched to receive the writer's marks, but also it is always already torn. Derrida claims that "the hymen is never pure or proper, has no life of its own, no proper name. Opened up by its anagram, it always seems torn, already, in the fold through which its affects itself and murders itself" (*DS* 229).

There is nothing proper to the hymen. But this supposed self-murder, this suicide, seems suspect. Is the hymeneal desire, woman's desire, self-destructive; does woman desire death? The question of woman's desire is always only mimed, even mimicked, in Derrida's texts. Repeatedly in *The Double Session*, Derrida refers to the hymen as "between desire and its fulfillment" (*DS* 209, 212, 213). "It is the hymen," he says, "that desire dreams of piercing, of bursting, in an act of violence that is (at the same time or somewhere between) love and murder" (*DS* 213). Whose desire is this desire to burst the hymen? Between whose desire and fulfillment does the hymen stand? Is this woman's desire? In her analysis of Derrida's use of the metaphor of hymen, Gayatri Spivak concludes that the "desire here must be expressed as man's desire, if only because it is the only discourse handy. The language of woman's desire does not enter this enclosure" (*DDW* 175).

In his analysis of Blanchot, Derrida says that the hymen affirms itself, which suggests the self-affirmation of woman's desire (*LG* 75). In Derrida's text the double affirmation, the hymen's "marriage with itself," comes from beautiful women. Yet this double affirmation, this Nietzschean "yes, yes" out of the mouth of beautiful women, is still only the masculine appropriation of a feminine yes. Soon we find out that Derrida is this affirming woman: "I am a woman and beautiful" (perhaps he is only quoting Blanchot) (LG 76). The double affirmation, the hymen's affirmation of itself, comes from the man posing as woman. The yes is nothing more than the miming of a yes. It is the masculine miming the feminine yes to the masculine: "Yes, I am a virgin; yes, I belong only to you." It is, therefore, a double affirmation; but it is a double affirmation of the masculine affirmation of the hymen that ensures his mastery and self-affirmation. Perhaps it is the masculine affirmation that the hymen is still intact—the nuptial affirmation, an affirmation that in fact destroys the hymen (see Weston). The hymen's so-called self-affirmation turns out to be its destruction.

The Logic of Castration: Derrida versus Lacan on Having and Not Having

The desire given voice in Derrida's texts is still a masculine desire for penetration and possession of the feminine. The hymeneal economy that Derrida proposes to substitute for the economy of castration has not escaped the phallic masculine economy of possession, in spite of his claims to the contrary. Miming Breton's definition of surrealism, in *Spurs* Derrida makes fun of Lacan when he says that one does not just happen onto the phallus "in a sewing-up machine on a castration table" (*S* 129–31). The Phallus is neither an accident nor natural. Rather, following Derrida, we could say that the phallus is placed in a sewing machine on a castration table. Yet where else is it that we find Derrida using the hymen besides in a sewing machine on a castration table? In *The Double Session* he even talks of stitching and pleating the hymen (272).

Has Derrida taken us much further than Lacan's phallocentrism? Indeed, the phallus, as Lacan says, is only effective when it is veiled, and its masquerading is always feminine. In *Spurs*, however, Derrida proposes to replace Lacan's economy of castration with a more fluid economy of the hymen. There he says that "at this point one ought to interrogate— and 'unboss'—the metaphorical fullblown sail of truth's declamation, of the castration and phallocentricism, for example, in Lacan's discourse" (*S* 59–61). Although in *Spurs* he mentions Lacan in connection with castration, his more developed criticisms of Lacan are elsewhere. Derrida's most well known criticisms of Lacan are in "*Le Facteur de la Vérité*," where he argues that Lacan reproduces phallocentrism by following too closely Freud's sexual theory, wherein there is only one libido and it is masculine (481–82, see note 60).

Derrida also points out that within Lacan's theory of meaning and signification, it is the phallus as transcendental signifier that guarantees the possibility of meaning. He argues that Lacan's postulate of the phallus as transcendental signifier reproduces phallogocentrism. Logos is anchored, centered, within the transcendental Phallus. The phallus is Lacan's "*point de capiton*," or "quilted stitch," which makes it possible to link signifier and signified to produce meaning and truth (cf. FV 464, 477). For Lacan the phallus signifies the process of signification itself. It signifies the link between signifier and signified. He calls the phallus the copula between signifier and signified (*Ecrits* 285). In other words, it is the *is* (or being) attributed to anything; it is the *is* that makes any thing a thing. But since Saussure, language or signification is the play of difference between signifiers, and the signified is merely the effect of this play. The phallus, then, also signifies the absence of the signified, or the loss of being—castration. This is why Lacan maintains that the Phallus is only effective when it is veiled (*Ecrits* 288). Once the phallus is unveiled it is nothing but the absence of the signified, a fraud, castrated.

We could say that Lacan uses the phallus as the metaphor for metaphor. Or in Derrida's terminology we could say that the phallus signifies the double effacement of metaphor. The first effacement is forgetting that the relationship between signifier and signified is only the effect of a play of signifiers. The second effacement is forgetting this forgetting of the signified effect. The phallus is erected on this double effacement. This is the same process through which the history of philosophy, as Derrida describes it in "White Mythology," has engaged in the double effacement of metaphor (*WM* 211). There Derrida claims that philosophers necessarily use metaphor in order to invoke the literal or real. The philosophers' first effacement is that they forget their dependence on metaphor. The second effacement is that they forget that they have forgotten the role of metaphor in philosophy. The memory of the role of metaphor would be the death of philosophy—philosophy would become poetry (Kant's worry). This is the same process that Nietzsche describes in "On Truth and Falsity in the Ultramoral Sense" when he claims that we hide truth behind a bush and then praise ourselves when we find it. This process operates through the negation of the negation of the literal/real/signified which yields the signified fortified against the metaphorical/fantastic/signifier.

Derrida criticizes Lacan's use of the phallus as the metaphor of metaphor because this transcendental signifier stands outside/for the operation of metaphor (see *P* 111). The phallus, then, is precisely the metaphor for which the theory cannot account. As Louis Mackey has said about Derrida's criticism of philosophers in "White Mythology," you can round up all the horses (or metaphors) in the corral except for the horse (or metaphor) that you rode in on.[8] Following Mackey's metaphor, we could say that Lacan is riding the phallus; this is the metaphor for which his theory cannot account.

The operation of the phallus, however, like the operation of affirmative deconstruction, is the "feminine operation." For Derrida the feminine operation is the operation of displacement and insofar as he performs the operation of displacement he takes up the feminine operation. According to this logic even his displacement of the place of woman, what Gayatri Spivak calls his "double displacement," is a feminine operation. It is strange that Derrida also identifies the operation of double-effacement as (on the) feminine. In "Living On: Border Lines" Derrida identifies deconstruction as a process of what he calls "double invagination" or double effacement (LO 100–101).

Double invagination occurs when a text folds in on itself. It is the self-reflexive, even self-effacing, operation of deconstruction. The difference, it seems, between deconstruction's double effacement of itself and philosophy's double effacement of metaphor is that while the philosopher is not self-conscious about effacing or forgetting the role of metaphor in his text, the deconstructionist is self-conscious; he is in control and intentionally effaces his own text. He is the master of double invagination. This presumption, which of course the deconstructionist text explicitly denies, runs counter to Derrida's criticisms of the intentional subject who stands in any sense outside the text. Yet the difference between traditional philosophy's effacement and Derrida's seems to be a matter of intention, which requires that the deconstructionist adopt a position outside of the text. Moreover, for Derrida, the outside is the position of the masculine while the inside, the vaginal folds of the text, is the place of the feminine. The deconstructor performs the refolding of the vaginal folds of the text. The deconstructor manipulates the vaginal folds in order to perform his double effacement. Following Derrida's metaphor, the effacement of the text is an effacement of the vagina.

For Derrida an operation is feminine if it is a masquerade, if it gives itself for what it is not. So the masculine becomes feminine by masquerading as the feminine. The masquerade itself makes the operation feminine. In this operation, however, the feminine is doubly had: she is possessed by the masculine as his attribute or character in the act of being mimed and she is possessed by the masculine as his property or object in the act of being appropriated to consolidate what is proper to him.

For Lacan, like Derrida, the masquerade is feminine. The phallus is feminine/feminized because it is a masquerade. As the signifier of the process of signification itself, the phallus creates the illusion of presence or being while at the same time it is absence or castration. It gives itself for what it is not. Derrida criticizes Lacan for proposing a phallocentric theory that revolves around the phallus as a transcendental signifier and is driven by castration.[9] In Lacan's scenario all desire is desire for the phallus. So the loss or lack of satisfaction is a type of castration. For Lacan, we are always already castrated: No one possesses the phallus and all signification is based on a primary lack of any signified. In a sense, desire is the gap between the signifier and the signified and desire is therefore inherently unfulfillable.

Derrida wants to displace the economy of desire based on castration and primary absence. He rejects what might be called Lacan's negative theology, which makes absence central rather than presence. He displaces the economy of castration by setting up the figures of undecidability within the position of the center/phallus. In *Spurs* and *The Double Session*, he replaces the operations of dissemination and the hymen for the operations of the phallus and castration. Derrida tries to escape creating any kind of Lacanian transcendental signifier by constantly changing his metaphors for the process of metaphor: *différance,* supplement, pharmakon, hymen, etc.

Yet the fact that Derrida maintains that these various figures of undecidability that re-present the process of signification itself are interchangeable places them within the economy of castration. For it is only within the economy of castration that terms are interchangeable, that one can be substituted for another. Within the psychic economy that Lacan describes, the logic of castration is based on substitution. Signification revolves around the phallus and threats of castration, which are effective only because one thing can be substituted for another. Within Lacan's scenario one of the first substitutions is that of the Law of the Father for the desire of the mother. Lacan calls this the paternal metaphor. Basically, by substituting the paternal law for the dependence on the maternal body, the child enters the social. From then on the child is engaged in a series of more or less successful substitutions. The child substitutes language, words, for the expectation that its needs will be automatically met; it asks for what it wants. Words are substituted for things. Words are substituted for each other. A whole network of exchanges is predicated on the possibility, however illusory, of substitution.

Derrida's use of the hymen, insofar as it is an interchangeable undecidable, operates within this same kind of economy of exchange, where one thing can be substituted for another and create the illusion of equivalence. He maintains in *Positions* that even though the graphic of the hymen, or what he also calls there "dissemination," "affirms" substitution, "in doing so, [it] runs all the risks, but without the metaphysical or romantic pathos of negativity" (*P* 86–87). So although we are still within the economy of substitution that characterizes the logic of castration, we do not have anything to fill the metaphysical position of Lacan's transcendental signifier, the phallus. There is a difference, then, between Derrida's substitutions and the Lacanian economy of castration because it seems that Derrida does away with the transcendental signifier.

Drucilla Cornell defends Derrida against the claim that, like Lacan's, his discourse operates within the logic of castration by claiming that "he moves within the myths and allegories of the feminine to expose the traditional role they are given within phallogocentrism" (*BA* 86). There is, however, a distinction between exploiting traditional myths and allegories and demystifying them. I have suggested that Derrida's use of the hymen does not acknowledge its traditional roles in patriarchy. I have also argued that Derrida uses the hymen within his own economy of substitutable terms for undecidability and thereby invokes the logic of castration.

In addition to operating within an economy of substitution, within a larger framework, Derrida's use of the hymen operates within an economy of castration. It operates within an economy of possession, which is, of course, the primary concern within the logic of castration—do you have it or not? What is at stake in Derrida's dispute with Lacan is precisely the question of propriety, property, ownership. Who stole from whom? To whom does the text or the concept belong? Who said it first? Who owns the copyright? Who has it and who does not? Some of Derrida's most telling criticisms of Lacan are in the interviews and their footnotes, especially note 44, in *Positions*. There Derrida complains that Lacan has reappropriated Derrida's own texts. This, he says, is why he does not engage Lacan:

> In the texts that I have published so far, the absence of references to Lacan,
> in effect, is almost total. This is justified not only by the aggressions in the
> form of, or with the aim of, reappropriation that Lacan, since the
> appearance of *De la grammatologie in Critique* (1965) (and even earlier, I
> am told), has proliferated, whether directly or indirectly, in private or
> public, in his seminars, and from 1965 on, as I was to notice myself
> reading them, in almost *each* of his writings. Such movements correspond,
> each time, to the argumentative framework precisely analyzed by Freud
> (*Interpretation of Dreams*) which I showed (*Grammatologie*, "Pharmacie
> de Platon," "*Le puits et la pyramide*") always informs the traditional
> proceedings against writing. This is the so called "kettle" argument, which
> meets the needs of a cause by accumulating incompatible assertions. (1.
> Devaluation and rejection: "it is worthless" or "I do not agree."
> 2. Valuation and reappropriation: "moreover it is mine and I have always

said so.") (P 107, n. 44)

What is striking in Derrida's criticism of Lacan's use of the so-called "kettle" argument in relation to his own texts is that Derrida turns around and employs the kettle logic against Lacan, a logic that he identifies in *Spurs* with the feminine operation (S 67). In Freud's story of the kettle, a neighbor borrows a kettle and breaks it. He makes contradictory excuses for the broken kettle: First he says, "The kettle is not broken"; then he says, "I did not break the kettle"; and finally he says "I did not borrow it" (*SE* VIII, 205). Derrida claims that Lacan uses this kind of argument against his own writings; he claims that Lacan both rejects his writings and claims the ideas in them as his own. Yet this is exactly what Derrida does in this note from *Positions*. He justifies the lack of reference to Lacan by first insisting that he had written *De la grammatologie* and "*Freud et la scéne de l'écriture*" before the publication of Lacan's *Ecrits*. He assures us that he had read very little of Lacan's work. Then he lists some of the motifs that he develops in his own writing which Lacan reappropriates from him (P 108–109). Next he excuses himself for not addressing all of the major motifs that Lacan addressed by saying that "at the time of which I am speaking, I—and certain others with me—perceived other pressing questions" (P 109). Finally, he proposes several objections to Lacan's work as his reasons for not engaging with that work: "Even if these reservations are far from exhausting Lacan's work, of which I remain persuaded, they were already important enough for me not to seek references (in the form of guarantee) in a discourse so different, in its mode of elocution, its site, its aims, its presuppositions, from the texts that I was proposing" (P 110). It certainly seems as if Derrida is claiming that he did not borrow the kettle and if he did he did not break it because it was already broken.

In spite of his undecidable concepts, some of them reappropriated from woman's body—hymen, invagination—Derrida's texts, on his own insistence, circulate within an economy of castration which privileges presence over absence and measures everything according to having or not having ownership. Derrida's concern for ownership could not be more blatant than in the recent squabbles over the copyright to an interview on Heidegger and Fascism, originally published in *Le Nouvel Observateur*, which was translated by Richard Wolin and published in his *The Heidegger Controversy: A Critical Reader* without Derrida's consent. Writing to the editor of the *New York Review of Books*, Derrida says: "I maintain that *Le Nouvel Observateur* does not have the right to authorize without my accord the republication of my text in translation. Any competent lawyer will confirm this to be the case. No contract was ever signed between this magazine and myself on the subject of a text of which I remain *the sole legal owner*" (*NYRB*, March 25, 1993, 65; my emphasis).

In addition to castration and the bursting hymen, another strange mark on the body that appears in *Spurs* is circumcision. There Derrida maintains that Nietzsche "ranks both Jews and women among those expert mountebanks, the artists . . . and the fact that Nietzsche often considers them in parallel roles might in fact be related to the motif of castration and simulacrum for which circumcision is the mark, indeed the name of the mark" (*S* 69). On Derrida's reading, what Nietzsche finds in common between women and Jews is that they are both masters of simulation, artists and actors. Both feign castration.

While it is true that Nietzsche does sometimes treat the Jew and the woman in a similar manner and to similar ends, there is another possible reading of his strategy. Perhaps it is not because both the Jew and the woman are fakers that he gives them a similar status but rather because they both occupy marginal positions within nineteeth-century German culture. Or perhaps they are fakers because they occupy marginal positions; simulation is their only power. A careful reading of Nietzsche reveals that it is possible that some of Nietzsche's remarks on Jews and women are not characterizations of these groups at all. Rather, they are stereotypes hurled back into the face of his anti-Semitic and sexist German contemporaries designed as insults. What better way to insult a sexist than to call him a woman or effeminate? What better way to insult an anti-Semite than to call him a Jew?

Nietzsche's writings are scattered with remarks about the effeminate German culture. And in *On the Genealogy of Morals*, for example, Nietzsche seems to goad his anti-semitic contemporaries by identifying Jesus, Mary, and Joseph as the Jews responsible for the slave revolt in morality (*OGM* I, §16, 53). In addition, Nietzsche praises the heroes of the Old Testament and criticizes the God of Saint Peter, the "pawing and nuzzling" God of the New Testament, whom he identifies as a Jewish God! (*OGM* III, §22, 144). Rather than joining the Jew and the woman because of their play with/at castration, Nietzsche seems to be playing the Jew and the woman in order to effect a castration of his contemporaries. He plays the supposed castration, powerlessness, or inferiority of Jews and women off the power of these two groups in order to enrage his contemporaries.

Irigaray addresses Nietzsche's association of the Jew and the woman in a perplexing section of the chapter entitled "Veiled Lips" in *Marine Lover of Friedrich Nietzsche*. She analyzes, and seems to criticize,

Nietzsche's association of the Jew and the woman as actors (*ML* 81–82; Irigaray refers to *Gay Science*, p. 361). Against Nietzsche (and Derrida) Irigaray argues that while the Jew simulates castration, the woman represents or threatens castration. Irigaray's criticism could be seen as a lesson in psychoanalytic theory. Irigaray points out that signs are safeguards against castration and the threat of castration. What she might be referring to is the Lacanian notion that the child is forced into the realm of signs by the castration threat, which it wards off with words. Recall that in the Lacanian schema the threat of castration is the threat of cutting off all possible gratification, which comes when the child realizes that it is separate from its mother and cannot expect her to automatically meet its needs. In order to ensure that it can have some gratification, the child resorts to words or signs to indicate to its mother what it needs. In this scenario the child protects itself from the castration threat by using signs.

Irigaray interprets circumcision as a (dis)simulation of castration within the realm of signs: "almost the reverse of castrating, this excision is what marks the body's entry into the world of signs" (*ML* 81). Circumcision, as part of a process of signification, a social ritual, wards off the threat of castration. The "Jewish operation," as Irigaray calls it, does not represent or simulate castration as much as it misrepresents or dissimulates castration in order to safeguard against it (See *ML* 82). Where Irigaray finds problems with Nietzsche (and Derrida) is in the association of this "Jewish operation" with woman or the feminine operation.

For Irigaray, woman, unlike the Jew, does not operate within the patriarchal economy except as the threat of castration. She does not simulate castration or the threat of castration; she *is* the threat; she *is* castrated: "As a result of being nothing in this theater [the theater of representation] but a nothing that resists representation, and also being an apparatus that sometimes gets in the way, she interprets the generalization of posing. . . . Because she is castrated, she is the threat of castration. She might act as prompter for the whole scene because she stays outside this way"(*ML* 83). Woman's operation, or the feminine operation, as it has been surreptitiously defined within the discourses of Western culture, is outside the realm of signs. It is her threat, however, that initiates the movement into the realm of signs. As Derrida says in *Given Time*, woman may be absent from the narrative but she is always behind the scenes marking its tempo.

Recall that for Freud it is the sight of the female genitals that initiates the little boy's fear of castration which eventually resolves itself by his entry into the social with its laws and taboos. I read Irigaray as saying that woman is left with pretending, because which is the place that she is assigned by a sign system that has made her the "prompter for the whole scene," insofar as she is always outside the scene of representation. Within Western culture, hers is the action at a distance that makes the movement into signification possible; but this necessitates her exclusion from the realm of signification. So, whereas the "Jewish operation" is performed within the realm of signs, within the social, the "feminine operation" is not. As Irigaray might say, woman remains the blank, the absolute spot, within the economy of signs (*ML* 82–3).

My arguments in this chapter indicate that Derrida's deconstruction of woman is nothing more than a blank shot into the binary man/woman. Derrida does not make a position for woman within the economy of signs. Rather, he tries to valorize her position outside that economy as the undecidable. Yet his attempts merely reproduce the classical logic of castration within which woman is nothing and no one because she does not have the phallus. All value is still defined in terms of having or not having the phallus. Woman's value is her castration and her castration threats. Even the power to castrate, however, is illusory; as it turns out, she can only simulate castration and play the part of the castrator. I argue that this is because within Derrida's scenario, woman is always only *his* subject. She is the passive hymen constantly being broken and torn apart by the masculine. And any self-affirmation that Derrida might try to attribute to woman turns out to be merely man's affirmation of his mime of the feminine. Derrida affirms or values femininity only insofar as it is mimed by men. In fact, on his analysis, femininity can only be mimed by men because femininity itself is the act of miming—of giving oneself for what one is not. And, when woman mimes woman or femininity, she is taken too seriously and called "feminist." Finally, in answer to the question "Where does woman belong in Derrida's discourse?" woman does not belong except as the possession of the masculine.

4 *The Plaint of Ariadne* [10]

Even though the English translation of Luce Irigaray's *Marine Lover of Friedrich Nietzsche* appeared in 1991, there has been little commentary or critical engagement with the text published in English. [11] Occasionally a critic plucks a line from the text, or groups this work with others by Irigaray, and makes some general remarks; but no one has published a sustained reading of this extremely difficult and poetic text. Certainly most Nietzsche scholars with whom I have spoken about this work don't know what to make of it. Irigaray doesn't even mention Nietzsche's name until the last few pages of the book! Throughout this chapter I will engage in the difficult task of constructing a way to read this text.

I read Irigaray's *Marine Lover of Friedrich Nietzsche* as the plaint of Ariadne against her appropriation by the god Dionysus, her appropriation by Nietzsche, and her appropriation by Derrida in *Spurs*, his reading of Nietzsche's woman. Irigaray attempts to reappropriate woman for/from woman by, among other things, appropriating Derrida's reading of Nietzsche. At the center of Derrida's text is the question of propriation and Irigaray turns this question into a question of appropriation. Using a version of what has become her well-known methodology of double mimesis, Irigaray both reappropriates the position of the feminine by taking up that position and speaking "from the other side" and at the same time appropriates Derrida's text by reproducing it in a debilitating way. Luce Irigaray's *Marine Lover of Friedrich Nietzsche* is an attempt to answer the question of propriation from the side of the feminine, from the side of Ariadne, from the immemorial waters out of which we were born—the sea and woman's womb.

In the first section of *Marine Lover*, Irigaray creates Ariadne's response to the men who have tried to appropriate her for their own purposes. It is written as the final love-letter to end a bittersweet affair, because the addressee, the male lover, is incapable of marrying/merrying an-other; he loves always only himself. In this "letter" Ariadne complains that in her face he sees only the mirror image of himself and in her voice he hears only the echoes of his own words. The feminine and the woman that he embraces so tightly (that he becomes confused about his own identity) is just a projection of himself; he is deluded if he thinks that he has really touched any other. The forlorn female lover of "Speaking of Immemorial Waters" writes to Nietzsche and the men who come before and after him that they have forgotten women. They have forgotten their mothers out of whom they were born; they have forgotten their sisters with whom they learned who they are; they have forgotten their lovers from whom they receive confirmation of themselves.

Irigaray's Violated Lips

Although his name is never mentioned, Derrida is an implicit addressee of *Marine Lover*. Derrida's *Spurs* is full of sails always passing over the surface of the immemorial waters without dipping in, sails ripped apart by sharp objects. With the question of woman, "the stylate spur (*éperon stylé*) rips through the veil. It rents it in such a way that it not only allows there the vision or production of the very (same) thing, but in fact undoes the sail's self-opposition, the opposition of the veiled/unveiled (sailed/unsailed) which had folded over on itself" (Derrida, *S* 107). Ripping renders everything equal; the folds are torn open so that all opposition and difference become the "very same thing." Irigaray's "Immemorial Waters" pleads that we no longer need to tear women apart with some spurring operation in order to annihilate their difference: "Let us be done with believing we need flints which only open up the solid shells of your ideas, or spurs to get your impassive things moving" (*ML* 37).

The midsection of *Marine Lover,* in French entitled "*Lèvres Voilées*" (veiled lips), reads like a response to Derrida's spurring operation: "believing he must crack this thing open, that he can only take possession of it through violence, by forcing her/it beyond the present appearances, man arms himself with some pointed object—probe, stiletto, sometimes a pen—so he can get inside her/it" (*ML* 105). [croyant qu'il doit ouvrir cette chose, qu'il ne peut se l'approprier que par effraction, la forcer au-delà des apparences présentes, "l'homme" s'arme d'objet pointu—stylet, poignard, parfois plume—pour pénétrer (Irigaray, *AM* 112)]. Irigaray suggests that man creates the distance between woman's lips and then does not know how to get from one side to the other. He creates the distance between himself and her and then he cannot figure out how to cross it. He resorts to violence and violates her "lips"; Irigaray repeatedly uses the metaphor of lips to figure the female sex. In *Marine Lover* she says that the violence against woman's lips can be seen most clearly in the figure of the Virgin Mary, whose two pairs of lips form a cross as they are sewn shut by patriarchy, silent without sex (*ML* 166). Also recall Derrida's knives and letter openers that violently separate the virginal "lips" of books (*DS* 259). In *Spurs*, Derrida resorts to violence when he arms himself with Nietzsche's spur; he uses this spur against woman in order to make her give up her property, which is the very limit to the question of property itself.

Derrida reads the multiplicity of women in Nietzsche's texts as a sign "that Nietzsche had no illusions that he might ever know anything of these effects called woman, truth, castration, nor of those ontological effects of presence and absence" (*S* 95). He cites the heterogeneity of Nietzsche's texts as his proof. With his analysis of the multiplication of women in Nietzsche's texts, Derrida both figures woman, in her multiple personae, as that which cannot be possessed—cannot be property—and uses this figure of woman to deconstruct the notion of property. In his deconstruction of property, Derrida makes the figure of woman (as the figure of the undecidable) his property.

Where Derrida reads multiplicity in Nietzsche's women, Irigaray reads homogeneity. All of these woman, however they are characterized, are "the feminine" only within the masculine imaginary. Nietzsche creates these various women so that he can avoid any encounter with woman as an other. His woman is not an other; she is his creation. Derrida goes further and maintains that Nietzsche occupies the positions of his women. Nietzsche becomes woman. And within his own discourse on the feminine/woman, Derrida himself claims to occupy her position. Recall Derrida saying "I am a woman and I am beautiful." While this remark may be merely for literary force in his analysis of Blanchot in 1973, he answers an interviewer that he likes to think that he writes like a woman:

> Fauzia Assaad: Could not one find, in light of your text, a possibility of doing philosophy which is feminine?
>
> Jacques Derrida: I said "the woman (of) Nietzsche," the "woman Nietzsche": at the point where he affirms, at the moment where he is, where he loves the affirmative woman, he writes, if one can say, "from the hand of woman." Were you asking me a personal question? I would love to write as, like (a) woman. I am trying. . . (*Nietzsche aujourd'hui*, 299; my translation).

Irigaray interprets the desire by a man to be a woman as the ultimate refusal to love a woman (*ML* 39). She says that "mimicking the maternal-female role is equivalent to hiding it/oneself as other in the strategy for establishing the royal sovereignty" (*ML* 161). If man becomes woman, then there is no woman/other, there is only man and the woman/other is merely a mask worn by the selfsame. There are not two, but only one.

It is intriguing that Irigaray criticizes the mimetic strategy when it is used by Nietzsche and Derrida (although she never mentions Derrida) and yet she adopts this strategy herself. This raises some important questions: What is the difference between Irigaray's use of mimesis and Nietzsche's or Derrida's use of mimesis? What is the effect of Irigaray's appropriation of Derrida? And, how can a man read Irigaray? I will take up this last question first and come back to the question of mimesis.

Some critics might want to charge that just as there is no place for woman in Derrida's text, there is no place for man in Irigaray's texts. While I think that this is a serious concern deserving of more investigation, and Irigaray's strategy is not without its problems, there are some important differences between Derrida's style and Irigaray's. My argument against Derrida has been that his discussion of the feminine and woman is a discussion directed to and from the masculine and man. He does devote much attention to the feminine and woman in his writing, but in the end they are continually constructed as objects and reappropriated. Irigaray, on the other hand, addresses her text to the masculine and man. She uses the pronouns "I" and "you" to designate the female author in conversation with the male Nietzsche/Zarathustra/reader. Here, Irigaray is following Nietzsche's lead in *Zarathustra* where Zarathustra uses personal pronouns to address the woman whom he loves, eternity (see *Z* III "The Seven Seals"). While the masculine does occupy a position that is being called on by Irigaray to account for itself, it is not constructed as an object. Irigaray attempts to construct a dialogue (albeit one-sided) between masculine and feminine. She does not present a discussion of the masculine directed to and from the feminine or feminists. In many ways, she takes up the position of object assigned to the feminine and woman in the classics of Western philosophy and talks back. This is why many of her texts are difficult to read. The reader is often positioned as eavsdropping on a conversation in which s/he hears only one side, unless s/he can determine whom Irigaray is addressing in her text.

For example, Irigaray mimes Derrida's *Spurs* by speaking from the position of the mirror/woman. She takes Derrida's questions about propriety and truth seriously, but she asks these questions from the position of the other which Derrida has already closed off by assigning her/its place. Irigaray does this, however, without ever mentioning Derrida or *Spurs*. She positions him and his text as "woman" in relation to her own text. That is, his text becomes the silent other from whom she steals (back what belongs to woman) in order to write. The problematic effect is that Irigaray usurps man's position in order to speak from/for the feminine.

When Nietzsche or Derrida attempts to mime woman by taking up the place of the other the effect is a recuperation of the other into the economy of the same. Because these authors mimic from and for their position as subjects, their mimesis can become a conservative strategy designed to maintain the status quo, which does not tolerate difference. In other words, they mime the other of the same. By miming the other qua mime, they merely represent woman as the mirror whose non reflective surfaces in principle cannot be seen. This becomes just another strategy to ensure that those surfaces that do not reflect the masculine will not be seen. Unlike Irigaray who speaks to, and not for, the masculine, both Nietzsche and Derrida speak for, and as, the feminine.

In her *Luce Irigaray: Philosophy in the Feminine*, Margaret Whitford describes the difference between Derrida's strategy and Irigaray's as the difference between "speaking as" a woman or man and "speaking like" woman or man (128). Whitford persuasively argues that while Derrida is concerned with speaking *like* a woman or like the feminine, he is reluctant to admit that he is speaking *as* a man: "Derrida, for example, is able to acknowledge that the transcendental subject is male, but is less willing to acknowledge that his own place of enunciation is male; he insists on his feminine voice" (*LI* 132). Whitford maintains, and I agree, that Derrida's feminine voice works on a slippage between speaking like and speaking as. Whitford powerfully describes this process in *Luce Irigaray*:

> Because of the slippage between speaking like and speaking as a man or woman, Derrida is in the position where he can speak like a woman (this is clearly important to him) but, since he has deconstructed the opposition male/female, he can glide over the fact that he is speaking as a man. He particularly does not want feminists distributing "sexual identity cards." So he is then able to point out that feminists are phallocentric in that they speak "like men" while at the same time refusing them the possibility of speaking "as women," which would be a phallocentric stance too. In both cases, women lose out. (128)

As Whitford points out, Derrida overlooks the fact that it is different for men to speak as men, like man, than for women to speak mimetically like man, as women. The effects are very different (*LI* 129). Derrida seems to think that men miming woman is more effective than either women speaking as woman or women miming man because it is subversive. While it is true that it produces a different effect, I am arguing that it does not necessarily produce an effect that undermines phallocentrism; rather it can produce the effect of further excluding women and the possibility of speaking as women from the discourse of philosophy.

In *This Sex Which Is Not One,* Irigaray points out that in Plato there are two types of mimesis, productive and reproductive mimesis (131). Productive mimesis, which she identifies with the realm of music, does more than merely reproduce the status quo; it can provide new meanings and languages. Reproductive mimesis, on the other hand, which she identifies with the history of philosophy, merely reproduces the status quo in various guises. As long as philosophical discourse "does not question its own hierarchical relation to the difference between the sexes," it is merely reproductive. So long as it is "defined," "practiced," "monopolized" by a single sex, asks Irigaray, "does not writing remain an instrument of production in an unchanged regimen of property?" (*TS* 131). While Derrida does question philosophy's hierarchical conceptions of sexual difference, he does so by "becoming woman," by taking woman's place.

Rather than use mimesis to reproduce the subject in the dominant position, either by insisting on the subject-object dichotomy or by denying it, Irigaray attempts to go beyond the economy of the masculine subject and show something of what has not been represented of/from the other in the "unchanged regimen of property."[12] This is why whereas Derrida reads the women in Nietzsche's texts as Nietzsche's triumph over the subject-object dichotomy, Irigaray reads them as his failure to go beyond it.

Derrida uses the multiplicity of women in Nietzsche's texts to show that the object, woman, is not unified and therefore the subject is not either. He intends to deconstruct the opposition subject-object, man-woman. Within Derrida's discourse, woman in all of her guises, and because of her multiplicity, becomes the sign of the undecidable. He recuperates her multiplicity by turning her into a formula for the undecidability of language itself. He imagines her outside the discourse of truth because she represents both truth and untruth. She becomes for him the very possibility of discourse, the mark of undecidability, the "hymen's graphic" that produces the ontological effects of opposition and dichotomy (see Derrida, *S* 107, 111). This is why it is funny that woman is *his* subject; especially since it is obvious in his text that she is never her own subject. She is always only the subject of the advice given from one man to another: "one must beware to keep one's own distance from her beguiling song of enchantment" (Derrida, *S* 49).

Irigaray reads in Nietzsche's uses of woman the desire to master the other by absorbing it and thereby annihilating it in its difference. She argues that positioning woman as the undecidable is still to position her within man's game; the only difference between this game and the more traditional games that men play with women is that these ambivalent boys up the ante: "That he should will himself to be feminine doubles the ante perhaps. Doesn't change the game" (*ML* 117). He merely steals from her so that he won't have to acknowledge his debt (see *ML* 79). The game remains the same because man always ends up playing the castration game, which Irigaray argues reduces all difference to a question of more or less (*ML* 80–81). Within the game of castration there is no other way to conceive of difference than in terms of quantity. And Derrida too falls into the game of castration, not only because within his discourse there is no alternative but to do violence to yourself—chew off a limb—in order to at least demonstrate your good faith attempt to go beyond the metaphysics of presence, but also because he explicitly engages in the debate over whether or not woman is castrated/castrating: "Unable to seduce or to give vent to desire without it, woman is in need of castration's effect. But evidently she does not believe in it. She who, unbelieving, still plays with castration, she is woman . . . . woman knows that castration *does not take place* [*la castration n'a pas lieu*]" (*S* 61). Irigaray responds: "And whether or not woman wants castration, whether or not she believes in that operation, and finds it casting her again as seductress, isn't this/the id still thinking on the male side? This is still what man's woman would be like. And, perhaps, the masculine's feminine?" (*ML* 85).

Irigaray argues that the economy of castration does not allow woman to have any relationship to herself or to other women. By defining her always in some relation to castration—even if her relation to castration is disbelief—she is always and only defined in relation to the masculine and never the feminine. Irigaray alludes to another "truth" beyond the economy of castration that has a place when women embrace themselves and each other (ML 85). Taking woman's sex as a metaphor, as she often does, Irigaray suggests that women are always touching themselves in such a way that it is impossible to separate the subject of the touch from the object of the touch. Man, on the other hand, cannot embrace himself in this way. For man, "to touch oneself" is what sets up the subject-object/subject-predicate distinction (*ML* 91). He touches himself as a subject touching an object.[13] And even when man takes woman as his other, he cannot embrace her: "should the other serve as a sheath for him, at best he will make a wrapping of it, but not an embracing" (*ML* 85). Between the sword and the sheath there is no exchange.

Irigaray is concerned with the economy of exchange. Like *Spurs*, "Veiled Lips" is full of metaphors of economy. Recall that at the center of *Spurs* is the question of propriety or property. Involved with property are the questions of "propriation, exchange, give, take, debit, *price*" [la propriation, l'échange, le donner, le prendre, la dette, *le coût*] (*S* 112–13). Irigaray takes up these questions from the other side and asks: How does man finance the death of his other? What belongs, is proper, to woman? (*ML* 79, *AM* 86–87).

Within the economy of castration, nothing belongs to woman; she is not allowed any possessions. "The possessive, the mark of belonging, does not belong to her" (*ML* 86–87). Within the economy of castration, "the question that would be appropriate to her is always and forever impossible to formulate even if one wanted to make the effort" (*ML* 88). Everything that she has belongs to man. "She stakes him in a new game without his needing to borrow from the kitty. And therefore go into debt, risk losing" [Elle lui redonne de l'enjeu sans qu'il se voie repuiser dans la cave. Donc s'endetter, risquer de perdre] (*ML* 79, *AM* 85).

His theft is all in the name of "love." Man takes from woman because he loves her. But Irigaray wants to know why he never gives anything in return. He demands that woman affirm his identity, but he does not even allow her an identity: "And if, to the whole of himself, he says yes and also asks her to say yes again, did it ever occur to him to say yes to her? Did he ever open himself to that other world? For him it doesn't even exist. So who speaks of love, to the other, without having even begun to say 'yes'?"[14] (*ML* 190). If love is always only love of the same, then love is the murder of the other (*ML* 188). Man finances the death of the other by stealing from her, becoming her, in the name of his "love" for her. If Derrida reads Nietzsche as suggesting that when "we" love a woman "we" risk death, Irigaray responds that the risk is only that by killing her, "your" other, you also kill yourself (see Derrida, *S* 45–47). As I will explain later, this is what Irigaray suggests happened to Nietzsche. By taking away everything that is woman's, man's mirror becomes a void.

Within the economy of castration man does not go into debt as he takes from woman. She gives herself and he gives nothing in return. Within this economy there is no reciprocal exchange between two. There is only exchange as substitution, which is always defined in terms of the masculine possession, having or not having the phallus, or some substitute for it. Yet how can Irigaray suggest that this economy of castration is operating within Nietzsche's *Zarathustra* when Zarathustra proclaims the gift-giving virtue as the highest virtue? And certainly Derrida explicitly rejects the economy of castration in favor of a hymeneal economy. In fact in *Given Time* does he not open up the possibility of imagining an economy beyond exchange as the circulation or substitution of goods, an economy where the gift is possible?

An Economy of the Gift

> This is your thirst: to become sacrifices and gifts yourselves; and that is why you thirst to pile up all the riches in your soul. Insatiably your soul strives for treasures and gems, because your virtue is insatiable in wanting to give. You force all things to and into yourself that they may flow back out of your well as the gifts of your love. Verily, such a gift-giving love must approach all values as a robber; but whole and holy I call this selfishness.
>
> —Friedrich Nietzche, "On the Gift Giving Virtue," in
> *Thus Spake Zarathustra*

The gift-giving virtue that Zarathustra describes seems to be a gift of oneself to oneself. Certainly, as he describes it here, the gift is a gift, even sacrifice, of the self, and all things are taken back into the self. Within this economy of the gift all things come from and return to the self. In addition, all gifts given out of the self are for the sake of taking something back in; they are forms of taking. Gifts move through complex circuits in *Zarathustra*, but are they ever given to an other? Is reciprocal exchange possible within the economy of the gift set out in *Zarathustra*?

Gary Shapiro analyzes the ambiguities of Zarathustra's gift-giving virtue in *Alcyone: Nietzsche on Gifts, Noise, and Women*. There Shapiro identifies scenes where Zarathustra engages in an exchange with his interlocutor. Specifically he cites Zarathustra's first encounter with the hermit and his encounter with the old woman who instructs him to take the whip when he goes to women. Shapiro argues that Zarathustra's encounter with the hermit/saint "could be taken as Nietzsche's transformation of the fable of the state of nature. Two isolated figures meet, figures who as hermits are represented as self-sufficient. But they enact neither the Hobbesian war of all against all nor the Hegelian battle to the death that is resolved only through the elementary social form of lord and bondsman. Instead they engage in a highly ceremonial and subtly orchestrated discussion of gifts, in which each verbal gesture is a giving or receiving" (24). We have to wonder after this encounter between the two hermits, Zarathustra and the saint, whether or not there is any exchange. In this scenario we have two charachters of the same type, one whose gift is his love of God, the other whose gift is the death of God. Yet neither of them gives his gift to the other; these are not gifts that the other is prepared to receive. The saint gives Zarathustra advice that he will not take; and Zarathustra leaves before he gives the saint a gift that would be a taking away. So Zarathustra leaves before stealing from the saint. Shapiro suggests that this is his gift; Zarathustra gives to the saint by not stealing from him his belief in God. But what kind of gift is a gift that is merely not a taking away?

Although, as Shapiro points out, the old woman is given gifts by Zarathustra while the hermit is only not taken from, perhaps the hermit receives more than the old woman. For what Zarathustra gives her is an assortment of aphorisms that indicate that woman uses man as a means to a child and that she should love her man more than he loves her and respect his will more than her own.[15] Zarathustra gives her things that take away from woman. Shapiro points out that within *Zarathustra* gift giving is always ambiguous. It is always both a giving and a taking away. It is violent and makes demands on the receiver. It is always an act of selfishness. It is the lust to rule (see Shapiro *A* 17, 22). Both giving and receiving are dangerous acts. And Zarathustra suggests that it is better to steal than to receive.

In "The Night Song" Zarathustra laments that he longs to accept gifts from another. He wants love and yet he cannot receive from another: "But I live in my own light; I drink back into myself the flames that break out of me. I do not know the happiness of those who receive; and I have often dreamed that even stealing must be more blessed than receiving" (*Z* II 218). In *Ecce Homo* Nietzsche says that this lonely dithyramb of the solitary lover expresses the suffering of Dionysus and that only Ariadne can answer such a cry (*EH* 308). "Who besides me" proclaims Nietzsche, "knows what Ariadne is!" (*EH* 308).

On my reading, Irigaray's "Speaking of Immemorial Waters" is Ariadne's refusal to marry the male lover—Nietzsche—Dionysus, Zarathustra, because he wants to marry only *his own* image of her; and it is this insistence on the selfsame that prevents their making merry together. The forlorn lover of "Speaking of Immemorial Waters" responds to Nietzsche/Zarathustra's night song by pointing out that she has always and only been whatever he made her out to be. Only he knows Ariadne, because he has made her in his own image. Ariadne's response is to demand her freedom:

> Let me go. Yes, let me go onward. Beyond the place of no return. Either you seize hold of me or you throw me away, but always according to your whim of the moment. I am good or bad according to your latest good or evil. Muse or fallen angel to suit the needs of your most recent notion. (*ML* 11)

> You meet Ariadne or Diotima or . . . You want to marry her. To chain her
> to your side, as guardian of your hearth, so that your work can be
> accomplished. She refuses. Stresses her freedom in the face of your will.
> You try to find your balance again, fail. Except in the eternal recurrence
> that creates an autological movement that cannot be reopened. By giving
> yourself up wholly to a center in which the other has no role except as
> counterweight or balance arm between you and yourself, you cannot get
> out of the circle. (ML 72–73)

On Irigaray's reading, within the circle of the eternal recurrence gifts are impossible. The circle maps the circulation of goods and property that always returns to its origin, in this case the male lover, and all giving is really a taking away. In *Given Time* Derrida describes this circular economy of exchange in which the gift is impossible (9). There Derrida maintains that the exchange of gifts cannot be reciprocal because the recognition of a gift, especially with the giving of a gift in return, annuls the gift as gift (*GT* 14). Once the gift enters the economy of exchange , or property, it is impossible. The gift, if it is possible, takes us outside of the economy of exchange. So, any gift is not a gift when it is acknowledged or recognized because acknowledgement puts the gift within an economy of exchange. On Derrida's analysis the only possible gifts are gifts that are not recognized as such by either the giver or the receiver.

Within the economy of exchange, on the other hand—an economy that Derrida also identifies with the economy of castration or property—a gift always returns to its giver. Derrida claims that through gift giving a subject wants to get his own identity back by reappropriating his identity as property (*GT* 11; cf. FV 448). The gift allows the subject to translate what is proper to him into property. By giving a gift the subject binds the receiver with debt and obligation; within the economy of exchange, the receiver is bound to return the gift (without literally *returning* the gift). Following Nietzsche's descriptions of the violence of giving and receiving in *Zarathustra*, Derrida interprets gift giving as a violent act that enslaves the receiver as soon as he accepts it (*GT* 147). Like Nietzsche's Zarathustra, Derrida sees gift giving as a selfish act whose pleasure, even the pleasure of surprising another, is always autoaffective. What the giver really takes pleasure in is his power over the receiver as the cause of the surprise (*GT* 146). On Derrida's analysis violence is the absolute of the gift: "Such violence may be considered the very condition of the gift, its constitutive impurity once the gift is engaged in the process of *circulation*, once it is promised to recognition, keeping, indebtedness, credit, but also once it *must be, owes itself to be* excessive and thereby surprising. *The violence appears irreducible, within the circle or outside it, whether it repeats the circle or interrupts it"* (GT 147).

At this point we could conclude that violence is perhaps the only absolute in Derrida's philosophy. As I suggested earlier, for Derrida reading and writing are violent operations. Philosophy itself is violence. Now gift giving is violence. Violence is irreducible *both inside and outside* the phallogocentric economy of exchange. Staying within the circle of phallogocentric exchange requires violence but so does breaking out. While everything else changes into its opposite to the point of undecidability, violence remains; yes, of course, it is also indistinguishable from its opposite, nonviolence, but this is precisely what makes it possible to say that all is violent. Both violence and nonviolence are violent. Does the converse—violence is nonviolence—have the same power within Derrida's discourse? In the end, is there nothing but violence?

Nietzsche identifies a violence at the heart of reason, language, and morality that levels all difference and turns it into the same. Freud identifies a violence necessary to enter the social that demands the exclusion of bodily drives and particularly of their association with the maternal body. And in the face of some attempts to think a nonviolent philosophy that does not begin with the Hegelian premise (for example, Levinas's philosophy), Derrida continues to insist on the primacy and inescapability of violence. In "Violence in Metaphysics" Derrida describes a discourse that is itself war and a philosophy that operates according to an economy of violence (116-17). Derrida maintains that Western philosophy cannot escape the violence of the Hegelian lordship/bondsman encounter (VM 119). Any engagement with an other, or with difference, is necessarily a war (VM 119, 130). Like the Hegelian violence, Derridian violence is constitutive and it is inherent in the self-other relation, or any relation across difference. Is our best hope in the face of violence, as Derrida suggests, to turn violence against itself? Or, can we risk imagining the possibility of nonviolence?

Derrida discusses the relation between violence and nonviolence in "The Violence of the Letter: From Lévi–Strauss to Rousseau." There he points out that anthropologist Lévi–Strauss becomes complicit with the very ethnocentric values that he is trying to undermine when he assumes that prior to the appearance of the anthropologist and writing that the Nambikwara were an innocent, nonviolent people (OG 114). Derrida shows that Lévi-Strauss's claim that writing is violence (which Derrida in fact believes, OG 135) presupposes that there is some pure and innocent presence in a speech before writing that is violated by writing (OG 119).

Derrida, of course, argues that there is an absence at the heart of speech that prefigures writing and for this reason speech already operates according to the logic of writing (OG 128, 139-40). If writing is violence, and speech is already writing, then there is violence prior to writing proper. But what is this violence? And why doesn't it presuppose some nonviolent presence that *it* necessarily violates?

Derrida is clear that his supposition that writing is violence is not like Lévi-Strauss's supposition that writing is violence. Derrida insists that his supposition does not presuppose the myth of presence: "Recalling in this introduction that violence did not wait for the appearance of writing in the narrow sense, that writing has always begun in language, we, like Lévi-Strauss, conclude that violence is writing. But, coming at it another way, this proposition has a radically different meaning. It ceases to be supported by the myth of myth, by the myth of a speech originally good, and of a violence which would come to pounce upon it as a fatal accident. A fatal accident which is nothing but history itself" (OG 135). Where as Lévi-Strauss identifies *writing proper* with violence, Derrida identifies what makes writing possible—what makes writing writing—with violence. Absence makes writing possible. While I agree with Derrida that language requires absence, I don't understand why this absence is necessarily violent. Nor do I understand how this absence can be violent or do violence without presupposing some presence which it violates. Is violence possible without violation? If presence is a myth and Derrida's essay is beyond the myth of this myth, then how is absence violent unless it violates presence? What is it that absence violates unless it is the myth of nonviolence or innocent presence?

Like Lévi-Strauss, we can do violence by seeing nonviolence where there is violence. This can become especially dangerous not only when we romanticize the other and thereby violate that other (as in the case of Lévi-Strauss's anthropologist) but also when we cover over our own violence by calling it nonviolence. We justify our violence by seeing it, or characterizing it, as nonviolent. We euphemize our violence away. On the other hand, however, can we do violence by seeing violence where there is none? Can we make something violent or create violence where there was none? Certainly, interpreting something as violent can in itself lead to empirical violence, war and retaliation. Yet, my neat distinction between two modes of violence—which tends to reduce everything to violence—presupposes presence, a reality, that is violated in its re-presentation (when it is misrepresented). Is representation necessarily violent? Is it violent because its presence is absence? Because it presents itself as something that it is not? Because it thereby performs the feminine operation?

In his early writings, "On Truth and Falsity in the Ultramoral Sense," and *The Birth of Tragedy*, Nietzsche suggests that all representation, especially in language, does violence to the world. In these texts, however, Nietzsche holds on to a trace of some reality or nature that is corrupted in its representation. Something is lost in the translation of this nature into language. This is why in *The Birth of Tragedy* Nietzsche says that he prefers music without lyrics (*BT* §6). In his later writings Nietzsche seems to give up this remnant of nature or reality and suggest that our belief in such a transcendental realm is an illusion affected by our language (see *OGM* I §13, 45). Now, rather than corrupt reality, language creates it. On this view, to characterize something as violent could make it so. In addition, throughout Nietzsche's writings there is the suggestion that language corrupts or distorts some more primordial bodily drive force and thereby does violence to the instincts. Nietzsche often suggests that communication, language and grammar are the products of human animals becoming social; he romanticizes a presocial innocence in which aggressive instincts were directly discharged (see *OGM* II § 16, 84–5). As I have suggested earlier, for Nietzsche there is always a violence involved in language, in speaking and listening, as well as reading and writing. Moreover, for Nietzsche it is not only the case that language is violent, but also language should become violent. Nietzsche prescribes violence. Violence is what separates strong language from impotent language. Everything creative must be destructive.

While Derrida might agree that everything creative must also be destructive, he would not prescribe violence except insofar as it is necessary, possibly in order to avoid greater violence. Can we only hope to fight violence with violence? Derrida suggests this conclusion in his analysis of Levinas in "Violence and Metaphysics":

> Discourse, therefore, if it is originally violent, can only do itself violence, can only negate itself in order to affirm itself, make war upon the war which institutes it without ever being able to reappropriate this negativity, to the extent that it is discourse. Necessarily without reappropriating it, for if it did so, the horizon of peace would disappear into the night (worst violence as previolence). This secondary war, as the avowal of violence, is the least possible violence, the only way to repress the worst violence, the violence of primitive and prelogical silence, of an unimaginable night which would not even be the opposite of day, an absolute violence which would not even be the opposite of nonviolence: nothingness or pure non-

sense. Thus discourse chooses itself violently in opposition to nothingness or pure non-sense, and, in philosophy, against nihilism (VM 130; cf. FL 49).[16]

Outside discourse, beyond all oppositions, including the opposition between violence and nonviolence, is absolute violence. Absolute violence is primitive and our only safeguard against it is violence, the violence of distinguishing one thing from another, of protecting and exposing the myth of presence and property, the violence of writing. For Derrida, in order to avoid absolute violence, the unspeakable violence, we must continue to speak/write and to risk doing violence to the world and each other. He suggests that we must continue to speak/write to one another even insofar as our language itself does violence (FL).[17]

We could imagine that language is violent because it is necessarily generating/generated from a fundamentally violent intersubjective relationship. Or, we could imagine the language is violent because it violates or misrepresents intersubjective relationships; it fixes what is fluid. The first position presupposes that either violence precedes language and that language merely carries within it the violence of the intersubjective relation or that the intersubjective relationship is already linguistic and this is what makes it violent. To say that the intersubjective relationship is violent because it is linguistic might be to say that language is violent because it is intersubjective. In other words, what makes language violent could be the fact that it is intersubjective, that it takes two (and therefore three, a mediating element). To be linguistic is to be intersubjective and to be intersubjective is to be violent. Derrida seems to adopt some version of this last argument when he says "If it is true, as I in fact believe, that writing cannot be thought outside of the horizon of intersubjective violence, is there anything, even science, that radically escapes it? Is there a knowledge, and, above all, a language, scientific or not, that one can call alien at once to writing and to violence? If one answers in the negative, as I do, the use of these concepts to discern the specific character of writing is not pertinent" (OG 127). Is intersubjectivity necessarily violent? Is it also essentially or fundamentally violent? Is there any way to escape the fundamental violence of the Hegelian master/slave relationship?

At this point in my analysis it is unclear what Derrida means by violence. For Derrida is violence necessarily violation? In Of Grammatology Derrida distinguishes three different levels of violence in relation to Lévi-Strauss's analysis of the Nambikwara. First, there is the originary violence of language which replaces the absolute proximity of self-presence ("which has never been given but only dreamed of and always already split") with the proper name (*OG* 112). The name breaks self-presence even while repeating the myth of self-presence. The second level violence is the prohibition of writing and the proper name which is legislated to protect the proper (self-presence) from its violation by the name. And "a third violence can possibly emerge or not (an empirical possibility) within what is commonly called evil, war, indiscretion, rape: which consists of revealing by effraction the so-called proper name, the originary violence which had severed the proper from its property and it self-sameness" (*OG* 112). The violation of the prohibition of speaking proper names operates on the level of empirical violence along with rape and murder. It is the violation of a legal prohibition that is enforced in order to return the property lost to language in the first place.

In a sense, in empirical violence it is what stands in for, and covers up, the original violence of language (absence) that is violated. Empirical violence is the violation of the law, the contract, the third party, that mediates social relations and both destroys and maintains the myth of presence. Since the third party or mediation is necessary for social exchange, self-presence is already absent; but self-presence is maintained in the third party who is positioned to mediate between two subjects supposedly present only to themselves. "This last violence is all the more complex in its structure because it refers at the same time to the two inferior levels of arche-violence and of law. In effect, it reveals the first nomination which was already an expropriation, but it denudes also that which since then functioned as the proper, the so-called proper, substitute of the deferred proper, *perceived* by the *social* and *moral consciousness* as the proper, the reassuring seal of self-identity, the secret" (*OG* 112).

The violation of the law can be complex in that the law can at once protect and violate the myth of presence or property. If, as Derrida maintains in "Force of Law," the law is born out of justice, then the law can never be just because the act of justice "must concern singularity, individuality, irreplaceable groups and lives, the other or myself as other, in a unique situation," while law requires a rule or norm that is not true to the singularity of the individual (FL 17). The law requires the mediation of a third party that both guarantees and prevents the myth of self-presence or the proper: "To address oneself to the other in the language of the other is, it seems, the condition of all possible justice, but apparently, in all rigor, it is not only impossible (since I cannot speak the language of the other except to the extent that I appropriate it and assimilate it according to the law of an implicit third) but even excluded by justice as law (*droit*), inasmuch as justice as right seems to imply an element of universality, the appeal to a third party who suspends the unilaterally or singularity of the idioms" (FL 17).

This brings us back to the necessary violence of all intersubjective relations. When in "The Violence of the Letter: From Lévi–Strauss to Rousseau" Derrida asserts that all intersubjective relationships are necessarily violent, and in "Violence and Metaphysics" he suggests that we cannot escape the violence of the Hegelian master/slave relationship, could he be referring to the necessity for appropriation in any intersubjective relationship? Is he arguing that insofar as every intersubjective relationship requires a third party, and every third party is necessarily engaged in the process of translation or appropriation of idioms, and appropriation is violent insofar as it takes away from the proper or singularity of the individuals, then all intersubjective relationships are violent? This argument operates on the myth of self-presence or the proper; what is singular is properly proper and what is universal is appropriation of the properly proper. The process of appropriation violates the proper. Appropriation is the misrepresentation of self-presence. I can never see you as you see yourself and your view is the proper view.

Certainly intersubjective relationships require communication and exchange, the third party. Yet, this exchange does not have to be violent in the sense of the Hegelian master/slave relationship. It does not have to be a struggle to the death. Even the terrain of the negotiation between appropriation and alterity can be altered if we replace the Hegelian model with a new model of intersubjectivity. Within the Hegelian model of intersubjectivity violence is necessarily directed towards the other and at the onset of subjectivity the negotiation between appropriation and alterity is a hostile attempt to annhilate the other; but if we replace the Hegelian model, perhaps we can envision a model of intersubjectivity that can account for the so-called violence of the negotiation between self and other without requiring that that violence be directed towards the other.

In some of his writings, for example, "Force of Law," and "The Laws of Reflection," Derrida talks about *force* and violence. With the introduction of the concept of force, following Nietzsche, Derrida can refigure the constitutive violence, that might be necessary for any creation, in terms of force. The discussion of force allows for a law or language that, although constituted through a certain violence or force, cannot be reduced to violence. Constitutive violence as force is neither just nor unjust (FL 13). Perhaps this type of violence as force, as constitutive, does not violate. Ceratinly it complicates the issue of violation. In fact, although as Derrida points out in "The Laws of Reflection," constitutive violence is always in danger of becoming excessive violence, the notion of force makes the always precarious, but necessary, distinction between constitutive and excessive violence possible.

In "The Laws of Reflection," Derrida maintains that this constitutional or constitutive violence can be forgotten so that the constitution or law can be effective only if certain conditions are met; included among these conditions are that the law be enacted and that the constitutive violence not *appear* too great or excessive (LR 18). In the case of South Africa, Derrida argues that the violence was excessive, or not excessive enough, because there were too many witnesses to the inequalities and constitutional violations. In other words, the white minority did not commit the genocide necessary to enable the forgetting of the constitutive violence. So either constitutive violence must be extremely and powerfully excessive or it must enact a law whose effect will make people forget the constitutive violence: those who suffer as a result of the law must be dead and their memories erased, and those who are alive must have no memory of injustice. Derrida claims that the excessive violence in South Africa allows Nelson Mandela to use the law against itself, since the constitution declares democracy and yet it did not produce democracy for all, but radical inequalities between white and black South Africans (LR 17–18).

Perhaps, then, when Derrida insists that Western philosophy cannot escape the violence of the Hegelian lordship/bondsman model, he is not suggesting that intersubjective relationships are *essentially* violent, but that they necessarily *risk* violence. Between Derrida and Levinas, we might imagine that language is an invitation to the other, which always necessarily runs the risk of violence. It makes no sense to think of language as essentially violence since we don't need language to do violence to each other, we need only sticks and stones. Yet, as Derrida reminds us, the invitation's double is "conductive violence" (ATP 65). Derrida indicates in his analysis of Levinas that to engage in conversation we must be willing to risk violence; we have to risk being victims and risk victimizing. More than this, engaging in a conversation always runs the risk of merely substituting words for weapons, or justifying the use of weapons with words that purify violence and try to turn it into a necessity or call it "justice" ("ethnic cleansing," "the final solution," "peace keeping missions").

While I agree with Derrida that in order to act or communicate, we always risk violence, I believe that we also need to imagine the possibility of nonviolence, even if this image is constantly called into question. The image of possibility is what continues to motivate action and communication. As Derrida insists, we must act in the face of these risks. In

"Force of Law" he maintains that the possibility of ethics is based on our uncertainty in the face of this risk: "A decision that didn't go through the ordeal of the undecidable would not be a free decision, it would only be the programmable application or unfolding of a calculable process" (FL 24). If we are certain in our action and face no risks, then we are merely following orders from some authority beyond ourselves; we are not free and therefore we are not ethical agents. This is Simone de Beauvoir's criticism of both Kant's and Plato's suggestion that to know the good is to do the good; doing the right thing becomes a matter of epistemology and not ethics (*EA* 33). Ethics requires the freedom to make mistakes, the freedom to do violence or refrain from violence. The problem, of course, is that it is not always easy to tell the difference. In spite of his own intentions, Nietzsche's texts become the ammunition of the Third Reich and for the good of the nation Heidegger joins the Nazi party. Although the risk of violence is essential to ethics, violence is not. Although every intersubjective relation brings with it the risk of violence, it is not reducible to violence.

Here again Derrida's distinction between constitutive and excessive violence might be helpful. Derrida suggests that constitutive violence or force is necessary in order to avoid the excessive violence of injustice. Every ethical and judicial decision must be both creative and destructive in order to be just: "In short, for a decision to be just and responsible, it must, in its proper moment if there is one, be both regulated and without regulation: it must conserve the law and also destroy it or suspend it enough to have to reinvent it in each case, rejustify it, at least reinvent the reaffirmation and the new and free confirmation of its principle. Each case is other, each decision is different and requires an absolutely unique interpretation, which no existing, coded rule can or ought to guarantee absolutely (FL 23). This unique interpretation is the violence as force which Derrida describes as neither just nor unjust in itself. Constitutive or interpretative violence or force is necessary in the name of justice, in the name of the necessary impossibility of nonviolence.

Derrida himself suggests that we need to imagine an impossible nonviolence towards which we aim, not as a horizon or a regulative principle, but as an immediate call to responsibility (FL 20). In "Force of Law" Derrida indicates that justice is outside of the law, outside of the mediation of language or law, because "as the experience of absolute alterity," justice "is unpresentable, but it is the chance of the event and the condition of history" (27). Justice calls language and law to account for their authority from the other side of the intersubjective exchange. Justice is both the motivation and limit to that exchange. Justice demands the impossible because it demands that we continue within the realm of language and law, the realm of the myth of presence and property, to cultivate justice: "the deconstruction of all presumption of a determinant certitude of a present justice itself operates on the basis of an infinite 'idea of justice,' infinite because it is irreducible, irreducible because it owed to the other, owed to the other, before any contract, because it has come, the other's coming as the singularity that is always other. This 'idea of justice' seems to be irreducible in its affirmative character, in its demand of gift without exchange, without circulation, without recognition or gratitude, without economic circularity, without calculation and without rules, without reason and without rationality" (FL 25).

How, then, are we to diagnose Derrida's insistence on violence and the impossibility of gift giving? Is he suggesting that in spite of the fact that nonviolence and giving to an other are impossible that we still must continue to give? Is he suggesting that we must continue to perform the feminine operation and give ourselves for what we are not, to risk violence, the violence of castration, in order to avoid the absolute violence of complete annihilation? In *Spurs* Derrida associates the impossibility of the gift with the impossibility of woman. There Derrida has described the feminine operation as that of giving oneself for what one is not. The feminine operation *is* the violent operation of giving, giving oneself for something one is not. Derrida realizes that to define woman in terms of the economy of exchange is to define her in terms of the feminine operation through which she pretends to give herself up as property to be possessed by the male. But woman is not property, because there is no such *thing* as a woman, which is to say that woman is not a *thing*. She is not property. To give oneself for, then, is to pretend to be a thing, a piece of property, which of course is always to give oneself for something that one is not. Within an economy that turns everything into a presence/present or an absence, it is impossible to give a gift because, as both Nietzsche and Derrida suggest, the only real gift is a gift of oneself; property is never a gift. This is why, as Gary Shapiro points out, the only real gifts from Zarathustra are his speeches; and language is taken for something that it is not when it is reduced to property (through copyright laws, for example). Also, Being cannot be reduced to property. Being gives itself as something that it is not when it gives itself as a thing. Derrida claims that there is no such "thing" as Being because, like woman or language, Being is not a thing. Being is neither a subject nor an object. And this is why Derrida follows Heidegger in saying that there is no such thing as an essence of the *es gibt Sein*: "Just as there is no such thing then as a Being or an essence of *the* woman or the sexual difference, there is also no such thing as an essence of the *es gibt* in the *es gibt Sein*, that is, of Being's giving and gift" (S 121).[18]

In addition to maintaining that the gift is given from/of oneself and cannot be reduced to property, a thing, or an essence, Nietzsche and Derrida maintain that it is a gift of oneself *to oneself*, but that is only because they are still negotiating the gift within the economy of presence/presents. Within this economy which seems to be based on exchange, there is, in the end, no real exchange or change because everything goes out of, and comes back to, itself. There is no exchange with, or of, an other. I want to try to imagine an economy in which gifts of oneself can be given to an other and in which reciprocal exchange is possible. Perhaps this is Derrida's vision, even Nietzsche's vision. By calling into question traditional notions of subjectivity, don't Nietzsche and Derrida make it possible to imagine a giving to "oneself" that can no longer be self-ish? Once we begin to rethink the self-other dualism, then isn't a gift to the other also a gift to the self?

In a fascinating comparison of Nietzsche and Hélène Cixous on giving and the gift Alan Schrift suggests that Nietzsche provides an alternative economy within which gift giving is possible. In "On the Gynecology of Morals: Nietzsche and Cixous on the Logic of the Gift, " Schrift sets out two possible economies which he figures, following Cixous, as masculine and feminine.[19] Within the masculine economy exchange is based on debt; every gift is really a debt that must be repaid. Schrift calls this an economy of reciprocal exchange. What he means by reciprocal is that every offer requires a counter-offer; no one gets something for nothing. On this model exchange is always a demand for something in return. He points out that what Cixous calls the masculine economy is grounded on Locke's definition of property, in the *Second Treatise of Government*, as whatever is taken out of nature and mixed with human labor. The masculine economy is based on an exchange of property.

Cixous makes a connection between property and the proper. In *The Newly Born Woman* she describes the Hegelian model of intersubjectivity through which one self-consciousness recognizes itself through another as an exchange of property (*NBW* 71, 78–79). On the Hegelian model, the self appropriates the other in order to acquire its own self-consciousness. Schrift continues Cixous's analysis: "The phallocentric desire that animates the Hegelian dialectic of self and other is a desire for appropriation: one confronts the other as different and unequal and one seeks to make the other one's own. The desire to possess, to receive a return on one's investments, animates an economy that Cixous suggests we call 'masculine' " (OGM). If the masculine economy seeks appropriation, it is because it is driven by the fear of expropriation. The masculine economy is driven by the fear of loss, the fear of castration. The masculine economy operates according to the logic of castration, which, as Schrift indicates, is an economy of scarcity wherein everything is defined in terms of loss and there is never enough to go around. Within this economy one person gains only at another's expense and every investment expects a return.

Within the feminine economy, on the other hand, the intersubjective relationship is founded on generosity and gift giving. Gifts of oneself are not property or possession, subjects or objects, that return over and over again to the self alone. Exchange takes place not in an economy of scarcity but within an economy of overabundance where giving of oneself does not require sacrifice and taking or receiving is not registered as debt only. Schrift associates this feminine libidinal economy with Nietzsche's discussion of generosity and plenitude. He argues that in spite of what Nietzsche explicitly says about the feminine, the economy endorsed in his text is a feminine economy as Cixous sets it out.

Schrift argues that Nietzsche proposes two notions of justice. One notion—the masculine—is based on debt and revenge: The creditor cannot forget the debt owed him and the debtor resents his debt. The second notion—the feminine—is based on generosity of forgetfulness: The creditor is rich enough to forget about debt. The difference between these two notions of justice is the difference between an economy of scarcity and an economy of overabundance. Schrift claims that two primary examples of gifts given from the spirit of overabundance are Zarathustra's gifts to his disciples and Nietzsche's gifts to his readers. Zarathustra presents his speeches as gifts and Nietzsche presents his texts as gifts. In both cases these gifts are gifts of the self that cannot be reduced to the realm of property. Yet a question still arises, "To whom are these gifts given?"

Nietzsche writes *Ecce Homo*, for example, as a gift to himself on his Forty-Fourth birthday. In fact he identifies all of his writings of 1888 as presents for which he is grateful, presents to himself (*EH* 221). And while Zarathustra is overfull, pregnant, with his gifts, who receives them without feeling indebted? Does Zarathustra steal from woman his gifts to others without acknowledging her? Do his gifts come from an other? Is his forgetting is an active forgetting of her, the first gift giver, the giver of life? Does he forgets that the gift of life comes from a woman, the mother? Hers was the first gift and to advocate forgetting is to justify forgetting her, the origin of life. From Socrates as midwife to a pregnant Zarathustra, philosophy is full of attempts to forget the connection between woman and life. The latest attempt to forget might be the poststructuralist scoff at the "nostalgia" for origins. Rather than trying to substitute a masculine mother for a feminine mother (ala Nietzsche), they advocate forgetting origins altogether. For example, Gary Shapiro sings praises for the images of waterbirds—specifically, the halcyon—in *Zarathustra*, because womb-born animals suffer from a nostalgia for a fixed place of origin (the womb) while nest-born animals, especially animals born in nests that float on top of the water, do not suffer from this nostalgia (*A* 134). This forgetting could be another example of what Irigaray calls the matricide committed by philosophy. Irigaray suggests that man forgets his maternal origin and invents instead a masculine birth.

Derrida's insistence on forgetting the gift is ultimately also an insistence on forgetting the womb and the mother's gift of life. If it is necessary to forget all gifts and all acts of giving in order for the gift to be possible, then we are to forget the gift of life given through the act of giving birth. What is the first gift, if not the gift of life? What is the first act of giving, if not the act of giving birth? Any debt to the mother must be forgotten and all gifts must be given from and to the (masculine) self, even the giving of birth. As Derrida points out (following Heidegger), for Nietzsche production is masculine and the productive or fertile mother is a masculine mother (Derrida *S* 77). As I will indicate later, in Nietzsche's texts the mother, in order to create culture, must be a manly mother; the feminine and woman are valued only insofar as they are procreative, but real creative mothers cannot be feminine or women. Maternal creation is taken over by man; he gives birth. Later I will analyze the final section of *Marine Lover*, "When the Gods are Born," where Irigaray argues that all of Nietzsche's gods—Dionysus, Apollo, Christ—have their ways of usurping their mothers' creative power. For now, however, I turn to another example that Irigaray cites of man forgetting his maternal origin, Nietzsche's eternal return.

The Eternal Return of the Same

Gilles Deleuze, in his influential *Nietzsche and Philosophy*, reads Nietzsche's eternal return as the return of difference. On Deleuze's reading the eternal return is both a physical doctrine and an ontological doctrine. He reads the physical doctrine as the return of the being of becoming and the ontological doctrine as the return of the being of becoming as the self-affirming of becoming active. In the first case the eternal return is the return of becoming (48). What returns is the process of change through which nothing is the same. This is the eternal return of difference not sameness. The eternal return as ontological selection is the return of only self-affirming active forces (72). In this reading the eternal return weeds out the reactive forces in favor of the active forces. The eternal return is the return of forces that multiply life rather than diminish life; only active forces return. The eternal return operates as the mechanism for the *self-overcoming* of reactive forces. In this way, the eternal return makes a gift of oneself possible insofar as self-giving is also always a process of self-destroying. Through the eternal return a new "self" is continually emerging. Through this process of continual self-destroying and self-creating, the never-ending process of othering takes place. The self becomes other.

Derrida offers the beginning of an interpretation of Nietzsche's eternal return in *The Ear of the Other* where, like Deleuze, he claims that the eternal return is a selective principle (45). What returns is the double affirmation, the self-affirmation of the hymen, the "yes, yes." Only the affirmative returns while the negative falls into the past. Like Deleuze, Derrida maintains that forces return; the eternal return, contra Heidegger, is not the return of beings, and it is not metaphysical (*EO*, 46). The force that returns is the "self's" gift to itself, its double affirmation, its "yes, yes" to itself.

Like Heidegger, and unlike her French contemporaries, Deleuze and Derrida, fathers of the so-called new Nietzsche, Irigaray reads Nietzsche's eternal return as the return of the same. On Irigaray's reading the eternal return is not the mechanism through which the self becomes other; rather it is a mechanism through which the other becomes reabsorbed into the self. Although as a student of Nietzsche's writings, I am more sympathetic to a reading of the eternal return as the return of difference over sameness, there is something fascinating, even compelling, about Irigaray's reading of Nietzsche's eternal return. For Irigaray, like Heidegger, the problem with Nietzsche's eternal return is a metaphysical problem, and it is a problem of difference. Unlike Heidegger, however, her concern is with the primacy of sexual difference and not the primacy of ontological difference. Irigaray's writings suggest that there is no ontological difference without sexual difference. Sexual difference is primary. And the history of the West is a history of only one sex; it is a history of the erasure of sexual difference. Now, with Irigaray, I ask, How and why has philosophy continued to forget, or cover over, sexual difference?

Nietzsche's Ressentiment
Irigaray describes Nietzsche's eternal return of the same as just a way of avoiding the difference of the female other: "And your whole will, your eternal recurrence, are these anything more than the dream of one who neither wants to have been born, nor to continue being born, at every

instant, of a female other?" (*ML* 26). She suggests that the eternal return is born out of resentment. Woman, the feminine other, is man's greatest resentment (*ML* 25). Like the slave morality of *On the Genealogy of Morals*, man affirms himself only indirectly through the denial of the feminine other. Compare Irigaray's analysis of the logic of Nietzsche's eternal return with the logic of the slave morality. Like the slave, man affirms only the selfsame and rejects to the point of annihilation everything different. This is the logic of Nietzsche's eternal return. On Irigaray's reading the eternal return is the return of the selfsame, which denies all difference and out of resentment appropriates and yet rejects the other—the feminine, the body, the earth.

For Irigaray, the *Übermensch* is another way to deny the other. She proposes that the *Übermensch* is just a "flying over life" that tears holes in woman's body and drains her blood drop by drop because it has forgotten that it is born out of the sea (*mer*), out of a woman, the mother (*mère*) (*ML* 18, 52). The *Übermensch* prefers the heights, the peaks, and bridges so that he can avoid contact with the sea, the immemorial waters of his birth; here Irigaray alludes to Nietzsche's metaphors in *Zarathustra* of going up to the mountains and hopping from peak to peak. Ellen Mortensen points out that for Irigaray it is not just the feminine other who is denied by Nietzsche's notions of the *Übermensch* and the eternal return. She suggests that Zarathustra appropriates difference or excludes it rather than recognizing it (IN 232). She sees this exclusion of difference as inherent in Nietzsche's notion of overcoming, which requires that the old perish for the sake of the new. Overcoming requires death, the death of the other. Mortensen says, "By focusing on death, the nothing and eternity in their so-called celebration of the body, of life and of the earth, Nietzsche's 'superior men' seem to flee that which they wish to reevaluate, claims Irigaray. They are on earth, but have no love for it" (IN 233). Zarathustra teaches death—the eternal, the beyond-man. Irigaray suggests that with the *Übermensch* and the eternal return, Nietzsche erects "idols even more fascinating because they are the work of an artist more and more gifted in lies" (*ML* 21). In this regard Nietzsche is like the nihilistic ascetic priest who sets up idols instead of valuing the earth.

Like Nietzsche's notion of the *Übermensch*, on Irigaray's reading, the notion of the eternal return denies the other—the feminine, the body, and the earth. The eternal return is the closed circle of the nuptial ring. Zarathustra says, "Oh, how should I not lust after eternity and after the nuptial ring of rings, the ring of recurrence? Never yet have I found the woman from whom I wanted children, unless it be this woman whom I love: for I love you, O eternity. For I love you, O eternity!" (*Z* III, "The

Seven Seals," 340–43). To Nietzsche's metaphor of the eternal return as the circle of a wedding ring, a nuptial celebration with eternity, Irigaray responds that "in the eternal return, she [woman] attends your wedding celebration, she takes part in it, but you yourself are bride and groom" (*ML* 32). She claims that Nietzsche/Zarathustra wants woman only under the guise of eternity (*ML* 43). Once again woman is turned into a metaphor or a language-body.

In addition, Nietzsche's description of eternity as a nuptial ring locks woman into either a closed circle or a bottomless well. Irigaray reads Zarathustra's eternal circle as a closed flat circle that has lost its roundness; it is two-dimensional, without depth: "That, for your eternity, everything should always turn in a circle, and that within that ring I should remain— your booty" (*ML* 11). If it is not a closed circle from which there is no escape and in which the same moves round and round, then it is a bottomless well: "For either your soul loses its wondrous roundness, or the place of turning back is merely a bottomless well" (*ML* 7).

The place of turning back is a turning back to "that from which one comes," the feminine other, the maternal body. This is Zarathustra's greatest resentment, that he was born of a woman:

> But your greatest sorrow and your greatest disgust are reserved for me.
> And in order to return to the depths of the earth, you still need to get back
> through the skin sickness that keeps you apart. That you covered her with
> to prevent you from wanting to move back inside her. That keeps you far
> away in ressentiment. . . . And your whole will, your eternal recurrence,
> are these anything more than the dream of one who neither wants to have
> been born, nor to continue being born, at every instant, of a female other?
> Does your joy in becoming not result from annihilating her from whom
> you are tearing yourself away? (*ML* 26–27)

For Zarathustra the return to the mother is a return to eternity, to a time before birth, a time without time. Irigaray sees this eternity figured only as a closed circle in which the mother is contained or as the threat of a bottomless well. Neither of these speak to the rhythms and cycles of a woman's time or a woman's body, or the time of the earth. The cycles of the earth are neither closed nor bottomless. They have rhythms. Becoming dances to the rhythms of the earth:

> And, for me, ebb and flow have always set the rhythm of time. But (they)
> come at different hours. At midday or midnight, at dawn or dusk. one
> moment is worth absolutely no more than the other, for the whole is
> present in each. At each hour comes fortune, multiple in the unwinding of
> its becoming.

And (I) have no need to turn around and round to come back to the same or to enter eternity.

For same have (I) been from all eternity, and, at the same time, ever different. And thus (I) come and go, change and stay, go on and come back, without any circle. Spread out and open in this endless becoming. (*ML* 14)

The rhythm of woman, the rhythm of the earth, is the rhythm of the sea with its ebbs and flows. It moves in cycles not in a circle. And although the tides are ever changing, they are not without their patterns. Irigaray compares the rhythms of the sea, which she suggests Nietzsche / Zarathustra forgets, to the movement of the sun, a central metaphor in *Thus Spake Zarathustra*.[20]

The sun's time is circular and unchanging. And even within time's circle Zarathustra prefers midday, the noon sun, a circle high in the sky. Irigaray asks, "Isn't your sun worship also a kind of ressentiment? Don't you measure your ecstasy against the yardstick of envy? And isn't your circle made of the will to live this irradiation—there will be no other but me?" (*ML* 15). The sea is dangerous because it is dark and does not just move according to the sun's movement (see *ML* 50). Everything is safer in the light of day when things can be perceived with the eye, at the greatest distance. Zarathustra, Nietzsche, and Derrida must shield themselves and arm themselves against the sea. They use sails as a defense against the sea; sails allow one to stay on the surface safe from the threatening depths and wild waters of the sea (*ML* 49). Sails allow one to stay above the sea, to keep one's distance.

Irigaray is not only concerned with time but also, perhaps more so, with space. While Derrida uses and repeats Nietzsche's advice to keep women in the distance because her power is in the distance, Irigaray criticizes this territorialism. Derrida goes further than Nietzsche to suggest that woman may not merely be a thing in the distance from which to keep one's distance, but that she may *be* distance itself (*S* 49). Recall that for Derrida she is not only in the background, she *is* the background. Irigaray diagnoses this positioning of woman as a fear of getting close to her (*ML* 39–40):

And what is that terror awaiting them in the shadow? That featureless memory of the terrible fight between the slashing breakers and the streaming sails? That peril of water coming from sky and land? And that horror they feel for the might of the sea when she sheds all masks and refuses to be calm, polite, and submissive to the sailor's direction? . . .

> If only the sea did not exist. If they could just create her in dreams . . .They prefer to dry up, and die of thirst, rather than run the risk of sinking . . . .
>
> To think of the sea from afar, to eye her from a distance, to use her to fashion his highest reveries, to weave his dreams of her, and spread his sails while remaining safe in port, that is the delirium of the sea lover . . . . —but at a distance. (*ML* 51)

Nietzsche (and Derrida) use metaphor in order to keep their distance from woman. They create what Irigaray calls a "language-body" in order to keep the body—especially woman's body, particularly the maternal body—distanced and under control. In *Marine Lover* Irigaray criticizes the triumph of Apollo over Dionysus in Nietzsche's writings as the "precedence of interpretation over the movement of life" (71). And although she never even mentions Derrida in that text, her criticisms seem like a response to his reading of Nietzsche. To Nietzsche/Zarathustra/Derrida Irigaray says, "(The) evil begins at birth—the birth of your language. You have to go farther back than the point where you saw the light of day. To set your coming into daylight within this language-malady, does that not already mean acceding in your decline? Believing that what gives you life is an obstacle to life? And wanting life to be engendered from a language-body alone?" (ML 65) Here Irigaray criticizes the tendency to turn everything into language and interpretation. This of course is the primary lesson that Derrida takes from Nietzsche.

By turning the female body into just so many metaphors, metaphors that no longer have anything to do with that body, the deconstructive philosopher can safely distance himself from the female body and maintain his mastery over it. Man can ensure that he has control over his own origins and birth by inventing this language-body as the source of life. But Irigaray asks: What is farther back than this language body? What is prior to the onset of language? If we begin with the onset of language, if that is the hallmark of culture, then haven't we forgotten the maternal body? And in addition, Irigaray asks. What was left for her/woman to interpret? Everything, including her hymen, has already been interpreted for her within the language of philosophy (see *ML* 71). Within these interpretations, she has become nothing more than a metaphorical body, a language-body, drained of its blood. "Something red was lacking, a hint of blood and guts to revive the will, and restore its strength." (*ML* 79). On Irigaray's reading of Nietzsche, the feminine, woman, and the maternal have all been appropriated by the masculine. They are drained of their lifeblood, turned into metaphors, and made to serve a patriarchal philosophical language.

Up to this point, I have been constructing an argument out of Irigaray's *Marine Lover* without evaluating that text as a reading of Nietzsche. At first reading it may seem inappropriate to hold Irigaray's text accountable as a reading of Nietzsche; *Marine Lover* is written in a personal voice as a love letter from a spurned lover. Yet, don't we usually accept the account of a painful break-up from one of the parties involved as only *one side* of the story? Even if we are sympathetic, don't we suspect that the situation was more complex than the "Dear John" letter suggests?

Perhaps Irigaray has been too quick to identify Nietzsche's eternal return with sameness. In order to understand Irigaray's strategy and in order to be fair to Nietzsche, it is necessary to return to Irigaray's supposition that the eternal return is the return of sameness. We could interpret Irigaray as maintaining either that Nietzsche proposes a theory that opens up the possibility of difference but his theory falls short of its goal, or that Nietzsche proposes a theory that promotes sameness and his theory achieves its goal. There are places in *Marine Lover* that suggest both of these interpretations. Given all of the places where Nietzsche praises difference, change, and flexibility and the places where he criticizes equality, permanence, and rigidity it would be extremely difficult to defend the thesis that Nietzsche proposes a theory to promote sameness. On the other hand, If Irigaray is suggesting that Nietzsche falls short of his own goals, she does so in a style as unorthodox as Nietzsche's own. In addition to Irigaray's problematic reading of Nietzsche, even with her unorthodox style, she has not escaped the resentment of the slave morality.

In order to assess Irigaray's interpretation of the eternal return, it will be useful to return to Nietzsche's first introduction of the notion of eternal return in *Gay Science* (*GS* §341, 273–4). There Nietzsche presents a test to determine whether or not we can affirm our lives as we live them, complete with joy and sorrow. He describes a demon who steals after us in our "loneliest loneliness" and tells us that we will have to live every detail of this life over and over again eternally. It is crucial that the demon appears at the moment of our deepest despair because as Nietzsche says in *Zarathustra* "joy wants the eternity of *all* things, *wants deep, wants deep eternity*" (*Z* IV "The Drunken Song" 436). The response to the demon's proclamation is decisive: "If this thought gained possession of you, it would change you as you are or perhaps crush you" (*GS* 274). As David Wood argues in "Nietzsche's Transvaluation of Time," the affirmation of the eternal return is transformative. The moment of an affirmation of the eternal return produces change and thereby the thought of the eternal return generates difference.

This "vision of the loneliest" appears again in *Zarathustra's* "On the Vision and the Riddle" when Nietzsche presents another version of the eternal return (Z III 267). Here Zarathustra speaks to sailors who embark "with cunning on terrible seas" until he is interrupted by a dwarf who tells him that he is a philosopher's stone that will fall back on himself (Z III, 268). The dwarf's mocking silences Zarathustra until he realizes that courage slays even death by proclaiming "Was *that* life? Well then! Once more!" Gathering his courage Zarathustra confronts the dwarf and tells him that he (the dwarf) could not bear the abysmal thought of the eternal return. Zarathustra points out a gateway between two paths, one future and one past, both eternal. Inscribed above the gate is "Moment." When the dwarf exclaims that "time itself is a circle," Zarathustra chastises him for making things too easy for himself. Zarathustra concludes: "And this slow spider, which crawls in the moonlight, and this moonlight itself, and I and you in the gateway, whispering together, whispering of eternal things—must not all of us have been there before? And return and walk in that other lane, out here, before us, in this long dreadful lane—must we not eternally return?" (Z 270). When Zarathustra asks "must not all of us have been there before?" he is standing at the gateway between past and future marked "moment." Is he asking haven't all of us been at this gateway, at the moment between past and future, before? And won't we all necessarily be at this place, this moment, over and over again eternally? Is what returns the moment? And if it is the moment that returns, what does it mean to call this a return of the same? Perhaps, like the dwarf, Irigaray's interpretation of the eternal return as merely the nuptial ring of recurrence, the circle of the same, makes things too easy for her. As David Wood suggests, perhaps the structure is the same but the content is always different (NTT 52-3). Moreover, like the version of the eternal return in *Gay Science*, Zarathustra's version is also transformative.

Zarathustra tells the riddle of a heavy black snake which crawls into the throat of a sleeping shepherd. This snake seems to represent the eternal return and the shepherd is gagging on it until Zarathustra tells him to bite its head off. Once the shepherd bites down on the eternal return, he is transformed: "No longer shepherd, no longer human—one changed, radiant, *laughing*!" (Z 272). Once again the eternal return generates difference in the decisive moment in which it is affirmed. The eternal return makes it possible to give one's life as a gift to oneself.

In *Marine Lover* Irigaray insists that both the eternal return and the *Übermensch* are forms of matricide which deny the gift of life that comes from the mother. She makes her point by relying primarily on metaphors from *Zarathustra*: circles, rings, sun, heights, peak, bridges. She laments that the *Übermensch* is afraid of the immemorial waters of maternal birth, the sea; it prefers the mountain tops and sunlight to the dark depths of the sea. But what of the prelude to *Zarathustra* in which Zarathustra not only associates the *Übermensch* with the earth but also the sea? "All beings so far have created something beyond themselves; and do you want to be the ebb of this great flood and even go back to the beasts rather than overcome man?. . . The overman is the meaning of the earth. . . *remain faithful to the earth*, and do not believe those who speak to you of otherworldly hopes. . . Verily, a polluted stream is man. One must be a sea to be able to receive a polluted stream without becoming unclean. Behold, I teach you the overman: he is this sea; in him your great contempt can go under" (Z I Prelude 3, 124-25). In addition, speaking of *Zarathustra* in *On the Genealogy of Morals* Nietzsche talks about an alternative to the slave morality born out of a resentment toward the earth and the body: "This man [*Mensch*] of the future, who will redeem us not only from the hitherto reigning ideal but also from that which was bound to grow out of it, the great nausea, the will to nothingness, nihilism; this bell-stroke of noon and of the great decision that liberates the will again and restores its goal to the earth and his hope to man. . . " *(OGM* II §24, 96). This *Mensch* of the future will restore our values to the earth and to our embodied existence on this earth.

There is the suggestion in *Marine Lover,* which is brought out clearly in Mortensen's reading of it, that if Nietzsche's doctrines of the eternal return and the *Übermensch* provide ways for man to give birth to himself, then this implies that man denies his relationship with the earth. In other words, implicit in Irigaray's analysis is the traditional association between the mother and the earth, mother-earth. Although I agree with Irigaray that the mother and birth are problematic in Nietzsche's texts— to the point that he proposes a masculine mother—my project at the end of this book is to disentangle traditional associations of mother with earth. I will argue that the philosophical matricide identified by Irigaray is possible only *because of* the identification of mother with earth. While, against Irigaray, I believe that Nietzsche does move us out of a metaphysics that annihilates the value of the body, at the same time he cannot admit the value of the feminine pregnant maternal body. But the issue is more complex than Irigaray's text makes it out to be. Why, then, is her text so compelling?

This question is a question of style. Recall that Irigaray maintains that her style is one of productive mimesis. In her response to Nietzsche she not only engages in a passionate dialogue with his texts but also accuses him of violence, of violating "her." She accuses him of not loving "her." She makes "him" out to be a hostile lover. Turning Nietzsche's genealogical method back on Irigaray's mimetic method, we could ask what is the meaning of the way in which she positions him as primarily the violent male lover? Why does she need to make him out as the villain in this affair in such a categorical fashion? If Irigaray claims that Nietzsche's doctrines of eternal return and the *Übermensch* are born out of resentment towards the mother, then what does it mean for her to mime that resentment? If, as Irigaray suggests in much of her writing, woman has been positioned as a reflective surface for man, then taking up her place of mirror Irigaray must reflect back in a productive, rather than merely reproductive, way the resentment in Nietzsche's text. She must make a space in which to create herself by taking up the place assigned to her as the resented woman. Yet, she does this by defining her lover as hostile and violent. Isn't this exactly the logic of resentment employed by the slave morality? The slave can define itself only in relation to a hostile other (*OGM* I §10, 36-7). Moreover, if, as Irigaray suggests in some of her other writings, she wants to engage a dialogue between different sexes, is the best way to do so to refuse to see anything but violence in the other? Perhaps it is obvious that *Marine Lover* is written not only out of pain but also out of love.

If Irigaray refuses to see any difference in Nietzsche, she does so strategically. The force of *Marine Lover* is Ariadne's lament, the voice of a woman. This lament is powerful because it is not only addressed to Nietzsche but also to all of the patriarchal traditions in philosophy. Irigaray wants this domestic fight, this lover's quarrel, to be out in the open (see *ML* 24-5). She suggests that by fighting on equal terms, we can break the mirror that woman has been forced to become (*ML* 66). By presenting her side of the story, Irigaray forces tensions in Nietzsche's work to an immediacy unprecedented in Nietzsche scholarship. She reflects violence back at itself in order to produce the possibility of something other. The fact that, like all revolutionary projects, she both succeeds and fails suggests that perhaps the eternal return is both the return of the same and yet the return of difference. If Irigaray's mimetic method is to succeed, then Deleuze is right that the eternal return must act as a selective principle that operates through the self-overcoming of reactive forces, the self-overcoming of resentment. Now, I too risk the repetition of the same for the sake of difference by continuing my analysis of Nietzsche's eternal return in its relation to woman's body.

Medusa and Baubô

Medusa and Baubô are two more of the metaphors of woman's body that Nietzsche employs in order to describe the eternal return. At one pole, Medusa represents the unrepresentable, the terrifying decapitated head swarming with snakes, the sight of which will turn men to stone, while, at the other, Baubô represents the equally terrifying exposed female sex, the sight of which is disillusioning at best and deadly at worst. These two poles are collapsed in Freud's imaginary when he interprets Medusa's head as the spectacle of the exposed female genitals.[21] He maintains that Medusa's head elicits in man the fear of castration; decapitation stands in for castration. When the male child sees his mother's pubis, he sees the spot of a missing penis surrounded by hair. On Freud's reading the Medusa's snakelike hair becomes a throng of penis substitutes which both evoke and protect against castration. Medusa's head becomes a fetish of sorts—it both acknowledges and denies castration by setting up a penis substitute.

In his "Nietzsche Medused," Bernard Pautrat presents a fascinating, if stretched, reading of Nietzsche's identification of the eternal return with Medusa, which turns the eternal return itself into a fetish. Pautrat points out that in various drafts for *Zarathustra*, Nietzsche refers to "the great thought as a Medusa's head: all features of the world harden, a frozen, mortal combat"[22] (160). Using this quotation from Nietzsche's notes for *Zarathustra* part IV, Pautrat is justified in interpreting "the greatest thought" as the thought of the eternal return. Then he proceeds to consider what it could mean to call the eternal return a Medusa's head and why Nietzsche did not mention Medusa in the final version of *Zarathustra*. He concludes that the thought of the eternal return has the same effect as a Medusa's head: it freezes the world in mortal combat; it is terrifying; it is impossible to look at (*NM* 160). The fact that Medusa's head is left out of the final version, he claims, makes it no less representative of the eternal return. His argument is that the eternal return is left out of *Zarathustra* and, by virtue of its displacement, it occupies the same place as the displaced Medusa. He maintains that throughout the text Zarathustra never describes the thought of the eternal return; he merely refers to it: "[Zarathustra] is never in a position to give an exoteric statement of [the eternal return]. The mode of representation of the eternal return is either the dream or the riddle, the responsibility for which is always left to others, dwarfs or animals. And each version which is given of it is immediately contradicted by the master of the return, who fails to see his truth in it, the truth he wants to transmit to his future disciples" (NM 162–63).

Pautrat's argument stretches when he moves from Nietzsche's identification of the eternal return with Medusa's head through an analysis of fetishism to the claim that the eternal return is Zarathustra's fetish. He argues that "the thought of the eternal return as thesis of identity and identifiable thesis, arises as a fetish against the world of difference which *also* seeks to think itself in the eternal return" (NM 167). If we return to the arguments that I have constructed out of Irigaray's poetic suggestions in *Marine Lover,* and take them together with Pautrat's thesis, a stronger case could be made for interpreting Nietzsche's eternal return as a fetish.

Recall that the Freudian fetishist both denies and affirms castration. Additionally recall that for the Lacanian fetishist castration is not cutting off an organ but cutting off the possibility of gratification. What gratifies the philosopher? Discovering an unchanging, eternal truth. But if the world is constantly changing and all identity necessarily gives way to difference, then any principle, including the principle that asserts this Heraclitean position, must give way to something else. Nietzsche's eternal return is such a principle. With the eternal return, especially on Deleuze's reading, as we have seen, Nietzsche proposes a principle that promises the eternal return of difference. By doing so, however, he has absorbed difference within this principle of identity. He both affirms and denies the possibility of philosophical gratification by acknowledging difference even while identifying it with a fixed principle, the eternal return. On this point my reading of the interpretations of the eternal return put forward by Deleuze, Derrida, and Irigaray work in concert. The eternal return is both the return of the difference and the return of the same simultaneously; what is the same about life is difference itself. The principle of return both denies and affirms difference. But, what kind of a principle is it that guarantees the return of difference? Doesn't this priniciple challenge or alter our very notion of priniciples? In addition, doesn't it complicate the relation between sameness and difference?

Sarah Kofman suggests that Nietzsche's figure for the eternal return and life itself, Baubô, steers clear of fetishism. Kofman relies on a passage from *Gay Science* in which Nietzsche says: "Perhaps truth is a woman who has reasons for not letting us see her reasons? Perhaps her name is— to speak Greek—Baubô? Oh, those Greeks! They knew how to live. What is required for that is to stop courageously at the surface, the fold, the skin, to adore appearances in form, tones, words, in the whole Olympus of appearance" (GS, Preface §4, 38). On Kofman's reading Baubô is the female double of Dionysus (B 197). She represents fecundity and the eternal return of life. Kofman notes that Baubô makes Demeter, the goddess of fertility, laugh by pulling up her skirts and showing her a drawing of Dionysus on her belly. Kofman says that "[t]he belly of the woman plays the role of the head of Medusa. By lifting her skirts, was not Baubô suggesting that she go and frighten Hades, or that which comes to the same, recall fecundity to herself? By displaying the figure of Dionysus on her belly, she recalls the eternal return of life" (B 196–97).

The role of Medusa in this case is to petrify by exposing her procreative powers. Kofman presents the connection between Baubô and fertility by pointing out that Baubô is "the equivalent of *koilia*, another of the 'improper' words used in Greek to designate the female sex" (B 197). Kofman overlooks what should be obvious in her analysis; the threat of Medusa may be this "improper" female sex itself and not merely its powers to reproduce. Baubô lifting her skirts, with Dionysus drawn on her belly, may also threaten castration. Kofman argues that the Baubô-Dionysus duo operates between castration and fetishism but cannot be reduced to either. She argues that because of his female double, Dionysus cannot be categorized: "Dionysus, a Greek god anterior to the system of theological oppositions, crosses himself out (*se rature*) of the distinction between the veiled and unveiled, masculine and feminine, fetishism and castration" (B 198). Kofman claims that like Dionysus, Nietzsche is his own double. He is both sides and therefore neither (B 187).

Following Derrida, Kofman seems to suggest that Dionysus is outside all dualism; he operates as the undecidable, neither one nor the other. Her discussion of the difference between fetishism and castration, however, seems confused. She maintains that they are opposites. While fetishism protects against the threat of castration by setting up a substitute for the maternal penis, at the same time it acknowledges maternal castration. So it makes no sense to say that fetishism is the opposite of castration, or that Dionysus is between fetishism and castration. Fetishism *is* the logic of the between.

It is odd that Kofman associates the skirt-lifting Baubô with Nietzsche's affirmative woman who is, above all "modest." She contrasts Baubô with Nietzsche's negative scientific woman who is not at all modest about what women want. For the affirmative woman, "modesty appears as a beguilement that permits the male to desire a woman without being petrified (médusé); it is a veil which avoids male homosexuality, a spontaneous defense against the horrific sight of female genitalia, and the opportunity for life to perpetuate itself" (B 191). It is also odd that Baubô as the female double of Dionysus, who has "unspeakable relations" with Proshymnos, can provide the veil that avoids male homosexuality.

At this point it is interesting to compare Eve Kosofsky Sedgwick's analysis of Nietzsche's relation to homosexuality in *Epistemology of the Closet*. Sedgwick interprets the phenomenon of the double or divided self as a camouflage for homosexual desire (161 n. 35). Using Sedgwick's thesis, Nietzsche's double character and Dionysus's double character could be veiled manifestations of an economy of homosexual desire. I can make the case for this reading stronger by addressing an issue implicit in this thesis, the relation between identification and desire. Sedgwick suggests that in Nietzsche's writing there is a conflation of the sense of "what I am" and "what I desire"; the object of desire is not other than the self (161). "In Nietzsche, for example, the unimaginable distance between the valetudinarian philosopher who desires, and the bounding 'masters of the earth' whom he desires, is dissolved so resolutely by the force of his rhetoric . . ." (161 n. 35). Sedgwick substantiates this claim by pointing to Nietzsche's identification with Dionysus, Christ, and "every name in history" (162–163). Nietzsche not only desires Dionysus, he identifies with Dionysus. He signs his name Dionysus. Conversely, Nietzsche not only identifies with Dionysus, he desires Dionysus.

The conflation of identity and desire in Nietzsche should not be surprising if we recall the logic of the master morality described in *On the Genealogy of Morals*. The master affirms himself directly without any relation to an other. Unlike the Hegelian dialectic, which requires a desire for recognition from an other, the master's recognition comes entirely and directly from himself. If we think of desire in terms of sexual desire, the master's desire for himself and others like him is a homosexual desire. Only the slaves require recognition from an other. Within the Hegelian scenario this desire for the other leads to the Unhappy Consciousness that is caused by a radical split between identification and desire. The Unhappy Consciousness desires what it is not. The master of Nietzsche's *Genealogy*, however, never reaches this level of Unhappy Consciousness, because he "idealizes" only himself; yet we cannot even say that he has any ideal insofar as he acts spontaneously from instinct, because he is not self-conscious. Self-consciousness, with its mate, bad conscience, is the disease of the slave.

In *Genealogy* Nietzsche is not suggesting that we return to master morality, if that would even be possible. Rather, the slave morality adds a psychological depth that could make the master's self-affirmation more meaningful and profound. The ascetic ideal is, after all, the ideal that requires life to be meaningful. Through the wedding of the master's sensuality and the slave's discipline, a true creative spirit can be born (see *OGM* III §2, 98). Bad conscience gives birth to great health (*OGM* I §19, II §24). Does Nietzsche suggest that the self-alienation of the slave morality is necessary to move to a healthier relationship between identification and desire? Perhaps it is only after this self-alienation that identification and desire can come together. Prior to self-alienation there is neither identification nor desire. Both self-identification and desire require self-alienation and the resulting self-consciousness. So what is Nietzsche's identification with Dionysus? Is it the identification of a master or a slave? Is his identification with Dionysus an acknowledgment of the other, or is it a denial of that other?

The Birth of Gods

Dionysus is born of the womb of a dead woman who is cut open so that he can, as Irigaray says, give birth to himself (*ML* 125). According to the traditional version of the myth, Dionysus is the child of Zeus and Semele, a mortal with whom Zeus was having an affair.[23] Zeus disguised himself as a mortal in order to deceive Semele into having an affair. When Hera found out, she took her revenge by disguising herself as an old woman and convincing Semele to ask Zeus to appear without his disguise. Semele got Zeus to agree to grant her a wish and then asked him to appear without his disguise. The splendor of his godly appearance annihilated Semele instantly in a flash of lightening. The unborn Dionysus, a god himself, was not annihilated. Zeus sewed the premature Dionysus into his thigh so that he might finish the gestation process and be born at the right time. Dionysus was not born of a woman, but of his father.

Dionysus is raised by various women, primarily Semele's sister, Ino. In the name of avenging his mother, Dionysus repays his aunt for her nurturing by stinging her with madness. In Euripides' *Bacchae*, Dionysus believes that Ino is responsible for the rumor that Zeus is not really his father. Dionysus has heard that his aunt was telling people that his father was really a mortal and that his mother's father, Cadmus, had made up the story that Semele was impregnated by Zeus. On Ino's version of the story, Semele is struck dead by Zeus when he finds out that they are falsely blaming him for the pregnancy. In the name of his mother, Dionysus punishes all the women of Thebes:

> Because of that offense
> I have stung them with frenzy, hounded them from home
> up to the moutains where they wander, crazed of mind,

and compelled to wear my orgies' livery.
Every woman in Thebes—but the women only—
I drove from home, mad. There they sit,
rich and poor alike, even the daughters of Cadmus.
beneath the silver firs on the roofless rocks.
Like it or not, this city must learn its lesson:
it lacks initiation in my mysteries;
that I shall vindicate my mother Semele
and stand revealed to mortal eyes as the god
she bore to Zeus.24

In the name of his mother, he defends his divine paternity and turns on the surrogate mother who raised him. In defense of his divine paternity, he turns on all women, mothers and daughters alike. He makes them carry the symbols of his potency and worship him. The intoxicated frenzy of his devotees, however, leads them to tear flesh and eventually rip him to pieces.

So although, as Irigaray says, Dionysus "sets flowing the water frozen into solid walls," the waters of passion and bodily desire, he does so with such violence that once again we have entered an economy of castration and self-sacrifice: "His crazy desire loosens all bonds, destroys all homes, overthrows all institutions, laughs at all stability. Lets out what is already walled up. Sets flowing all the water that is frozen into solid walls. But he betters and wounds everything he opens up. And as he frees the fluid energies, he fractures the place they flow out of. As he lets the springs leap up once again, he annihilates the place from whence they come. By recalling desire, does he not destroy the body?" (*ML* 129).

With Dionysus the tension between divine and human is too great and he goes to pieces. Human desire is violently destructive; and the god of fertility and the desiring body destroys that very body with his desire. Even Nietzsche's favorite god, the god of sensuality, sacrifices the body; with Dionysus the body is sacrificed to desire. The body is not strong enough for desire. The phallus, Dionysus's symbol of potency, becomes an instrument of death as well as a symbol of life; and, for Irigaray, worshipping the fertile phallus is merely another means of forgetting the mother and her fertility (*ML* 136–37).

In Nietzsche's texts, Dionysus overshadows Ariadne, without whom his life has no meaning. Irigaray suggests that Ariadne is called on merely to echo and mirror the masculine (*ML* 117). Her voice is never heard. It is also significant that Ariadne is a goddess of childbirth and erotic love.[25] Nietzsche's focus on Dionysus with his fertility and potency blinds us to

Ariadne's fertility and potency. In fact in *Twilight of the Idols*, Nietzsche gives all of Ariadne's powers over childbirth to Dionysus. In Nietzsche's text Dionysus represents procreation, pregnancy and birth (*TW* "What I Owe," §4).

And what about Demeter, goddess of procreation and the earth, whose daughter is kidnapped and raped? Demeter will only produce in the company of Persephone, her daughter.[26] Separated from her, she is barren. Her daughter is her source of life. The company of her daughter ushers in the seasons of life. Persephone is the midwife, of sorts, for her mother. Artemis, twin sister to Apollo, is also a midwife for her mother. And she, too, has been forgotten in Nietzsche's texts in favor of her brother, Apollo.

In Nietzsche's texts Apollo counterbalances the violent frenzy of Dionysus. Apollo provides stability, temperance, and individuation to the Dionysian chaos. For Irigaray, Apollo's *jouissance* is the fight with Dionysus or tension itself; Apollo is the god of resistance and restraint (*ML* 145). In Apollo the divine is always mediated by this restraint which holds everything at a distance: "The whole is always already wrapped in a protective membrane that isolates it from a return to the rapturous undifferentiation within one unique orgasm with that originary mother. Everything is separated from everything, each thing inhabiting and inhabited by a dream that takes and gives shape. The poetry of the god shines forth and covers the whole with a still springlike, still matutinal gold. Still close to the solar illumination, but soon melted down into words that will generate and maintain a new, a patriarchal order. The sky will soon be solid bronze" (*ML* 149). Apollo's restraint resists any identification with the originary mother or nature. He insists on giving order to the chaos of nature by turning fluid nature into solid words. The mother's passion becomes the father's words.

Irigaray argues that in the shadows of Apollo's sun is his sister Artemis. From her, Apollo steals light; from her he steals creativity. Irigaray admits that "only the backing on which he weaves the miracle of his advent and of his Olympian gift of measured restraint can be interpreted thus." She claims that she interprets "only a thread through the myths of his rise to power" (*ML* 152). Then she proceeds to weave the story of Apollo and his twin sister, Artemis, who must stay in the shadows of the forest with only animals for companions so that her brother can shine. She is his underside, without whom he could not be who he is; his identity is dependent on his contrast with her. They are two parts of the same whole; they are twins who share not only their parents but also their identity.

In order to make sense of Irigaray's analysis of Apollo, it is necessary to recall some of the myths surrounding this god and his sister. Apollo is the son of Leto and Zeus. Hera, jealous as usual, sends Python to pursue the pregnant Leto; she decrees that Leto should not give birth anyplace where the sun shines. As the story goes, Leto, on the run, gives birth first to Artemis, who immediately helps her mother across the water to safety on the island of Delos where Leto gives birth to Artemis's twin brother, Apollo. Artemis acts as the midwife to her own twin brother. He owes his life to her. Because of her role in Apollo's birth and the fact that, unlike Apollo, she caused her mother no pain during childbirth, Artemis becomes a goddess protector of pregnant women as well as (some) virgins.[27] Unlike Artemis, who protects pregnant women from pain, Apollo pays no debt to the mother.

In fact, it is Apollo's oracle at Delphi that commands Orestes to kill his mother Clytemnestra. Later, when Orestes wants to spare his mother, he is reminded of Apollo's words. After Orestes commits the matricide ordained by Apollo, he is pursued by the Erinyes, Furies with snakelike hair and eyes dripping blood, sent by Clytemnestra's ghost. Driven to distraction and pursued unto death by these castrating women, Orestes once again seeks Apollo's help. In Aeschylus's *The Eumenides,* as Apollo vows to help him, the chorus, howling with the furies, scorns Apollo: "Shame, son of Zeus! Robber is all you are. A young god, you have ridden down powers gray with age, taken the suppliant, though a godless man, who hurt the mother who gave him birth. Yourself a god, you stole the matricide away. Where in this act shall any man say there is right? . . . You gave this outlander the work to kill his mother."[28] Apollo sends him to Athens to plead his case before Athena. As Apollo points out in Orestes' defense at the trial before Athena, she has no allegiance to the mother, born straight from her father's head: "The mother is no parent of that which is called her child, but only nurse of the new-planted seed that grows. The parent is he who mounts. A stranger she preserves a stranger's seed, if no god interfere will show you proof of what I have explained. There can be a father without any mother. There she stands, the living witness, daughter of Olympian Zeus, she who was never fostered in the dark of the womb yet such a child as no goddess could bring to birth" (Aeschylus, *E* 158; cf. Irigaray, *ML* 94).[29] Apollo persuades Athena that the mother is not a parent but merely an altogether unnecessary nurse or soil within which the child grows. Athena accepts Apollo's plea and transforms the Erinyes into the Eumenides, who now serve as protectors of all supplicants who beseech the gods.

So while Dionysus is born of a dead mother, Apollo orders the murder of the mother. He commands the death of the mother and forgets about his sister. While I have emphasized Apollo's matricide, Irigaray is concerned with his annihilation of his sister, Artemis. Irigaray argues that his identity is dependent on his annihilation of his sister. She maintains that Apollo's balance and harmony against Dionysian chaos are bought at Artemis's expense: "And he who entertains and realizes the dream of achieving peace in equilibrium, of overcoming the pain of living and of insoluble tragic dilemmas, also reveals himself to be the master of duels in which no violence breaks out, because one of the terms has been removed" (*ML* 152). Artemis has been removed. In fact, within the Apollonian economy all women are abandoned, denied, and used so that the sun god can create "his dreams or works of beauty" out of them (*ML* 155). Irigaray suggests that Apollo, god of truth and light, denies the other to the point of denying his own body (*ML* 157). The body is too dark, unstable, and chaotic; he requires order and restraint. He insists on the one, the selfsame, the truth. He represents everything that the body is not. Extending Irigaray's suggestive remarks on Apollo's denial of the body, I maintain that the body to whom he owes his life, the body of the mother, is the real target of Apollo's arrow. He denies the body altogether; and by so doing, he denies the significance of his birth out of the laboring body of a woman. He forgets that through her pain and nurturing he was given the gift of life. He repays his debt, however, with matricide.

For Irigaray, these male gods forget their debt to the maternal-feminine by miming the maternal-female so that they don't have to acknowledge woman's existence. They usurp women's procreative powers in order to ensure the power of the masculine order: "The fight and the compromises with the ancestress, the mothers, sometimes even the mistresses are on display. The brother-sister couple remains unresolved. Is this the deepest layer of the mimesis hidden in the night of truth? . . . In this way the god-men may defend themselves from the archaic forces: with Zeus mimicking the mother, Apollo the sister, Dionysus the mistress? Even as they ensure the power of the masculine order, which they aim to keep" (*ML* 161).

The last god-man that Irigaray reads as the mime of the maternal-female is Christ. Her stunning argument is that Christ "takes upon himself, mimics, the female in order to effect the passage back and beyond that creature whose flesh constantly incites men to lose control" (*ML* 166). He performs his mime on the cross when through the wound in his side he gives eternal life. His wound mimics the life-giving womb of the mother; hers is the flesh that incites men to lose control. And by so doing, he takes us beyond the flesh into a world under the reign of the Father to whom the human body has been sacrificed. Christ reenacts the sacrifice of Mary, the virgin mother whose body is also sacrificed in order to give life. Irigaray calls Mary's yes to the word of the Father a no to herself (*ML* 167). Once again the body of woman is sacrificed to the truth of the Father: "What Truth supports such a respect for life? The word made flesh? Or the power of patriarchies that works by the repression, seduction, and legal rape of the body of women who know the value of gestation and childbearing? . . . Liberate fleshly encounters from the taboos that pervert them. Leave the Christians to their crosses!" (*ML* 170).

Following Nietzsche, and yet going beyond him, Irigaray argues that Christians have forgotten the most important part of Christ's message: incarnation. They have forgotten that Christ is a bodily incarnation of god. Like Dionysus he is god-man; like Dionysus he represents the unity of the human and the divine. But whereas with Dionysus, Eros is too violent and rips up the body, with Christ, Eros disappears altogether (*ML* 176–177). Irigaray reminds us that Christ did not heal with words but with touch. His divinity is his incarnation (*ML* 181). Like Nietzsche, Irigaray laments the death of God; she agrees that man has killed God. And she asks, "If for men their God is dead, where can the divine be spoken without preaching death?" (*ML* 20). She imagines a divinity beyond this economy of death and sacrifice.

In the last section of the last part of *Marine Lover*, when Irigaray finally mentions Nietzsche by name, she suggests that he reenacts the Christian tragedy of death that requires sacrificing the body. In the end she says that Nietzsche could not perform a revaluation of values because he does not go beyond the father-son relationship, in which he insists on being both the father and the son (*ML* 34). He loves only the other of the same in his "echonomy" of sameness; he loves only himself. And without a proper other, "he plunges into the shadows" (ML 187). "Sensing the impotence to come, Nietzsche declares he is the crucified one. And is crucified. But by himself" (*ML* 188). He kills himself when he kills the other.

Irigaray maintains that without acknowledging the difference of the other there is nothing beyond the violent economy of castration, in which the masculine is substituted for the feminine: "Only through difference can the incarnation unfold (*se déploie*) without murderous or suicidal passion. Rhythm and measure of a female other that, endlessly, undoes the autological circle of discourse, thwarts the eternal return of the same, opens up every horizon through the affirmation of another point of view whose fulfillment can never be predicted. That is always dangerous? A gay science of incarnation?" (*ML* 188).

Rather than ripping through the folds of the other with some sharp object in the way that Nietzsche and Derrida do in order to make her yield what might belong to her, which will ensure that she does not exist, Irigaray proposes a nonviolent exchange without the fear of debt or loss: "Instead of tearing, let it [our embrace] return to something that has never taken place. The embrace of earth and air and fire and water, which have never been wed. Forget the knife-cut, the chalk-line partitions. Forget the appropriations at frontiers that belong to no one and are marked by arbitrarily solid lines that risk the abyss at every moment. The forfeit of the will, the insecurity of debt" (*ML* 21). For Irigaray the model for this new economy is not the master-slave relationship but rather the relationship between the infant and the maternal body and between the sexes.

The plaint of Ariadne is the plaint of the mother in childbirth. In this chapter that plaint has been heard as the cry to remember the mother. The last three sections, "The Eternal Return of the Same," "The Birth of Gods," and "The Economy of the Gift," have all given voice to that cry. Taking up Irigaray's powerful suggestions at the end of *Marine Lover*, I have elaborated the ways in which Nietzsche's gods—Dionysus, Apollo, and Christ—all appropriate the power of their mothers, sisters, or lovers without acknowledging their debt. They invent ways to give birth to themselves in order to forget that they were born of their mothers. Nietzsche's doctrine of the eternal return of the same is another way of telling a story in which man gives birth to himself without woman. By weaving together several readings of Nietzsche's doctrine of eternal return, I have suggested how it can be read as a fear of the feminine and a desire to give birth to oneself rather than acknowledge any maternal gift. In addition, the economy of the gift presented in *Zarathustra*, and endorsed by some Nietzsche scholars, prevents any acknowledgment of the maternal gift of life. The impossibility of the gift and giving within this economy is at its limit in Derrida's account of the gift in *Given Time*. I read his theory of the impossibility of the gift and the necessity of forgetting gifts and giving as yet another way to the mother's gift of life and her act of giving birth. The Greek myths of the gods, Nietzsche's stories of self-creation and Derrida's eulogy to the gift, all participate in what Irigaray has identified as the matricide committed by Western culture.

THREE

THE ETHICS OF MATERNITY
Giving Birth to the (M)other

INTRODUCTION

Why the Woman Is Not (merely) a Mother

Up to this point, I have only alluded to differences between the feminine, woman, and the maternal. Following the literature that I was criticizing, I have not made distinctions between the three concepts. There are, however, significant differences between them. In fact, conflating the three concepts is often used as a way to exclude all three from culture. In order to diagnose philosophy's relation to the feminine, it is necessary to delineate the differences between the feminine, woman, and the maternal, specifically in the case of reading Nietzsche. In the past I have argued that it is a mistake to conflate these three concepts when interpreting Nietzsche's relation to the feminine, woman, or the maternal.[1] My analysis in chapter 5 will further indicate that the results of interpreting Nietzsche's relation to the feminine are significantly different if we make a distinction between the concepts of the feminine, woman, and the maternal.

In terms of our ordinary language, "woman" refers to a subset of all adult human beings—those who are female. "Femininity" is a characteristic that is associated with females but is not a necessary characteristic of females and can be a characteristic of males. The relationship between femininity and woman has been complicated by contemporary feminist theory. Simone de Beauvoir, for example, claimed that "one is not born a woman." She maintained that being a woman is not the same as being female. The concept "woman" is a social construction that normalizes females to exhibit feminine characteristics and inhibit masculine characteristics. Beauvoir introduces a notion of gender apart from sex, through which women and femininity are not naturally identical with being female.

In *The Second Sex*, Beauvoir argues that "no biological, psychological, or economic fate determines the figure that the human female presents in society" (SS 267). Beauvoir says that "it is civilization as a whole that produces this creature, intermediate between male and eunuch, which is described as feminine" (267). Her distinction between sex and gender has become fundamental to feminist theory. For Beauvoir sex is the facticity of the body—one is born female or male—while gender is the cultural meaning that the body acquires. Still, the characteristics that are associated with woman and the feminine are generally seen as natural outgrowths of the female body.

For Beauvoir one is not, and should not be, defined in terms of gender. We are all persons first, persons capable in varying ways of transcending our physicality. Beauvoir argues that in spite of the cultural associations with woman or the feminine, women qua persons are identical to men in their "natural" ability to take a transcendental position in relation to their experience. Like many feminists before and after her, Beauvoir argues for the social, economic, and political equality of women because they are persons just the same as men. This may seem obvious, but in this country as late as 1971, states could use the U.S. Supreme Court ruling in the 1894 case of *In re Lockwood* (154 US 116) to confine their definition of "person" to males only. Beauvoir suggests that women should leave behind the burden of the category "woman," with the cultural associations of passivity, weakness, nurturance, emotionality, and so on, to enter the world of men as equal persons—active, strong and rational ones.

This kind of argument, however, has left bell hooks and other black women wondering, with Sojourner Truth, "Ain't I a woman?" In *Ain't I a Woman? Black Women and Feminism* bell hooks points out that black women have traditionally worked alongside men. Black women have traditionally been associated with strength and hard work. So who is this "woman" that "women" are to leave behind? And more than that, who is this "man" with whom "women" are to become social, economic, and political equals? Poor women, black women, Chicana women look around themselves and see that their men are not much better off economically or politically than they are. This leads them to ask: Who are these men? Who are these women? The men with whom these women want to become equals are not poor or black or Chicano. The women who will be liberated by throwing off their gender identity are white women and the men with whom they will become equals are white men.

So to what does the concept "woman" refer? One is not born a woman. And different women are not constructed as "woman" in the same way. Additionally, as Judith Butler points out, one is never just a woman: "If one is a woman, that is surely not all one is; the term fails to be exhaustive, not because a pregendered person transcends the specific paraphernalia of its gender, but because gender is not always constituted coherently or consistently in different historical contexts, and because gender intersects with racial, class, ethnic, sexual, and regional modalities of discursively constituted identities. As a result, it becomes impossible to separate out gender from the political and cultural intersections in which it is invariably produced and maintained" (*GT* 3).

If gender is inseparable from race, ethnicity, class, and sexuality, then it can't be women's identity as women or a shared experience of oppression that unites them. As Chandra Mohanty says in "Under Western Eyes," "sisterhood cannot be assumed on the basis of gender; it must be forged in concrete historical and political practice and analysis. . . . Beyond sisterhood there is still racism, colonialism and imperialism" (339, 348).

What, then, is a "woman"? Who are women? Is there anything that all women have in common? Do we at least share, as Beauvoir suggests, the facticity of our sex, regardless of what has happened to cultural constructions of gender? Judith Butler answers no. She extends Beauvoir's distinction between sex (the physical facts), and gender (the cultural representation of those "facts"). Butler argues that sex is actually a construction of gender. Sex is always already gendered. She compares Beauvoir's distinction between sex and gender to Levi-Strauss's distinction between the raw and the cooked. It seems to us that sex is the raw fact of the matter and gender is what we get when we cook sex up a bit. Butler argues that if sex is to the raw as gender is to the cooked, then sex is always already cooked (GT, 37-38).

If sex appears as an already given, Butler wants to know through what means it is given. She asks: "What is 'sex' anyway? Is it natural, anatomical, chromosomal, or hormonal, and how is a feminist critic to assess the scientific discourses which purport to establish such 'facts' for us? Does sex have a history? Does each sex have a different history, or histories? Is there a history of how the duality of sex was established, a genealogy that might expose the binary options as a variable construction? Are the ostensibly natural facts of sex discursively produced by various scientific discourses in the service of other political and social interests?" (*GT* 6–7). If "sex" is already gendered, the cause turns out to be merely an effect (*GT* 7). Butler argues that the identification and maintenance of two sexes serve what she calls the "heterosexual matrix." She maintains that the category of woman is necessary to maintain this heterosexual matrix.

Ultimately for Butler gender and sex are performances, masquerades. Femininity is a masquerade, and insofar as sex is already imbued with gender, femaleness is also a masquerade. Femininity is a performance that constitutes femaleness. She develops her account of performative gender in *Bodies that Matter*. Butler agrees with the Lacanian assertion that femininity is a masquerade. It is this assertion that leads Derrida to maintain that there is no such thing as a woman. Both woman and femininity are cultural creations. The concept "woman," like any other concept, does not correspond to some thing in the world. The word "woman" does not have one referent; rather it is set up in a network of other concepts, for example, femininity and maternity. In Western culture woman has been identified with both femininity and maternity.

In *Marine Lover* Irigaray insists on the difference between femininity, woman, and the mother. She argues that femininity is a concept that allows patriarchy to cover over the experience of both women and mothers: "The law of the father needed femininity—a replica of woman—in order to take the upper hand over the mother's passion, as well as the woman's pleasure" (*ML* 97). The appeal to, or belief in, femininity makes it possible to avoid any encounter with the mother's passion or the woman's pleasure. Here Irigaray alludes to Athena, the ideal of femininity and the ultimate judge in the case of Orestes' matricide (*ML* 94). Athena, born of a father alone, without a mother, owes her loyalty to the patriarch. In Aeschylus's *The Eumenides*, Athena approves of matricide while Apollo denies the mother any place in generation. Athena's femininity gives her the right to condone matricide. Her femininity becomes a means by which the father can enforce his law at the expense of the mother: "Femininity—the father's indispensable intermediary in putting his law into force. The simulacrum that makes the false pass into the true, obscures the difference between, substitutes for it a spacing of pretense: the neutrality of femininity. Which even God needed in order to pass for, to give himself out to be the only creator. To make himself out to be— what he is not. Which will be attributed to woman. And she need only forget that she owes life also to her mother for that loan to become her most divine reality. Life as femininity—the opposite" (*ML* 95).

This femininity is not/no longer an attribute of the woman; rather it is the father's creation. It is a concept with which women and mothers are fettered. Within the father's law there is no pleasure outside of the pleasures of femininity. And the bloodthirsty femininity of Athena justifies the son's matricide. Not only does a god command his matricide, but also a goddess, the ideal woman, condones it. Athena's birth itself, the birth of femininity, is a form of matricide; she is born without the mother.

As Irigaray points out, the power of femininity is seductiveness (*ML* 96). If the father uses femininity to pass for what he is not, the only creator, it is because femininity itself is the art of dissimulation. Femininity uses dissimulation in order to attract and ensnare. Witness centuries of warnings against feminine wiles. Recall that it is this act of passing oneself off for what one is not that Derrida calls the feminine operation. In *Spurs*, however, he distinguishes this feminine operation from femininity: "That which will not be pinned down by truth is, in truth—*feminine*. This should not, however, be hastily mistaken for a woman's feminin*ity*, for female sexual*ity*, or for any other of those essentializing fetishes which might still tantalize the dogmatic philosopher, the impotent artist or the inexperienced seducer who has not yet escaped his foolish hopes of capture" (*S* 55).

For Derrida the feminine is the feminine operation of dissimulation. It is the feminine operation that makes the feminine what it "is," that which will not be pinned down. Femininity and female sexuality, on the other hand, are manifestations of the dogmatic need to pin everything down. The dogmatic philosopher needs to identify things and their essences. Femininity and female sexuality, then, mitigate against the effects of the feminine operation. They are ways of trying to identify what the feminine *is* in its essence. What the dogmatist cannot see is that the feminine "is" always what it is not.

Implicit in Irigaray's discussion of femininity and its relation to the feminine, I find a criticism of Derrida's "notion" of the feminine. Making an analogy between Heidegger's use of Being and Irigaray's use of the feminine, in spite of his distinction between the feminine and femininity, we could criticize Derrida for treating the feminine as a characteristic of femininity, just as Heidegger criticizes the metaphysicians for treating Being as a being.[2] Irigaray identifies passing oneself off as what one it is not as a traditional characteristic of femininity. Recall her remarks about the simulacrum and pretense of femininity in the passage that I quoted above (*ML* 95). The idea that the feminine gives itself for what it is not is merely another stereotypical characteristic of femininity: because of their femininity, women shouldn't be trusted. It is with their femininity that women control and seduce men.

Irigaray's analysis of the relation between the feminine and femininity suggests an implicit rejection of Derrida's identification of the feminine operation with dissimulation and masquerade. Dissimulation and masquerade merely compound stereotypes of femininity that can be used by the father "in putting his law into force" (see *ML* 95). Irigaray might agree with Derrida that within the discourse of metaphysics the feminine can only appear as what it is not, which says more about the discourse of metaphysics than it does about the feminine. But unlike Derrida, Irigaray deploys "the feminine" in ways that call into question the metaphysics that excludes her instead of redeploying "the feminine" as the excluded. Whereas Derrida uses the exclusion of the feminine in order to try to undermine metaphysics, Irigaray tries to formulate a metaphysics from the side of the feminine. Like Derrida, Irigaray is concerned not merely with deconstructing metaphysical categories like woman and man but also with constructing new identities that do not operate within binary oppositions.

Where does the mother operate in the binary man/woman? Both men and women, males and females, have mothers. And obviously all women are not mothers and many are not capable of becoming mothers. In spite of patriarchal associations between women and their reproductive capacities, the mother appears to be a foil to binary sexual oppositions. As Derrida says in *Glas,* "the mother (whatever forename or pronoun she may be given) stands beyond the sexual opposition. This above all is not a woman. She only lets herself, detached, be represented by the sex" (134). Kristeva makes a claim similar to Derrida's when she says that the mother is "alone of her sex" (*TL* 253). Kristeva suggests that woman and the feminine operate independently of what she calls the maternal function (*DL* 237–270). By identifying the maternal as a function, she distinguishes between the child's relationship to its mother qua mother and its relationship to its mother qua woman. The maternal function cannot be identified with either woman or femininity. Kristeva maintains that the mother is neither masculine nor feminine (*TL* 234–63). The child's relation to the mother is pre-Oedipal and operates before any sexual difference. To conflate the feminine, woman, and the mother is to overlook the uniqueness of the mother-child relationship. Moreover, such a conflation subjects both woman and the feminine to an "abjection" that is appropriate only to the mother fulfilling the maternal function.

Kristeva introduces the notion of abjection in *Powers of Horror*. She develops the term *abject* in its ambiguity; in her verbalization of this adjective, it can mean to jettison, repel, repulse, throw out or to be revolting, disgusting, repulsive. The abject is not a "lack of cleanliness or health that causes abjection but *what disturbs identity,* system, order" (*PH* 4; my emphasis). The abject threatens identity. It is neither good nor evil, subject nor object, ego nor unconscious, but something that threatens these distinctions. In the child's relation to the mother, abjection shows up as the struggle to set up borders between the maternal body, the maternal "container," and itself.

The experience of abjection is founded in birth itself (*PH,* 10). In birth, one body is violently separated from another. This separation is necessary for the continuation of the species. Yet, it is with the experience of maternity and birth that identity is most powerfully called into question. Certainly the maternal body challenges notions of autonomous individuals. The controversies around abortion are evidence of this challenge. And even at the experience of birth, before the umbilical cord is cut, it is problematic whether there are two autonomous individuals or one. The abject, that which is abjected and gives rise to the experience of abjection, is related to the mother: "Defilement is the translinguistic spoor of the most archaic boundaries of the self's clean and proper body. In that sense, if it is a jettisoned object, it is so from the mother" (PH 73). The child is this jettisoned object, violently expelled from the mother's body. During the process of weaning and the stage at which the child first becomes conscious of itself, it engages in the struggle to separate from the maternal body, even while identifying with it. On Kristeva's analysis, the child hates that body but only because it can't be free of it; it is a horrifying, devouring body.[3] It is a body that evokes rage and fear. Yet Kristeva maintains that it is necessary for every child to "abject" its mother to become an autonomous subject. The child abjects the mother in the process of weaning and separation. Through this process the mother herself is made abject. In other words, because she is seen as abject she can be abjected. The child must see its mother as something undesirable in order to separate from her.

In Western culture, with the conflation of the feminine, woman and the maternal, it becomes difficult for the child to abject its mother *as a mother* performing her maternal function. Instead, as a culture we abject the feminine and woman when we abject the mother. The feminine, woman, and the mother all become undesirable. Because the feminine, woman, and even the maternal have been reduced to reproduction only, the maternal function, they have all been excluded from culture as that abject which challenges the border between culture and nature.

The maternal reproductive function is a threat to culture, even as it is necessary for the continuation of culture, because it is associated with nature. The ambiguity between culture and nature, and the autonomy of individuals, in the maternal body results in the latter's abjection by culture. It is a threat to borders and identity. For Kristeva, this abjection is necessary, but it is not necessary to conflate the feminine and woman and the mother with the maternal body only. To do so makes it possible to abject them all and exclude them all from culture. As I will elaborate in chapter 6, Irigaray suggests that we need to reconceive of maternity so that we do not imagine it as undesirable or a threat to autonomy or culture. Whether or not the abjection of the maternal body is necessary to culture, the conflation of the feminine, woman, and the maternal have contributed to the exclusion of them all. Only by delineating these concepts can we begin to understand philosophy's relation to them. In the case of Nietzsche, the affirming woman, as Derrida refers to her, is always only the mother. More than this, at her most productive she is always only a masculine mother.

5   *Emasculate Conception*

Who of us is Oedipus here? Who the Sphinx?
— Friedrich Nietzsche, *Beyond Good and Evil*

Nietzsche's Abjection

*With the riddle-solving and mother-marrying Oedipus in mind,
we must immediately interpret this to mean that where prophetic
and magical powers have broken the spell of present and future,
the rigid law of individuation, and the real magic of nature, some
enormously unnatural event—such as incest—must have occurred
earlier, as a cause. How else could one compel nature to surrender
her secrets if not by triumphantly resisting her, that is, by means
of something unnatural? It is this insight that I find expressed in
that horrible triad of Oedipus' destinies: the same man who
solves the riddle of nature—that Sphinx of two species—must
also break the most sacred natural orders by murdering his father
and marrying his mother. Indeed, the myth seems to whisper to us
that wisdom, particularly Dionysian wisdom, is an unnatural
abomination.*
—Friedrich Nietzsche, *The Birth of Tragedy*

Interpretations of Nietzsche's relation to the feminine range from David
Krell's claim that Nietzsche "writes with the hand of woman" to Ofelia
Schutte's insistence that Nietzsche "maintains what can be characterized
fundamentally as an antifeminist position both on gender difference and
on the issue of social and political equality."[4] These interpretations overlook an important difference in Nietzsche's writings between the feminine
and the maternal. Some of the ambiguity in Nietzsche's relation to the
feminine can be explained by separating the feminine from the maternal
and analyzing the position of the mother in Nietzsche's writings.

Kristeva's account of the abject mother can be very useful in diagnosing the ambiguous position of the feminine and woman in Nietzsche's writings as an ambiguous relation to the maternal. Nietzsche's writings portray

a fascination with the figure of the mother as both attractive and repulsive; the womb is both devouring and horrifying and procreatively powerful. At this point it will be helpful to expand on Kristeva's theory of abjection in order to use it to diagnose Nietzsche's writings. For Kristeva abjection operates differently in males and females. Her account of the male child's abjection in *Powers of Horror* can be applied to Nietzsche's writings. The male child feels rage against his mother because her having carried him in her womb compromises his identity. How can he become a man when "he" was once part of a woman's body? "He" inhabited her womb. Additionally, how can he become a man and love a woman, that abject and threatening hole "represented" by his mother? One way to deal with the threat of the "castrated" mother, the mother as hole, is fetishism. Fetishism is not a denial of *woman's* castration, but a denial of the *mother's* castration—the fetishist seems to say, "If mom is castrated and I was once her, then I, too, am castrated."

In *Powers of Horror* Kristeva describes an alternative to fetishism. The male child must split his mother to take up his masculine gender identity. The mother is spilt in two, into the abject and the sublime (*PH* 157). Making the mother abject allows the male child to separate from his mother and become autonomous. But if the mother is only abject (and not also sublime), then she becomes the phobic object, the child himself becomes abject, and the Oedipal situation is thrown out of alignment. In this scenario, it is either the mother or the child: either the child abjects the mother ("she is horrifying, so I am sublime") or the child abjects itself ("I am horrifying, so she is sublime"). If the mother remains abject, however, she never becomes the object, and certainly not the object of love. As Kristeva describes it, the abject is a preobject, a phobic object. At this stage prior to the object, there is no sexual difference because there is no border between mother and child.

The experience of abjection is not only horror at that which defies borders but also fascination at the impossibility of identity. In this fascination, the child sees its mother as sublime. If she is only sublime, however, the child will not separate from her. He will have no subject or object identity whatsoever, no primary repression and thus no secondary repression. In other words, the Other will have been completely foreclosed, never set up, and the child will be psychotic. He will still be unable to love a woman, or anyone else. For the psychotic, there is no one else, no object, no other(s). When the child does not properly go through the stage of abjection and take his mother as a proper object, when he remains at the stage of abjection and abjects himself, then the maternal body becomes a phobic "object." The phobic is on the "borderline," on the edge of psychosis, but not mad. Whereas the neurotic (the fetishist) has displaced or denied the Other to maintain its ego, and the psychotic has foreclosed the Other and therefore the possibility of an ego, the phobic has confused the Other with itself and upholds its "ego" within the Other (*PH* 15). In some sense, the abject "subject" is too precocious. It realizes that it can be constituted as a subject only by virtue of the Other—that its identity rests on separation—even before it undergoes this process. So rather than identify with the other, or with its own image in the other, the phobic identifies with the process itself; he identifies with the undecidable place between the self and the other.

For Kristeva, the child can only properly go through the stage of abjection with the support of what she calls a loving "imaginary father." Without the loving "imaginary father" the child abjects himself rather than separating from the mother. If he doesn't have some imaginary construct that enables him to both separate from her and separate the maternal function from the mother, then he misplaces abjection. Rather than perceive the "maternal container" as a horrible threat from which he must separate, he perceives women as a threat. Without the imaginary wherewithal to turn the threat into a representation of mother as Other, he turns women into the Other. To avoid this misplaced abjection it is crucial to differentiate between mother and woman.

Jean Graybeal uses Kristeva's notion of abjection in *Language and "the Feminine" in Nietzsche and Heidegger* to analyze Nietzsche's relation to his mother. Graybeal argues that Nietzsche abjects his mother, Franziska.⁵ She reads the opening line of the first chapter of *Ecce Homo*—"The happiness of my existence, its uniqueness perhaps, lies in its fate: I am, to express it in the form of a riddle, as my father already dead, while as my mother I still live and grow old" (*KS* 6:264)—as Nietzsche's failed attempt to articulate his relation to the feminine, specifically his relation to his mother. Graybeal points out that there are two versions of this section of *Ecce Homo*. There is a revised version that was discovered only relatively recently, because it had been suppressed by Nietzsche's friend Peter Gast after Nietzsche's collapse in January 1889. As Graybeal explains, Nietzsche collapsed very shortly after sending this revised version to his publisher. After his collapse Peter Gast edited the manuscript and omitted the revised version. Graybeal suggests that there could be a correlation between this later version of the chapter of *Ecce Homo* and Nietzsche's collapse.

Graybeal describes the significant differences between the earlier and later versions of the first chapter of *Ecce Homo*. She maintains that both versions are Nietzsche's attempts to come to terms with the influence of his mother on his life. She argues that his first attempt to look directly at his mother paralyzes him, whereas the second attempt plunges him into rhetorical excess and frenzy. In the first version, after his riddle, Nietzsche says only that his mother is "very German." The rest of that version describes his father. In the later version, however, Nietzsche launches into a miniature diatribe against his mother and sister, calling them "rabble" and a"hell-machine" (*KS* 6:268; *EH*). Graybeal concludes that had Nietzsche been able to articulate the sublime and the horror he experienced in relation to his mother, he might have retained his sanity longer: "As his father he is dead, beyond life, and as his mother he is abjectly implicated in the horrors of 'human, all-too-human' existence" (*LF* 92–93).

Graybeal doesn't develop her thesis that Nietzsche might have retained his sanity had he been able to articulate his relationship to his mother, but her hypothesis is intriguing. Perhaps she could develop it in the following way. Kristeva claims that if the child cannot abject the mother through the support of a loving imaginary father, then the child abjects himself. The mother becomes a phobic object for the child because he cannot separate himself from her. Perhaps Graybeal is suggesting that when Nietzsche tried to face the mother, he could not separate himself from her. After all, if the abject is a jettisoned object, "it is so from the mother." As the phobic, Nietzsche abjects himself when he abjects the mother; the identification is too strong. Her abjection was his abjection. Unable to separate from the mother, teetering on the edge of psychosis, his failed attempt to articulate his relationship to the mother might have sent him over the edge.

Although I find Graybeal's analysis provocative, and this is why I engage it here, I do not think that psychoanalytic theory can be applied to texts in order to diagnose the neuroses of their authors. Rather, I think that psychoanalysis can be applied to texts themselves in order to diagnose the psychic economies manifest in those texts. This type of textual analysis is very useful in determining the effects of particular texts. Leaving Graybeal's speculations on Nietzsche's relation with his mother, Franziska, behind, Kristeva's theory of abjection can be useful in identifying and understanding the axes of psychosexual relations in Nietzsche's texts.

The Manly Father

Kristeva diagnoses problems with abjecting the mother and then overcoming this abjection as the lack of any loving imaginary father to support that process. The father of traditional psychoanalytic theory is a stern father of the law, but this father provides no support for giving up an identification with the maternal body. The father figure in Nietzsche's writings also seems to be characteristically stern and demanding, Caesar or Napoleon.[3] Nietzsche's writings are full of hard warriors, fathers who demand the impossible from their sons, fathers who demand that their sons separate from the womanly mother to become manly: "Truths that are *hard* won, certain, enduring, and therefore still of consequence for all further knowledge are the higher; to keep to them is *manly*, and shows bravery, simplicity, restraint. Eventually, not only the individual, but all mankind will be elevated to this *manliness*, when men finally grow accustomed to the greater esteem for durable, lasting knowledge" (*KS* 2:25–26; *HATH* §3, 15; my emphasis).

Here Nietzsche identifies with the eternal *manly* truth and looks forward to the day when all of mankind is manly. In *Twilight of the Idols* he says that "freedom means that the manly instincts which delight in war and victory dominate over other instincts" (*TW,* "Skirmishes," 38). In *Gay Science.* Nietzsche welcomes signs of a more "virile, warlike age" (*KS* 3:526; *GS* §283, 288). In "How to Philosophize with a Hammer," Nietzsche orders us to become "hard!" And Zarathustra tells others, or is told, to become "hard," to become "manly." He tells us that all creators are "hard" (*KS* 4:166; *Z* II, 202; *KS* 4: 268; *Z* III 326).[4] Remember Zarathustra's proclamation: "Brave, unconcerned, mocking, violent—thus wisdom wants us: she is a woman and always loves only a warrior" (*KS* 4:49; *ZI*, 153). Nietzsche envies this warrior, this conqueror, this image of the manly hero. For Nietzsche impotence is the real enemy of life. "One is today ashamed of hardness," says Nietzsche (*KS* 5:358; *OGM* III §9, 114). It is no wonder that he chooses the god of fertility, Dionysus, whose symbols are blood-red wine and the tumescent phallus, to represent life's force. And repeatedly, degenerate life is figured in terms of castration, emasculation, effeminacy, and impotence.

Nietzsche suggests that philosophy castrates the intellect: "to eliminate the will altogether, to suspend each and every effect, supposing we were capable of this—what would that mean but to *castrate* the intellect" (OGM II §12, 119). He calls philosophy "the will to truth as the *impotence* of the will to create" (WTP §585; OGM II §7). Those motivated by the will to truth claim to discover reality because they are too weak to create it. For Nietzsche, detached objective truth is "castrated" because it is "impotent" to create truth. "Supposing truth is a woman," begins *Beyond Good and Evil*, ". . . all philosophers, insofar as they were dogmatists, have been very inexpert about women" (BT 2). Philosophers lust after woman (truth), but they don't have the potency to possess her. Their "*emasculated* leers," says Nietzsche, "wish to be called 'contemplation'" (Z 235).

Nietzsche wages the same attack against religion as he does against philosophy. He criticizes the Christian treatment of sexual excitation, the consequence of which, he says is: "...not only the loss of an organ but the *emasculation* of a man's character—And the same applies to the moralist's madness and demands, instead of the restraining of the passions, their extirpation. Its conclusion is always: only the *castrated* man is a good man" (*WTP* §343, 207). Nietzsche's attack against philosophy and religion is couched in the language of an anxiety about castration and impotence. Nietzsche criticizes the ascetic ideal because it denies the body, and yet his criticism displays a condemnation of the body because it is weak and impotent and does not perform. Nietzsche criticizes philosophy's will to truth, but he does so in the name of a masculine bodily anxiety, castration anxiety. His criticism speaks a fear of the limitations of the body and ultimately the death of the body. It speaks a fear of the impotent, castrated body. Ultimately it speaks the fear of the emasculated, feminine body.

Yet in *Ecce Homo* Nietzsche claims that as his father he is dead and as his mother he lives on. For him the masculine-paternal is death but the feminine-maternal is life. How is it that Nietzsche negotiates this fear of the emasculate feminine body and the life that it provides for him? What aspect of the feminine body is horrifying and what aspect is sublime? He can live on as his mother only by identifying with maternal procreativity, with the phallic mother. He must abject the castrated mother, a feminine mother, and affirm the phallic mother, a masculine mother. He cannot identify with the castrated mother and maintain his identification with the virile and potent body of the warrior. And identification with the feminine mother is an identification with castration.

If the son identifies with the castrated mother and the castrated mother is abject, then the son must be abject too. Kristeva suggests that if the child cannot separate from the mother then it will abject itself. In fact, in some cases the child will abject itself so that it doesn't have to abject its mother. To hate the mother is to hate yourself, hating yourself so that you won't have to hate the mother. Even Nietzsche claims that misogynists really hate themselves (*KS* 3:238; *D* §346, 165). So the mother's sex is horrifying because it is castrated and it is sublime because it is linked to powerful reproductive organs. Recall from Freud's analysis that it is because the mother's sex is castrated that it also threatens castration. Nietzsche's texts speak a fear not only of the castrated mother but also of the castrating mother who will cut man to pieces.

Unless she is domesticated in her pregnancy, the woman is dangerous. Nietzsche suggests that women exist to be pregnant. "Everything about Woman," says Nietzsche's Zarathustra, is a "riddle" solved by "pregnancy," and you can "cure" a woman by giving her a child (*KS* 6:306; *EH* §5, 267; *KS* 4:84; *ZI*, 178). Women's profession, says Nietzsche, is "to give birth to strong children" (*KS* 5:177; *BGE*, 177; KSA 2:267, *HATH* 197). Certainly woman's desire and feminine sexuality apart from her reproductive capacities are dangerous: "Even now female voices are heard which—holy Aristophanes!—are frightening: they threaten with medical explicitness what woman *wants* from man" (*BGE* §232, 163). But it is not just the *scientific* nature of the explication of woman's desire that frightens Nietzsche. He maintains that the "Eternal-Feminine" is designed to induce fear in men (BGE §232, 163). And it is not just the *eternal* feminine that frightens. Rather, woman's desire and feminine sexuality themselves in their various forms are dangerous seductions for strong men: "the danger for artists, for geniuses . . . is woman: adoring women confront them with corruption. . . . In many cases of feminine love, perhaps including the most famous ones above all, love is merely a more refined form of parasitism, a form of nestling down in another soul, sometimes even in the flesh of another—alas, always decidedly at the expense of 'the host'!" (*CW* §3, 161). Women devour, and tear at, the flesh of men. Nietzsche says that the tragedy of woman "tears to pieces as it enchants" (*KS* 5:178; BGE §239, 170). He worries that like Dionysus he will be torn apart by the woman/mother whose desire has not been domesticated: "May I here venture the surmise that I *know* women? That is part of my Dionysian dowry. Who knows? Perhaps I am the first psychologist of the eternally feminine. They all love me—an old story—not counting *abortive* females, the 'emancipated' who lack the stuff for children.—Fortunately, I am not willing to be torn to pieces: the perfect woman tears to pieces when she loves.—I know these charming maenads.—Ah, what a dangerous, creeping, subterranean little beast of prey she is! And yet so agreeable!" (*KS* 6:305–6; *EH*, 266). In spite of Nietzsche's identification with women, or perhaps because of it, he claims that he cannot be ripped apart by them. Fertile women, mothers, love him because he knows them. He identifies with these mothers. Yet he won't return their love; to do so is to risk dismemberment. Unlike Dionysus, he won't be torn apart by this mother in some phallic frenzy. While Nietzsche identifies with the phallic mother—reveres her as the sublime metaphor for the will to power—he is afraid that she will tear him apart. She is the terrifying abject mother who threatens to devour his unity and autonomy. She threatens to tear up his unified self. She threatens to dismember him. The beloved phallic mother becomes the feared castrating mother.

In *Language and "the Feminine" in Nietzsche and Heidegger,* Jean Graybeal argues that Nietzsche feared castration from his own mother. She quotes the latest version of the first chapter of *Ecce Homo*: "Here works a perfect hell-machine, with unfailing certainty about the moment when one can bloodily wound me—in my highest moments . . . for there all strength is lacking to defend oneself against poisonous vermin." Graybeal interprets this passage as a sign of Nietzsche's fear of a castrating mother: "This hell-machine has unfailing (hence inhuman) certainty about the *Augenblick*, the precise instant "when one can bloodily wound me." When could this be but in his *highest Augenblicken*? This entire fantasy suggests the association of erection and castration. The hellish perfection and inhuman, unfailing certainty of this female machine, a machine that knows exactly when to attack, when the victim is at the height of his exaltation. . .A castrating mother awaits him at the bottom of his ladder of life" (*LF* 87; *KS* 6:286).

We can move Graybeal's analysis from the level of personal psychology to the level of textual positionality. If Nietzsche's metaphorical mother is not castrating, then she is not the all-powerful phallic mother of his fantasies. And she cannot be the revered sublime mother. If she is not the castrating mother, then she is the castrated mother. She is the mother against whom the fetish becomes a shield. When Nietzsche looks at the mother whom he has created—the masculine mother, the *Übermensch*, Zarathustra—he sees that she is not the all-powerful mother of his fantasies. He can no longer deny the mother's castration; she is not the phallic mother. But to admit it is too much for him to bear because of his narcissistic identification with his mother. He cannot separate himself from her; if she is castrated, then so is he.

Much of his writing can be read as an attempt to escape his mother, his mother-land, his mother tongue, and maternal security in order to give birth to himself. He envisions a motherless child, the *Übermensch*, who gives birth to itself as a dancing star, a self-propelled wheel. His free spirit is one who flies alone without women, without his mother:

> The free spirit will always breathe a sigh of relief when he has finally
> decided to shake off the maternal care and protection administered by the
> women around him. What is the harm in the colder draft of air that they

had warded off so anxiously? What does one real disadvantage, loss, accident, illness, debt, or folly more or less in his life matter, compared with the bondage of the golden cradle, the peacock-tail fan, and the oppressive feeling of having to be actually grateful because he is waited upon and spoiled like an infant? That is why the milk offered him by the maternal disposition of the women around him can so easily turn to bile. (*KS* 2:281, 279–80; *HATH* §429, 426)

The free spirit flies free of the women around him only if he can abject his mother, only if for him her sweet milk turns to bile. Nietzsche's texts abject all women and femininity because he cannot abject the maternal. He misplaces abjection onto women and femininity in general as a defense against his own identification with the maternal body. In his writings, Nietzsche is not the free spirit. He cannot completely leave the safe haven of the maternal body. Without the support of a loving imaginary father, haunted by a perfect dead father, Nietzsche cannot imagine a creativity that is not an identification with the mother: "To be the child new-born, the creator must also be the mother who gives birth and endure the pangs of the birth-giver" (*KS* 4:111; *Z* II 199). Perhaps his writings manifest a guilt for his mother's pain and for the "matricide" necessary to separate from her. He must experience her pain, the pain that he caused her to feel. He cannot abject the mother and make her abhorrent; he feels too guilty. Yet feminine love is "maternal love" (*KS* 2:276, *HATH*, 203). And since love is associated solely with the maternal, to abject the mother is to live without love.

Nietzsche's writings are full of struggles to separate from the maternal. In his writing Nietzsche struggles with the boundaries between individuals, between categories, between opposites. His struggle often returns to the boundary between the child and the mother during birth. Birth is a process of individuation. Through birth, the child is separated from the mother and becomes an individual. For Nietzsche, individuation always covers over the chaos and arbitrariness of what was before individuation. The Dionysian womb of being gives birth to the Apollonian individual only through Apollonian control: "I see Apollo as the transfiguring genius of the *principium individuationis* through which alone the redemption in illusion is truly to be obtained; while by the mystical triumphant cry of Dionysus the spell of individuation is broken, and the way lies open to the *Mothers of Being*, to the innermost heart of things" (*KS* 1:103; *BT* §16, 99–100; my emphasis).

He argues that procreation is a reactive process because it is the inability, "impotence," to deal with excess (*WTP* §654, 345–347). This excess can only be tolerated if it is broken off, if it is separated into another individual, if it is born and the process through which it is born is forgotten. In fact, Nietzsche suggests that this is how truth is born. Truth is born out of chaos that we forget was once chaos. For him, it is Apollonian individuation that cures the eye hurt from staring at this chaos, the womb of being. Only individuation can make this creative/destructive life bearable. Nietzsche is fascinated and repulsed by the process of individuation, the process of birth and weaning. He is repulsed and yet fascinated by the abject, the in-between, the inability to distinguish; he is troubled by borders.

Perhaps the trouble with borders explains why Nietzsche's ideal womb is an impossible womb that does not give birth. For Nietzsche, individuation, like childbirth, is too painful. Therefore, he invokes Silenus' s wisdom: it is best not to be born at all (*KS* 1:35; *BT* §3, 42). If, however, one must be born, it is necessary to forget the repellent aspects of birth. To enjoy the child, one must forget the more repellent and painful aspects of pregnancy; it is necessary to forget the womb out of which one is born (*KS* 5:343; *OGM* III §4). Ultimately, it is the womb itself, this creative/destructive force, which must be forgotten to enjoy the child, or more precisely, so that the child can enjoy. The child (Nietzsche?) cannot bear to imagine its unity with the mother. He cannot tolerate an identification with the abject mother. The undifferentiated fusion is horrifying. The indeterminate identity between mother and child is too much to bear, especially for the male child. How can this child be a man if he was once part of a woman? In order for the child to be autonomous, he must forget that he was once part of his mother, expelled from her womb.

The *Übermensch* has no need for a mother; he gives birth to himself. The masculine Dionysian womb of being, unlike the weak feminine womb, creates *without* individuation. It is only the weak who need to individuate in order to make life bearable. Nietzsche's Dionysian *Übermensch*, on the other hand, is a strong new type who can bear the excesses of pregnancy without individuation. The *Übermensch* has no need for truth or individuation. These are for the impotent and the sick who cannot bear life's excess, for those who cannot affirm pain and difference. Zarathustra says that "whoever has to give birth is sick; but whoever has given birth is unclean" (*Z* IV, "On the Higher Man," §12). The *Übermensch*, on the other hand, is *eternally pregnant* with himself, a great health who does not need to give birth to anything other; the creator without creations; the artist without works of art; life become creative; son become mother, both sublime and abject.

The Masculine Mother: Giving Birth to Oneself

Nietzsche praises maternity because it is creative. In addition, Nietzsche repeatedly figures the will to power using metaphors of wombs and pregnancy, and the "eternally creative primordial mother" (*KS* 1:108; *BT* §16, 104). His Dionysian type is the "eternally pregnant mother"—she affirms herself continually through procreation. The womb becomes, for Nietzsche, a symbol of the phallic mother, the force of life, of life's potency. In fact the phallic mother becomes a masculine or manly mother. Perhaps this explains why the artist is stronger in his pregnancy than the "hysterical" woman is in hers. He's "man enough," she's not. The artist, says Nietzsche, cannot be expected to "become a woman—that he should receive" (*WTP* §811; cf. *WTP* §817; *WTP* §864). The artist's potency is not passive. Also, the artist, unlike "hysterical females," should be able to bear the excess which would be harmful to weaker sorts (*WTP* §812). This excess is associated with sexual potency in the artist which must be sublimated in artistic creation. In the artist chastity and sensuality come together in order to give birth to something creative (*OGM* III §8; *WTP* §811).

Like the ascetic priest who imagines a virgin birth, Nietzsche imagines a chaste conception that in the name of sexual desire replaces all bodily drives with creative products, *children*: "Making music is another way of making children; chastity is merely the economy of the artist—and in any event, even with the artists fruitfulness ceases when potency ceases" (*WTP* §800). Potency begets offspring only through an economy of chastity or self-discipline. The ascetic ideal becomes creative when it is wed to sensuality and gives birth to something beyond itself (OGM III §2). But as we discover, in Nietzsche's texts, this birth is an auto-birth as self-overcoming.[8] It is the birth of the self for the sake of the self; it is the ultimate gift to oneself. Only a masculine mother can give birth to a manly age of humanity.

Nietzsche's writings are full of masculine mothers and manly pregnancies. From his first book, *The Birth of Tragedy*—in which Apollo and Dionysus "continually incite each other to new and more *powerful births*"—to his last book, *Nietzsche contra Wagner*—in which "the Dionysian god and man, can afford not only the sight of the terrible and the questionable, but even the terrible deed and luxury of destruction, decomposition, and negation. . . because of an *excess of procreating*, restoring powers which can yet turn every desert into luxurious farm land"—and nearly every book in between, Nietzsche's Dionysian spirit usurps the powers of procreation, pregnancy, and birth (*BT* §1 33; *NCW,* "We Antipodes," in *PN* 668; my emphasis).

Nietzsche alludes to his Dionysian prophet Zarathustra's pregnancy. In *On the Genealogy of Morals* Nietzsche describes bad conscience as pregnancy (*OGM* II §19, 88). He talks of an animal soul that has turned against itself as "pregnant with a future" (*OGM* II §16, 85). And finally he talks of a great health and a *Mensch* of the future, the victor over god and nothingness, who must come some day. But at this point he stops himself because he says that he will "usurp that to which only one younger, 'heavier with future' [pregnant?], and stronger" has a right, Zarathustra (*OGM* II §25, 96).

Zarathustra experiences nausea as a kind of morning sickness. Out of a cycle of nausea, something is born. Man makes Zarathustra nauseous because man abjects life: "The great disgust with man— *this* choked me and had crawled into my throat" (*KS* 4:274; *Z* III 331). Man's longing for another world, a higher purpose, is the result of a nausea with life. Nausea at life leads to Christian redemption. And any type of redemption that denies the finite life of the body overcomes the nausea at life by denying life: "Christianity was from the beginning, essentially and fundamentally, life's nausea and disgust with life, merely concealed behind, masked by, dressed up as, faith in 'another' or 'better' life" (*BT* 23). Zarathustra's is the "great nausea" at man's nausea; his nausea is overcome through another "redemption," Dionysian redemption, a redemption of the earth, the *Übermensch*'s redemption: "He must yet come to us, the *redeeming* man of great love and contempt, the creative spirit whose compelling strength will not let him rest in any aloofness or any beyond. . . . This man [*Mensch*] of the future, who will redeem us not only from the hitherto reigning ideal but also from that which was bound to grow out of it, the great nausea, the will to nothingness, nihilism" (*KS* 5:336; *OGM* II §24, 96).

Out of nausea grows something beyond nausea: Out of man's nausea at life grows the life beyond, Christian redemption. Out of the nausea at man's nausea grows the beyond man, the *Übermensch*, Dionysian redemption. "close beside this sickness stand signs of an untested force and powerfulness of soul. *The same reasons that produce the increasing smallness of man* drive the *stronger and rarer individuals up to greatness*" (*WP* §109, 68). Nausea produces both smallness (Christian redemption) and greatness (Dionysian redemption). This nausea is a pregnancy that gives birth to something beyond it. Nietzsche describes this pregnancy as an illness out of which something grows, nausea as self-overcoming. "Bad conscience," he says is "an illness but . . . as pregnancy is an illness" (*KS*

5:327; *OGM* II §19, 88). The nausea of pregnancy is necessary to get beyond sickness, to give birth to health.

In *Ecce Homo* Nietzsche says that *Zarathustra* was gestating for eighteen months, the gestation period for an elephant, which suggests that he is a female elephant (*EH* 295). In her book *Nietzsche,* Lou Salomé quotes Nietzsche's *Beyond Good and Evil* where Nietzsche claims that "there are two kinds of genius: above all, one which begets and another which will gladly allow itself to become fertile and will give birth" (*BGE* §248). She comments, "Undoubtedly, he belonged to the latter. Nietzsche's spiritual nature was something—in heightened dimension—that was feminine" (29–30). Salomé sees Nietzsche as a fertile womb that gives birth; he is not the father who merely begets or plants the seed.

In a somewhat peculiar argument, Gary Shapiro concludes that Nietzsche has multiple pregnancies during the gestation of Zarathustra, that Lou Salomé is the father of at least one of his "children," and that she may be the father of *Zarathustra* (*A* 128). He maintains that "the entire narrative of *Zarathustra* is the story of Nietzsche's pregnancy" (*A* 126). Shapiro claims that, "like some other mothers," Nietzsche is a bit uncertain as to the father of *Zarathustra*. Yet he suggests a couple of likely candidates by going back to *Ecce Homo*, where Nietzsche describes the genealogy of *Zarathustra*. There Nietzsche describes a phenomenon typical of expectant mothers, a change in his tastes. At the time when Zarathustra was conceived, Nietzsche says that he experienced a change in his tastes in music; and he discovered "that the phoenix of music flew past us with lighter and more brilliant feather than it had ever displayed before" (*EH* 295). Shapiro suggests that Nietzsche's insemination may have been the result of his encounter with this bird. He points out, however, that Nietzsche goes on to describe his creations during this gestation period, and Shapiro is particularly keen on identifying the party responsible for his pregnancy. Nietzsche claims that "Hymn to Life" is the inspiration of a young Russian woman, Lou Salomé. Yet in his attribution, as Shapiro indicates, Nietzsche is ambiguous about whether or not *Zarathustra* is also the result of his encounter with Lou Salomé. Shapiro concludes: "The text was an inspiration, certainly Lou Salomé's, but was it also the inspiration of the whole composition? The language hints at this but does not confirm it. If so, Lou would be the father of the work and Nietzsche would have had multiple pregnancies in the same period of time" (*A* 128).

Shapiro presents a fascinating analysis of male pregnancy in *Zarathustra*. He discusses "The Seven Seals," in which Zarathustra sings seven praises for eternity, the only woman from whom he wants children.

He points out that Zarathustra says, "blessed is *he* who is thus pregnant" (*Z* III 340; my emphasis). Shapiro reads this as an inversion of "the usual (Aristotelian) conception of generation," in which the man impregnates the woman (*A* 134). In "The Seven Seals" woman (eternity) impregnates man. As Shapiro mentions in passing, "'The Seven Seals' alludes to the *Apocalypse*" (*A* 134). Could it be that the Apocalypse is brought on by this masculine appropriation of birth? By the forgetting of the mother/woman? By usurping woman's voice, Ariadne's, Alcyone's? Shapiro suggests that Alcyone's voice sings in Nietzsche's texts (*A* 10). He asks, "Is the mouth of *Thus Spoke Zarathustra* the mouth of a woman?" (*A* 122). Is it Alcyone's mouth? (see *A* 142–43).

Shapiro makes a distinction between the woman whom Zarathustra espouses and "the mouth of the book" (*A* 122). He suggests that the halcyon tone in *Zarathustra* could come from either. It could be merely Zarathustra's woman, or his impersonation of woman, or the book could speak with the mouth of woman. In spite of leaving the question open, the latter seems to be Shapiro's preference in *Alcyone*. He hears a woman in *Zarathustra*, possibly a masculine woman who is strong enough to impregnate the male mother. What kind of woman is this inseminating woman? Is she the phoenix of music, once again the brilliantly colored masculine bird? Or is she merely the feminine in the service of the father who helps to cover over matricide?

Further imbricating birds and pregnancy, recall Shapiro's distinction between womb-born animals and birds, especially birds that nest at sea, like the halcyon. While seabirds are born onto a constantly moving sea in no fixed location and consequently cannot feel nostalgia for a fixed origin, the mother's womb (*A* 135). With this claim, Shapiro proposes another reason for Zarathustra's bird metaphors, overcoming nostalgia for the womb. Yet if one reads the bird metaphors as a denial of the womb as origin through Irigaray's analysis of *Zarathustra*, they become another tactic for forgetting the mother and our maternal origins. Recall that for Irigaray the sea metaphors in *Zarathustra* are metaphors of the mother's womb and the immemorial waters of birth. So Shapiro's story of the halcyon can be read as another cover for the matricide that makes it possible to fly and leave the sea below. All of Nietzsche's male pregnancies may be what Shapiro calls his "hysterical pregnancy" (*A* 136). Shapiro suggests that Nietzsche's pregnancy may be hysterical because he continues to announce his pregnancies and never his births. Yet the strong, masculine mother has no need of birth; all Nietzsche's pregnancies are hysterical because he lacks the wherewithal to give birth. The "hysterical females'" pregnancies may not be so artistic, but at least they give birth. Whose pregnancy is hysterical, in its "fullest" or "heaviest" sense?

Forgetting the Mother

Forgetting both masculine and feminine mothers, some of Nietzsche's poststructuralist critics have emphasized, perhaps overemphasized, Nietzsche's identification with woman. Very few of these critics mention the importance of the figure of the mother in Nietzsche's texts. Recall that in *Spurs* Derrida argues that Nietzsche performs the feminine operation by identifying with three different types of women: the castrated woman, the castrating woman, and the affirming woman. "At once, simultaneously or successively, depending on the position of his body and the situation of his story, Nietzsche was all of these" (*S* 101). Derrida describes Nietzsche's relationship to these three woman as ambiguous: he identifies with them yet dreads them. Are these three women just any women? Or are they three faces of the mother? The castrated mother, the castrating mother and the phallic mother? Derrida does not identify any of these three women with the mother; he barely mentions the mother. Yet behind of the masks of Nietzsche's women, we find the mother with whom Nietzsche struggles. In *Human All Too Human,* Nietzsche himself says that our relationship to women is determined by our relationship to our mothers (*KS* 2:265; *HATH* §380, 195).

Following Derrida's *Spurs,* Sarah Kofman makes a similar mistake in *Nietzsche et la scène philosophique.* There she defends Nietzsche against the charge of misogyny by maintaining that there are at least two women in Nietzsche's writings and that he hates only one of them. She argues that while Nietzsche is critical of the theological woman who searches for the truth of woman-in-herself, he affirms the modest woman, Baubô, who does not expose her truth (NSP 246–47, 252–54). Like Derrida in *Spurs,* Kofman sets out a typology of Nietzsche's women. Unlike Derrida, she identifies a good and a bad woman. The good woman is the modest Baubô, lifting her skirts to amuse Demeter! The bad woman is the feminist who "assert[s] equality of rights, engage[s] in politics, or write[s] books" (B 191). These are the women who instead of bearing children "seek to gain a penis" (B 191). These are the immodest women. And while Kofman mentions the mother, she does not position her in this typology.

The most developed Derridian account of the typology of Nietzsche's identification with woman is David Farrell Krell's *Postponements: Woman, Sensuality, and Death in Nietzsche.* With *Postponements,* Krell pushes Nietzsche further into Derrida's "feminine operation." He claims that Derrida and Nietzsche save real women from dogmatic philosophy by writing with "the hand of woman": "It is the male philosopher who believes in 'woman' and 'truth' alike, the male philosopher who, according to both Nietzsche and Derrida, proves credulous, dogmatic, and mistaken. Writing now with the other hand, as it were, both Nietzsche and Derrida record the plaint of women against 'the foolishness of the dogmatic philosopher' " (10 85). Does Krell see himself writing with the "other hand (P 85)," the hand of woman?

Re-reading Krell's unpublished Nietzsche, I will attempt to answer the question that Krell raises, but cannot answer: "Why is Nietzsche's transition to woman always postponed and agonizing?" (P 23). Although Derrida in *Spurs* and Krell in *Postponements* both mention Oedipus, and Nietzsche's fascination with Oedipus in *The Birth of Tragedy* (BT §9), neither sees the Oedipus in Nietzsche. Enamored by Nietzsche's "skirts," Krell skirts Nietzsche's Oedipus. In *Postponements,* Krell does not distinguish between Nietzsche's desire for woman as mother and woman as lover. This is why he does not distinguish Nietzsche's desire for the eternally procreative mother and the sensual lover. He also does not distinguish between Nietzsche's desire to *become* woman and this desire to *impregnate* woman or *usurp* her pregnancies by inventing the masculine mother. The incestuous/matricidal nature of Nietzsche's postponement, however, can be read back into Krell's Nietzsche. Although Krell forgets the mother, she is floating on the surface of every one of the women that Krell skims from Nietzsche's unpublished manuscripts. It is Oedipus who can answer Krell's riddle: "Why is woman always postponed?"

Even Drucilla Cornell, who presents an extremely sympathetic reading of Krell's *Postponements*, suggests that Nietzsche's postponement, and the connection between woman and death, can be explained by man's nostalgia for the lost phallic mother, whom he seeks and yet with whom he cannot live: "The fundamental duplicity inherent in masculine desire . . . is the inability to live with what one seeks. We also have a clue to Krell's puzzlement as to why all the magnificent heroines Nietzsche gives us must be deserted in sensual love and end so badly" (T 52). Readers familiar with Cornell's "Disastrologies" will see that my reading of *Postponements* is not as generous as hers.

Krell begins his account of Nietzsche's postponements with "The Plaint of Ariadne," which was originally "The Travail of the Woman in Childbirth" (P 19). Krell points out that "The Travail of the Woman in Childbirth' " or the "Plaint of Ariadne," shows up as "The Magician" in part IV of *Zarathustra*. Here the gender of the speech changes. Ariadne's plaint is appropriated by a charlatan wizard whose fakery is exposed by

Zarathustra when he pummels the faker with a stick. The movements of Nietzsche's charlatan wizard are not so dissimilar from Nietzsche's own. Like the wizard who fakes Ariadne's lament, Nietzsche/Zarathustra fakes woman's lament, the lament of woman in childbirth. Krell asks, How could anyone suggest that we take a stick to beautiful Ariadne? He uses this implausibility to show that the stick is punishment for fakery. The stick is not intended to punish woman, but to punish the transvestism of the wizard. This may be so, but Nietzsche maintains that even beautiful women want the stick: "Good and bad women want a stick" (*BGE*, "E&I," §147).[6] What kind of a "pummeling" would Zarathustra give Derrida if he heard him claim "I am a woman and I am beautiful?"

Even when Ariadne's lament (the lament of the mother giving birth) is not appropriated by an old wizard, it is appropriated by Dionysus. In response to Ariadne's lament, Dionysus tells her "I am your labyrinth" (Krell 19). We are told that "a labyrinth human being never seeks the truth, but—whatever he may try to tell us—always and only his Ariadne" (Krell 26). From this Krell concludes that woman is labyrinth. If this is so, then every human being tells only his woman. Now Dionysus's response becomes an appropriation. He tells Ariadne, "I am your labyrinth. I am your woman." Dionysus becomes the woman in woman, just as Krell's Nietzsche becomes the woman in woman. Krell argues that the Dionysian dithyramb, "The Nightsong," takes over the language of "The Plaint of Ariadne." Once again appropriating Ariadne's lament, Dionysus exposes *his own* desire for love, maternal love, when in "The Nightsong" he longs to "suck at breasts of light!" The mother's lament during childbirth is replaced by the child's nostalgia for the maternal body.

Zarathustra's imperative— "become hard!"—addressed to Ariadne after her lament, takes on a new meaning. Ariadne must become hard for the sake of her woman, for the sake of the woman in woman, for the sake of Dionysus. Yet the woman in woman, like the procreative powers of the maternal, turns out to be masculine. Although woman's lament is appropriated by Nietzsche/Dionysus, woman's desire is figured only always in terms of masculine desire. Woman becomes hard only as a displaced man for the sake of his woman.

The second postponement diagnosed by Krell is that of Corinna, the mother of tragedy. We meet Corinna in Nietzsche's notes for the never written tragedy about Empedocles. Krell claims that Corinna is a symbol of rebirth (*P* 45-6). Corinna dies and Empedocles restores her through the heat that remained around the middle of her body (*P* 45, 86). Krell's suggestion that Corinna is the mother of tragedy and a symbol of rebirth already transforms the desire for her into an Oedipal desire for the mother. Also, it is through the heat in the middle of her body, the womb, that she is revived. Woman lives only through the activation and reactivation of the womb. Woman needs man to give her life through her womb.

It is also important that Empedocles' restoration is not sexual. He does not desire Corinna except through her life-giving womb. Dionysus, on the other hand, is infatuated with Corinna, yet he runs away (Krell 50, 86). So too do Nietzsche's texts run from erotic desires for the feminine or women unless they are transferred to desires for procreation. It is interesting that "Empedocles feels like a murderer, deserving of unending punishment; he hopes for a rebirth of penitential death" (Krell 49). He feels like a murderer although he has (literally) killed no one. Could his guilt be for his incestuous desire? The desire which demands the death of the father?

Krell's next postponement is that of Pana. Like Nietzsche's other postponements—those of Ariadne, the goddess of childbirth, and Corinna, the mother of tragedy—Pana represents maternity. Krell introduces Pana with a note from Nietzsche's plans for *Zarathustra*: "I want to celebrate *reproduction* and *death* as a festival" (P 54). For Zarathustra, Pana is both death and reproduction. Woman represents the life cycle: "woman as nature" (P 45, 46). This woman is not just any woman, she is once again the mother. Zarathustra's woman, Pana, symbolizes both the birth of the *Übermensch* and the death of Zarathustra. Once again Oedipus will solve the riddle of how woman is related to death. In all of the various plans for Zarathustra's death—the death always postponed—Zarathustra dies for the sake of his union with woman.

In part I, "On Free Death," Zarathustra wants to die out of love for the earth in order to "find rest in her who bore me" (Krell 42). He wants a reunion with the mother who bore him. He wants to climb back into the womb of the earth. Death is the ultimate union with the womb of being. Krell argues that Zarathustra realizes that he must die in order for the *Übermensch* to be born (P 65, 54). Zarathustra wants children with eternity; he wants to father the *Übermensch* (P 56). It is Zarathustra who must become hard for the sake of the *Übermensch* (P 59, 64). He must be hard enough to love eternity and beget their children. Yet Zarathustra realizes that, as the father, he must die so that his son can come into power. This is why in all of the postponed plans for Zarathustra's death, it is his union/identification with woman, the original mother, that demands his death. Or he dies among children for the sake of the child who will result from his union with the original mother. He dies for the sake of his son, the *Übermensch* (Krell 60–62, 67). Zarathustra's union with woman is postponed for fear of death. Or perhaps he is afraid that he is not man enough to sire the *Übermensch*. Zarathustra's desire to both possess and usurp the mother brings with it the fear of punishment—the fear of castration.[7] In addition, the "son," the *Übermensch*, demands Zarathustra's death as the father—the *Übermensch* is beyond all fathers. He has no need for fathers or mothers; he gives birth to himself. Nietzsche's writings exhibit this complex of fear and desire, the oedipal desire, full of patricidal-matricidal fantasies and fear of death.

The last of Krell's postponements, that of Calina, displaces Medusa and re-places Ariadne. Although Krell had made several references to Medusa in his first three chapters, the first line of Calina's chapter is "Medusa's chapter will have to wait" (*P* 72). But since Calina's chapter is the last in the book, it seems that Medusa's chapter will have to wait indefinitely. Perhaps she is Krell's own postponement. Why does he shy away from Medusa? Is Medusa Nietzsche's only woman who cannot be turned into a mother? Is she the woman who would rather lose her head than succumb to man? The woman who cannot be possessed? Feminine creativity which does not depend on man's fertilization?

At one point Krell claims that he does not want Nietzsche's destiny as his own (*P* 85). Yet, only the hand of woman, the writing hand, he exclaims, can loosen the grip of that destiny (*P* 85). What is Nietzsche's destiny that Krell wants to avoid? Writing with the hand of woman or postponing woman? In any case, it is Medusa who forces Krell's hand. She is the feminine power still cut off from the writing hand. So instead of Medusa, in Krell's text we get Calina.

Calina stands in for Medusa as the woman who cannot be forced (*P* 84). While it might be true that Calina cannot be forced, I suspect that Calina is no woman (although not *because* she cannot be forced). Moreover, because "she" cannot be forced, "she" is to be feared. We meet Calina in the plans for *Zarathustra*: "*Calina*, brown-red, everything too acrid nearby in high summer. Ghostly (my current danger!)" (Krell 80). In this note there is nothing to suggest that Calina is a woman. Calina sounds like a place, a desert. Especially given the next note: "Sipo Matador . . . Nothing there that would not poison, allure, gnaw, overthrow, transvalue" (Krell 79). Sipo Matador, says Krell, is identified in *Beyond Good and Evil* as a poisonous Javanese plant (*P* 79). Calina sounds like a desert full of tempting poisons.

If Calina is a woman, she is a desert, a barren womb. She is the greatest danger—the woman who cannot be possessed through pregnancy. She is one of those "*abortive* females, the 'emancipated' who lack the stuff for children," who tear men apart when they love (Nietzsche, *EH* §5).

Although alluring, she is not fertile. That is why she is a threat to Zarathustra's manliness. The final postponement, that of Calina, to whom Krell gives thanks in his preface, is not the woman that he takes her for.

Krell does not, however, claim to know Calina. "Somewhere," he says, "someone sees clearly and distinctly with Maenadic sharp sighted-ness—who or what Calina is . . . We ourselves will be patient, trusting in science. We will not mislay our umbrella, will not lose our leg" (P 25, 84). Here Krell, like Nietzsche, prefers to remain protected by the paternal umbrella "we," by the [paternal] science, than risk "losing our leg," the paternal leg. Looking once again through Oedipus, Krell's association with the paternal scientific tradition, and fear of losing "our leg," can be read as a castration fear. It is the fear of castration, of impotence, that drives Krell, along with Nietzsche, to return to the paternal identification. In fact, here Krell invokes the paternal tradition against Nietzsche, who, for him, poses as woman. Krell does not want Nietzsche's destiny, that is, his identification with woman. Rather, Krell prefers to stay under the safety of the paternal umbrella, science. Out of fear of losing "our (paternal) leg," Krell denies his connection to woman (Nietzsche): "I do not want Nietzsche's destiny as my own. Would prefer to lose him. Yet only the hand of woman, the writing hand, the hand back to which the trace of thread always leads us, can loosen the grip of that destiny. Gingerly. Derrida believes that Nietzsche possesses such a hand, So do I. Must it wither?" (P 85).

Could Krell's "oversight" of the maternal be due to the fact that the mother has no writing hand? Could it be due to the fact that the mother always operates as merely a nostalgia for the original womb, a lost home-land, a time before time? Could it be that within the patriarchal tradition, remembering the mother results in dismembering her? Contemporary philosophers ask: Is this text written with the hand of woman? Does this text's voice come from the mouth of woman? Is this text an example of double invagination or the logic of the hymen? Is the nostalgia for origins a nostalgia for the womb? These questions cut the mother-woman into pieces—hand, mouth, hymen, vagina, womb.[8]

Dis(re)membering the Mother
Derrida discusses the relationship between the mother and writing in "Otobiographies" in *The Ear of the Other*. In this peculiar text, he dis-cusses the connections between the graphical and the biographical, the name and the mother, writing and woman, and Nietzsche and Fascism. There, completely turning away from his typology of woman in *Spurs*,

Derrida claims that the only woman in Nietzsche's text is the mother: "No woman or trace of woman, if I have read correctly—save the mother, that's understood. But this is part of the system. The mother is the faceless figure of a *figurant,* an extra. She gives rise to all the figures by losing herself in the background of the scene like an anonymous persona. Everything comes back to her, beginning with life; everything addresses and destines itself to her. She survives on the condition of remaining at bottom" (*EO* 38). It is necessary to retrace and analyze the moves which Derrida makes in this text that lead him to these conclusions about woman and mother. He begins his discussion of Nietzsche with the claim that "the name of Nietzsche is perhaps today, for us in the West, the name of someone who . . .was alone in treating both philosophy and life, the science and the philosophy of life *with his name and in his name*" (*EO* 6). This is not only because, as Derrida points out, the name of Nietzsche is always a dead man's name and therefore no living person can inherit the returns on the signatures of his texts. Whatever returns come to his texts are inherited by his name (*EO* 7). Obviously, like all dead authors, Nietzsche lives on through his name and not through his body.

Yet, Derrida argues, what makes the name of Nietzsche important to his texts and their histories is Nietzsche's use of his name in the particular way in which he binds himself to his readers and their histories. Derrida cites a passage from the preface to *Ecce Homo*, Nietzsche's autobiography, "I live on my credit; it is perhaps a mere prejudice that I live," to substantiate his claim that Nietzsche writes for a future readership and therefore does not expect any returns in his lifetime from his contemporaries; rather, he expects returns to his name after his death (*EO* 8–9). Nietzsche anticipates the importance of his texts after his death. Derrida claims that "he has taken out a loan with himself and *has implicated us in this transaction through what, on the force of a signature, remains of his text*" (*EO* 8). In a sense, Nietzsche draws up a contract, a loan, with himself through his future readers to determine the significance of his texts. It is our responsibility to make his name what it will become. It is through his future readers, then, that Nietzsche becomes who he is.

It is through the "ear of the other" that Nietzsche becomes who he is and his signature has its currency. In writing for the other, Nietzsche writes for himself and vice versa. He writes *Ecce Homo* as a gift to himself; he tells his life to himself. But Derrida suggests that he can address himself in his text only by addressing his own eternal return. He addresses himself for the sake of his own eternal return, the return of his name, Nietzsche. His name with return over and over again only through generations of future readers. Nietzsche writes in order to give birth to himself through the eternal return, which he figures as a woman. Derrida concludes that "you cannot think the name or names of Friedrich Nietzsche, you cannot *hear* them before the reaffirmation of the hymen, before the alliance or wedding ring of the eternal return" (*EO* 13).

It follows, then, strangely enough, that the woman whom Nietzsche weds in order to give birth to himself is his own mother. Derrida interprets Nietzsche's riddle "already dead as my father, while as my mother, I am still living and becoming old" as a clue to the doctrine of eternal return. He suggests that the eternal return is a selective principle that guarantees that life returns as the living feminine who says "yes, yes" (*EO* 14). Life's "yes, yes" turns out to be a double affirmation of the birth of her son: she says yes to him by giving him birth and she says yes to him after his birth. The author's "yes, yes" is the acceptance of the gift of life and the acknowledgment of the debt from this gift (*EO* 15). What Derrida does not mention is that the author's double affirmation is possible only through the living feminine through which he continues to live; she says yes, and insofar as he says yes, he is living on as her. And the author's "yes, yes" is not a yes to her, but a yes to himself. Derrida describes the debt as a debt to oneself (*EO* 14). As a result, any debt to the mother is only a debt to oneself; ultimately there is no debt to the mother. The loan is from oneself and repaid to oneself.

Derrida maintains that if in Nietzsche's writing as his mother he lives on and as his father he is already dead, then the name of Nietzsche lives on as the name of the mother (*EO* 16). In fact, the signature on his writing is the name of the mother since at the point of writing he is dead as the embodied heir of his father; once the text is written it takes on a life of its own that leaves the embodied life of its author behind. Derrida develops this argument by pointing to a connection between the mother and language. Living writing takes place in the mother tongue. So too do all agreements and contracts, including marriage, take place in the mother tongue (*EO* 21). In fact, to speak the mother tongue is to engage in a contract of sorts, a marriage, that binds one to the rules of that language. The mother-tongue brings with it certain obligations that result from the very laws of grammar within it.[9] Derrida concludes that "[t] he repeated affirmation—like the contract, hymen, and alliance—always belongs to language: it comes down and comes back to the signature of the maternal nondegenerate, noble tongue" (*EO* 21).

Derrida spins his analysis out of Nietzsche's *Future of Our Educational Institutions*, in which he discusses the living body of language, of the mother tongue to which the student has certain obligations. The lesson that Derrida takes from Nietzsche is that the revitalization of language "must first pass by way of the tongue, that is, by way of the exercise of the tongue or language, the treatment of its body, the mouth and the ear, passing between the *natural*, living mother tongue and the scientific, formal, dead paternal language" (*EO* 26, my emphasis). I will return to this natural, living mother tongue after retracing Derrida's detour into Fascism; as we know, everything returns to her.

Following his fascinating maneuvers with the mother, Derrida's asks: How could Nietzsche's texts lead to Fascism? What is there in the structure of Nietzsche's texts that can lead to opposite sorts of interpretations of those texts, particularly the Fascist interpretation? Derrida indicates that this is not a question of Nietzsche's intentions but a question of the texts as they are read. The signature of Nietzsche, how he becomes what he is, is determined through the ear of the other. That ear, as we have seen, is always ultimately the ear of the mother, the mother tongue. What do we hear in our own mother-tongue? Yet, as Nietzsche reminds us, even asses have ears. And, as Derrida makes it out, Fascism's ears mistake the living mother tongue for the dead paternal system. Implicit in Derrida's text is the suggestion that the state gains the kind of authority that it had in the Third Reich when it passes itself off as the mother:

> Not only is the State marked by the sign and the paternal figure of the dead, it also wants to pass itself off for the mother—that is, for life, the people, the womb of things themselves. (*EO* 34)

> In fact the mother—the bad or false mother whom the teacher as functionary of the State, can only simulate—dictates to you the very thing that passes through your ear and travels the length of the cord all the way down to your stenography. This writing links you, like a leash in the form of an umbilical cord, to the paternal belly of the State . . . . all its movements are induced by the body of the father figuring as alma mater. How an umbilical cord can create a link to this cold monster that is a dead father or the State—this is what is uncanny? (*EO* 36)

> The ear can close itself off and contact can be suspended because the omphalos of a disjointed body ties it to a dissociated segment of the father. (*EO* 36)

What I hear in Derrida's text, and perhaps the ears of feminist suspicion are always too large for deconstruction's subtleties, is the suggestion that Fascism is linked to Nietzsche's texts through the umbilical cord of a bad or false mother. The state poses as the mother, natural and living, who demands certain obligations. This charade makes those obligations appear to be natural insofar as they emanate from the mother, language (the mother tongue), and life itself. If we look behind the charade, it becomes obvious that the patriarchal state is not natural, nor does it necessarily protect life. Yet the relation between paternal culture and mother nature is far from obvious in Derrida's text.

Unlike Lacan, who associates the name with the father, Derrida here associates the name with the mother. It seems that we might expect some kind of deconstruction of the opposition between father-name and mother-body or paternal culture and mother nature. But this is not what we receive from *The Ear of the Other*. As the mother *tongue*, language is identified with the body; and it lives only through this identification with the body. But in the end, the woman/mother, and the maternal body turns out to be an extra in Nietzsche's texts and in Derrida's as well. With Derrida's analysis of the eternal return of the name of the mother, we have come full circle back to mother-nature. The name of the mother is always only alive as a trace of her body (tongue) that remains locked into the crypt of nature. Recall the quotation from *The Ear of the Other* with which I began and with which Derrida concludes his text: "No woman or trace of woman . . . save the mother . . . the faceless figure of a *figurant*, an extra . . . the background of the scene like an anonymous person...Everything comes back to her, beginning with life. . . . She survives on the condition of remaining at bottom" (*EO* 38). Life is born out of her and returns to her; she is "mother earth;" she is nature. She is the background and the tongue that make language possible and yet she cannot write or speak. There is no trace of woman in Nietzsche or Derrida, save the mother, and she has no writing hand.

Drucilla Cornell defends Derrida and praises his remembrance of the mother. She maintains that Derrida remembers that the mother comes first and that he comes to himself only by recalling her: "The subject is 'there' for himself only in and through the dialogue with the Other who is never fully present and, yet, who calls him to mourning by her very absence" (*PL* 75–76). She lauds Derrida because he says "I follow" rather than "I am" (*PL* 75). In *Glas*, however, Derrida says that the mother follows and he suggests that he not only follows his mother, but that he *is* his mother: "I am (following) the mother. The text. The mother is *behind*—all that I follow, am, do, seem—the mother follows" (*Glas* 116). The mother is in the background, setting the stage. Like the woman in *Given Time*, she stands outside of time setting its tempo. Cornell says that the mother comes before and remains after the subject; in this way the mother also opens up the possibility of diachronic time or history (T 53). She is the nature, the background, out of which time is born. We are born out of the earth and when we die we return to the earth. The mother's identification with nature is precisely what distinguishes remembrance of the mother from nostalgia for the mother. Nostalgia is always for something that is forever lost because it was never present. Nostalgia for the mother is a longing for an impossible return to the peace of the maternal womb, a return to the earth. This longing for a return to the earth is what Freud calls the death drive. Remembering the mother, on the other hand, is recalling her as a desiring, speaking subject, to whom we are indebted for life.

In Derrida's *Glas*, man's dialogue with the Other is always a dialogue with himself set against the background, and on the back of, the mother who remains at bottom, speechless. He addresses his text to her, but she calls herself only through him: "I call myself my mother who calls herself (in) me. . . . I bear my mother's name, I call my mother to myself, I call my mother for myself, I call my mother in myself, recall myself to my mother" (*Glas* 117). Where is the mother's call? It is always his own calling to himself. And how does he pay his debt to his mother and settle his account? (see *Glas* 262). He remembers her by giving birth to himself through his text: "I give birth to myself, and I write myself" (*Glas* 193). He is blind to the body out of which he was born and turns it into the text, which lives and speaks only because the mother barely subsists and is mute.

Cornell claims that Derrida's is not the castrated mother and that by identifying with his mother and taking on her name, he avoids castration: "To take on the name of the Other, to recall the trace of the Other in one's self, to be dialogical, is to refuse castration" (*PL* 78; see also *T* 52). The dialogue with the Other in the self not only constitutes the subject but also protects himself from fragmentation or castration. By taking on her name, however, Derrida protects himself against the mother's body. Cornell argues that for Derrida the mother's body is not castrated. But Derrida does not, and cannot, identify with her body and escape castration. So he identifies with her name.

And what is her name? As Cornell points out, her name is the name of a plant or a flower, or possibly the name of a man, Jean Genet (Derrida *Glas* 34–35; see also Cornell, *PL* 77). Hers is the name of either nature or man. As either nature or man, she is the all-powerful phallic mother. An identification with her protects against castration only because she is the phallic mother, the masculine mother. Derrida describes the mother with whom Genet identifies, the mother in Genet with whom he identifies: "No longer his mother but his mother, no longer the bad mother, the one that cannot be erected, but the phallus ejaculating on the cross, the right mother, that is, normal, square, who shines, she, forever, whose sex glistens upright, trickling sperm" (*Glas* 148). As the phallus, the mother protects against castration. As the phallic mother, she makes love possible. Cornell claims that "love is the hope that the acceptance of exile from the Phallic Mother makes possible" (*T* 53).

This love, however, is the love of oneself, the love of one's ability to give birth to oneself. It is the love of the maternal power appropriated by the masculine. Man no longer needs the (m)other. His mourning is a deadly nostalgia that turns the mother into silent nature, a name without a body, an absent unnamed body. And his own pregnancy becomes more than metaphorical. Once the distinction between literal and metaphorical can no longer be trusted, his pregnancy can take the place of his mother's. He can become "fe-male," become mother. Speaking of Blanchot in "The Law of Genre," Derrida says: "'I,' then, can keep alive the chance of being fe-male or of changing sex. His transsexuality permits him, in a more than metaphorical and transferential way, to engender. He can give birth" (76). Man can give birth in a more than metaphorical way; his pregnancy is as "real" and as valuable as the mother's. Speaking of Nietzsche's pregnancy in *Spurs*, Derrida suggests that pregnancy is "no less praiseworthy in a man than it is in a woman" (S 65). As Derrida says in *Glas* (speaking of Kant), "Nature is good, is a good woman, that is in truth, by her reproductive force, her reason, her profound logos that dominates all the feminine chatterings, her imperturbable and always victorious logic, her educative resources, a father. The good woman is a father; the father is a good woman" (128).[10] The mother is either nature or man; and in both cases she becomes a good father.

As in *The Ear of the Other*, there are signs in *Glas* and other texts that the mother is still associated with a nature that stands outside culture and language as its silent source and telos.[11] In *Glas* Derrida says that "the breast [*sein*] of this mother steals away from all names, but it also hides them, steals them; it is before all names, as death, the mother fascinates from the absolute of an *already*" (*Glas* 133–34). Here the mother occupies the traditional role as nature, before all names, that makes the name possible. Within this economy, as nature she is necessarily silent and as speaking she is necessarily masculine. There is no trace of woman, save the mother. But there is no feminine mother.

If the maternal body is a blind spot in Derrida's texts, it is because he associates that body with nature. This is why he hides the maternal body behind the mother-tongue and the mother's name. Even in his most intimate text to/on the mother, his own mother Georgette Safar Derrida,

"Circumfession," the maternal body stands behind the name and the mother's tongue becomes the basis for the social contract. Yet, in this text the mother's position is so complex that I will not try to read it as a reduction to nature, or the name, or a language-body that hides mother nature. At this point, I will merely suggest some images that "Circumfession" calls forth.

"Circumfession," written as a eulogy to Derrida's dying mother, is so intimate, beautiful, and shocking that it is difficult to know how to respond to it. Except in the photographs were his mother's body is young and beautiful, when it makes an appearance in the text of "Circumfession," his mother's body appears as scarred, immodest, already dead (C 24, 25, 82, 101, 108). In this text her body is slipping away, already gone: "Now she is becoming—I'm with her this 18th of June—what she always was, the impassability of a time out of time, an immortal mortal, too human inhuman, the dumb god the beast, a sleeping water in the henceforth appeased depth of the abyss, this volcano I tell myself I'm well out of . . . " (C 80).

Even more upsetting than the slipping away of his mother's body in this confession of his mother is the fact that she no longer recognizes the son, no longer remembers, pronounces, his name(s). His name has slipped her mind. It is this slipping away of the name for the mother that shakes Derrida. It is the double sense of the slipping of the name *for* the mother that rocks him: her name like the name of god is unpronounceable (C 58, 264), and his name no longer exists for her—for the rest of her life he has no name (C 22). Although (because) she has forgotten, throughout the "Circumfession" he remembers the mark of the name on his body, his Hebrew name, Elijah, given in the ceremony surrounding his circumcision. "Elijah, the most 'eschatological' and thus the most awaited of the prophets, had condemned the Israelites for breaking the alliance. God supposedly then appointed him to be present at each circumcision as at the renewal of the alliance" (C 81).

The renewal of the alliance is foreshadowed in Exodus 5: 24-6 when Zipporah circumcises her own son in order to save Moses from God's wrath. Images of Zipporah appear in "Circumfession": the mother with the foreskin of her son in her teeth (C 97), the loved woman circumcising the son in an act of fellatio (C 218). In Derrida's images in "Circumfession" Zipporah circumcises her son with her teeth by biting off the foreskin. In the simulated castration of circumcision the mother wounds her baby in order to inscribe his name, the name that connects him to his community, on his body, on his sex (see C 66, 72, 153). She is responsible for this ritual which inscribes the proper name on the body and insures its proper entrance into the social contract. In this text, the mother's tongue is the guarantor of the mother-tongue; the mother's tongue marks the male body, makes it proper, so that the alliance, the social contract, can be renewed. Has the mother's tongue become the mother-tongue, a language-body? Has the maternal body slipped away? Is her body always necessarily a dead body, a body that is identified with nature? Is she, therefore, always a castrating mother threatening to use her tongue and mouth in the most violent and deceptive way? Does she pose as the lover in order to castrate? Does she give herself for something that she is not, perform the feminine operation? Is she the only woman, the sorceress of the feminine operation? No woman or trace of woman. . . save the mother.

6   *Save the Mother*

Many feminists are wary of emphasizing the mother or the maternal function. They are suspicious of theories that return to the mother because maternity and reproduction have traditionally been used to oppress women. Because women have been reduced to reproduction and maternity, they have been excluded from production and culture. Rather than neglect or deny maternity, however, I think that, as feminists, we need to reinvestigate how maternity has been constructed such that it stands opposed to production and culture. Rather than accept patriarchal images of maternity that induce us to avoid the issue of maternity in feminist discussions, we need to reconceive of maternity. In this chapter I will examine the way that maternity has been traditionally conceived in psychoanalytic theory. I will relate this conception of maternity to my earlier discussions of philosophy's relation to the mother, particularly in the writings of Nietzsche and Derrida. I will problematize the traditional associations with the mother and nature in order to suggest a notion of maternity as the foundation of the social rather than as a threat to it. Finally I will suggest that this new model of maternity can provide the ontological foundations for a new conception of the ethical relationship. In the context of this project this chapter will have to remain merely suggestive and preliminary. In my next book, tentatively entitled "Family Values," I will continue to develop this new model for ethics.

Philosophy is full of metaphors that associate women *qua* mothers with nature and the body in opposition to culture and the mind.[1] Earlier I indicated that even nontraditional philosophers such as Nietzsche and Derrida presuppose the link between the mother and nature. Because of this association between mother and nature, traditional psychoanalytic theory emphasizes the need to break off an identification with the maternal body in order to enter culture. The maternal body, and identification with it, poses a threat to culture. Both Freud and Lacan propose very violent scenarios filled with threats to explain how the infant must separate from the maternal body.

Traditionally, psychoanalysts maintain that the child's relationship to its mother (or mother surrogate) is the model for all subsequent relations. While I accept this thesis, I argue that the way in which that relationship has been conceived precludes the possibility of any subsequent intersubjective relationship between two people. If the traditional account of the child's relation to its mother is taken as a prototype for all other relationships, then we need an account of the mother-child relationship that sets up, rather than cuts off, the possibility of a reciprocal relation of exchange. We need to reconceive of the child's relation to its mother as a social relation rather than a relation to nature. Indeed, we need to call into question the relationship between mother/nature and father/culture.

Challenging the Paternal Metaphor

For Lacan the move from "nature" to "culture" is possible through what he calls the "paternal metaphor" which sets up what he calls the "metonymy of desire," the social relation. The move from the maternal body to the paternal culture is figured as a move from metaphor to metonymy. In "The Agency of the Letter in the Unconscious," Lacan associates the logic of metaphor with Freud's condensation and the logic of metonymy with Freud's displacement (*Ecrits* 298). Freud identifies displacement and condensation as two of the mechanisms used in the dream work that allow repressed unconscious material to make its way, in disguised form, into the dream. These mechanisms are also at work in jokes and slips of the tongue. Lacan takes over and revises Roman Jakobson's association of metaphor with substitution, which is regulated by the linguistic code, and metonymy with combination, which is regulated by the linguistic context.[2] Lacan argues that the way in which Freud describes the unconscious primary processes, particularly in dreams, is the same way that modern linguistics describe the most radical operations of language. Condensation is the process by which one symbol or word is substituted for another, "word *for* word," or metaphor (*Ecrits* 158). Condensation presents consciousness with a composite image that eliminates different features and compresses similar features. Displacement, on the other hand, is when one dream image substitutes for several unconscious thoughts, "word *to* word," or metonymy. Displacement presents consciousness with what appears to be an insignificant image onto which the unconscious wish transfers its intensity.

In terms of the "grammar" of the psyche, metonymy is the model for desire whereby one wish is associated with and covers over another wish but never completely replaces the original wish. Metaphor, on the other hand, is the model for repression whereby the symptom is substituted for the original trauma (*Ecrits* 166). In terms of the Lacanian model of psychic development the Name of the Father is substituted for the desire of/for the (absent) mother (*Ecrits* 200). This paternal metaphor is the foundational metaphor of the social. It is only once this substitution—The Name of Father for desire of/for mother—is made that the infant becomes a subject proper and enters language. It is only on the basis of this paternal metaphor that Lacan's logic of the metonymy of desire can be set up.

In the Lacanian model the paternal metaphor is necessary to ensure that the infant moves away from its attachment to the mother's body and into the social. The mother-infant dyad is antisocial and must be prohibited and repressed by the Law of the Father so that society might exist. Once the infant realizes that its narcissistic identification with its mother is imaginary and that its mother can be absent, it must substitute symbols for its missing mother. In other words once the infant realizes that its needs will not be met automatically by the mother, it must substitute demands (words) that indicate what it needs for the imaginary unity with the all-gratifying maternal body. Lacan calls the gap between need and demand "desire." Desire is unfulfillable; it is the remainder when you subtract the demand from the need. In other words, once you have to ask for what you need you cannot get what you need because what you need is to have your needs automatically met without having to ask. In Lacan's version of the Oedipal story, the infant moves from need to desire or from the maternal body to the Name or Law of the Father. The Oedipal situation is a struggle to the death between mother's body and father's name/law in which, if the resolution is successful, the father always wins. This struggle is the battle between nature and culture. The child must leave nature behind in order to enter culture. The maternal body is sacrificed for the sake of culture.

Irigaray maintains that the traditional Oedipal story in which the son murders his father covers over the primordial murder of the mother: "Hasn't the mother already been torn to pieces by Oedipus's hatred by the time she is cut up into stages, with each part of her body having to be cathected and then decathected as he grows up? And when Freud speaks of the father being torn to pieces by the sons of the primal horde, doesn't he forget, in a complete misrecognition and disavowal, the woman who was torn apart between son and father, between sons?" (*IR* 38).

Traditional psychoanalytic theory maintains that "matricide" is necessary for the existence of culture. Even Kristeva claims that matricide is our "vital necessity" (*BS* 27–28). This matricide is necessary, however, only within patriarchal culture and patriarchal psychoanalytic theory. In her 1981 lecture "The Bodily Encounter with the Mother," Irigaray calls on us to give new life to the mother through language: "We must give her new life, new life to that mother, to our mother within us and between us. We must refuse to let her desire be annihilated by the law of the father. We must give her the right to pleasure, to *jouissance,* to passion, restore her right to speech, and sometimes to cries and anger. . . . We have to discover a language which does not replace the bodily encounter, as paternal language attempts to do, but which can go along with it, words which do not bar the corporeal, but which speak corporeal" (IR 43). Against Lacan, Irigaray maintains that we don't have to substitute the Law of the Father for the body/desire of the mother. It is not the case that language necessarily replaces the corporeal relationship to the mother. Rather, we need to find a language with which to speak the corporeal. This speech is possible because the mother is not what Lacan and traditional psychoanalytic theory take her for.

Within traditional psychoanalytic theory the mother is seen as the infant's first object or partial object. She is merely the container that meets the infant's needs. The primary identification with the mother is seen as a threat to the autonomy and normal psychic development of the child. Only when the mother's body is associated with needs and not with desire, however, can she be a threatening, phallic, all-powerful mother. She is phallic—all powerful—only if she is associated with nature; if she embodies the power of nature that gives life to the child, then she seems all-powerful or phallic. If, on the other hand, the mother's body is a desiring body—if she is social and has relations outside of the mother-child dyad—then she has a relationship with a third party; she is not and never was a phallic mother. If she never was a phallic mother then she cannot undergo castration. And she cannot be the representative of lack that Freud and Lacan take her for.

Irigaray criticizes Lacan's notion that the mother's body operates as a kind of partial object for the child, an *objet a,* and that the child operates as what he calls a "pleasure cork" for the mother. Certainly the Lacanian model relationship between this partial object and this pleasure cork is not a desirable model for social relations. In *This Sex Which Is Not One* Irigaray quotes Lacan: "for that pleasure in which she is not-all, that is, which makes her somewhere absent from herself, absent as subject, she will find the cork in that little *a* that will be her child" (102). The mother-woman's body is full of alterity; it cannot be reduced to Lacan's partial object that has no alterity and therefore needs the specular image to lend it "its clothes" (see *Ecrits* 315–16). The mother-woman's body no longer needs to be covered up because it is lacking or antisocial. "Woman," says Irigaray, "remains several, but she is kept from dispersion because the other is already within her and is autoerotically familiar to her. . . . She herself enters into a ceaseless exchange of herself with the other without any possibility of identifying either" (*TS* 31). The mother's body is always a desiring erotic body, a woman's body. Rather than lacking something, especially sexual potency, the mother-woman's body is full of excess sexuality and indeterminate erogenous zones.

Irigaray proposes uncorking Lacan's *objet a* and letting bodily fluids, along with the mother's desire, flow. By turning bodily processes—milk, saliva, blood, urine, feces—into partial objects, Lacan turns fluids into solids, especially since the paradigmatic partial *objet* is feces. Irigaray criticizes Lacan's notion of desire as it relates to the *object a*, because it ensures that the object of desire results from the successful passage from fluid to solid (*TS* 113). Within the phallocratic economy of solids, fluids remain the excess that cannot be turned into an object, partial or otherwise (IR 64). The phallocratic economy of desire is operated by a mechanics of solids. Desire, through a closed circuit of metaphorical substitutions, always takes us back to the solid phallus. Irigaray seems to dispute Lacan's thesis that his desire operates according to a logic of metonymy—it is, after all, his paternal metaphor which sets the metonymy of desire into motion. She suggests that Lacan's theory gives priority to metaphor over metonymy (*TS* 110). And the logic of metaphor requires a mechanics of solids—one object is substituted for another. With fluids, on the other hand, a smooth substitution cannot take place. Irigaray suggests that fluids operate according to a logic of metonymy. They can be associated, touch each other, but can never be completely substituted for each other.[3]

Irigaray attempts to recover the repressed mechanics of fluids which lies behind the mechanics of solids in the traditional psychoanalytic account of desire. She enlists the penis in order to show that it is operated by a mechanics of fluids and sperm (and blood). Behind the mechanics of solids which erects the ideal of the phallus are bodies operating according to another mechanics, the mechanics of fluids. The phallocracy, however, covers over the exchange of fluids in both male and female bodies. It prefers form to matter because only in a formal system can one object be substituted for another, can relations be seen in terms of substitution. Within the economy of substitution, there is no reciprocal exchange *between* one and another. There is only exchange of one *for* another. For

Irigaray, wherever matter is concerned, individuals are not substitutable. Which is not to say that they have no relation. Rather, there can be relations only between two different sexes which are not reducible to one another, operating within an economy of desire which does not substitute/sacrifice one for the other. Desire cannot operate according to the patriarchal logic of subject and object. This logic fixes everything and turns all into one selfsame, and it kills the possibility of anything dynamic or fluid. It destroys desire by turning it into a metaphysical category. Irigaray imagines an economy of desire that is not dependent on a metaphysics of presence or the logos of patriarchal discourse. She imagines alternative discourses that come from the "side of the feminine" which do not turn woman into a subject or an object. These discourses do not ask "*what* is woman" (*TS* 78–79). Rather they allow for the possibility of fluid meaning.

Irigaray imagines desire as an exchange, the interval, between two that cannot be reduced to one. This is why she insists on discussing the *morphology* of the sexed body.[4] The morphology of the sexed body designates the interval between form and matter. This morphology operates according to the logic of metonymy, association, matter touching form. The body becomes a site in which need, desire, and demand cannot be separated. Rather, within the body they are always touching. As this *between* form and matter, *between* divine and earthly, the "body" can "speak." In particular the body of mother-woman can be reborn and it can find a voice to speak what has become, within patriarchal discourse, expressible only through the bodily contortions of hysterical symptoms. In *This Sex Which is Not One* Irigaray suggests that if we listen with attentive ears through these hysterical gestures we can hear the beginnings of an articulation of a new desire which gives life to the mother-woman rather than killing her (134).

For Irigaray, this new desire is not locatable; it *is* difference. This difference is not Lacan's lack, which always leads to opposition and hierarchy, and in which one sex becomes a mere reflection of the other. Irigaray figures desire as "the interval," "the residue," "the between," "a dynamic force," "wonder," as "angels" (*ESD*). So if for Lacan desire is the gap or lack between need and demand, for Irigaray it is the wonder-full excess between two different sexes. Recuperating elements from patriarchal culture—Aristotelian philosophy and contemporary physics—Irigaray tries to open a space for a new desire, a place (interval in space/time) "that could be inhabited by each sex, body or flesh" (*TS* 128), a desire which acts "upon the porous nature of the body" and includes "the communion that takes place through the most intimate mucous membranes" "a love so scrupulous that it is divine" (*TS* 128–129). Desire is the result of two different sexes encountering each other in their difference; it is the divine.

Going further than Irigaray, I propose that the divine is the result of an encounter between two different people. It is not merely the case, as Kristeva and Butler point out, that there is something extradiscursive that has been abjected and thereby circumscribed by discourse as the outside, something perhaps even inconceivable within dominant discourses. In addition to this constitutive absence "within" the social and discourse, there is a constituted transcendental that is produced through our communications with each other and yet goes beyond them. Through our embodied dialogues with each other, especially through the wonder of love, the divine is engendered. The divine is the meeting of two different people. Perhaps it is what Irigaray calls the "sensible transcendental": "This creation [of a 'we live here' together] would be our opportunity, from the humblest detail of everyday life to the 'grandest', by means of the opening of a sensible transcendental that comes into being through us, of which we would be the mediators and bridges. Not only in mourning for the dead God of Nietzsche, not waiting passively for the god to come, but by conjuring him up among us, within us, as resurrection and transfiguration of blood, of flesh, through a language and an ethics that is ours" (*ESD* 129).

Strangely enough, while Irigaray rejects Lacan's model because it emphasizes metaphor over metonymy, Kristeva rejects Lacan's model because it emphasizes metonymy over metaphor. Whereas Kristeva argues that Lacan makes desire operate according to the logic of metonymy and overlooks the metaphoric operations of love, Irigaray argues that Lacan makes desire operate according to a logic of metaphoric substitution and overlooks the metonymic operations of a true bisexuality. I will play one theory off the other in order to subvert the dichotomy between metaphor and metonymy. Through the subversion of this dichotomy, I will not only make the case that needs cannot be separated from demands and desire, but also that the fluidity of language makes it possible to reconceive of our relationship to the world.

Like Irigaray, following Melanie Klein, Kristeva argues that the infant's relation to the mother is not primarily a relation to an object or even a partial object. Klein emphasized the pre-Oedipal relation to both parents as a relation to part-objects, body parts, in a combined parent figure. Kristeva's notion of abjection with its preobject and her notion of the imaginary father as a mother-father conglomerate are both reminiscent of Klein. Unlike object-relations theorists who also emphasize pre-Oedipal relations to the mother, and ego psychologists, Kristeva insists that both objects and subjects remain in process through the Oedipal situation. There is neither a fixed and static object nor a fixed and static ego or subject.

Kristeva takes Klein's thesis of part-objects even further and suggests that the pre-Oedipal relation to both parents is a metaphorical relation with a nonobject. Traditional psychoanalytic theory purports that language comes through the Law of the Father, which guarantees that the primary prototype of the object, the mother, is signifiable by denying that she is desiring. In *Powers of Horror* Kristeva suggests that if we look closely at this thesis—that the mother is the first object—we see that "no sooner sketched out, such a thesis is exploded by its contradictions and flimsiness" (*PH* 32). For behind this mother-object, is the mother's semiotic body, filled with drives and preobjects. Behind this mother-object is the anti-Oedipus, semiotic negativity, which takes us beyond Oedipus and the unitary subject. Primary identification is not with an object or a partial object (*TL* 29). Like Irigaray, Kristeva maintains that the mother cannot be reduced to the primary object and that the infant's bodily exchanges with the mother cannot be reduced to Lacan's *objet a*.

Whereas Lacan identifies objects of desire with partial objects associated with bodily functions only because they represent what is forever cut off from signification, Kristeva wants to bring this lost body back into signification. Lacan claims that the *objets a* are objects of want; they are partial not because they are only part of a total object, the body, but because they represent the gap inherent in signification between the body/object and language (*Ecrits* 315–16). Kristeva objects that Lacan makes the body and identification intrinsically symbolic by making them dependent on a metonymical structure. She quotes Lacan's "The Agency of the Letter in the Unconscious": "It is the connection between signifier and signifier that permits the elision in which the signifier installs the want-of-being in the object relation, using the value of 'reference back' possessed by signification in order to invest it with the desire aimed at the very want it supports" (*TL* 387, quoting *Ecrits* 164). Within the Lacanian framework subjectivity, desire, and the entrance into language are based on this "reference back" through which signification can set up the lack upon which it is founded and which gives rise to its necessity in the first place. Kristeva, on the other hand, wants to avoid this circular logic that forces us into "the field of desire" and the "reign of the signifier" (TL 387). She describes a pre-Oedipal metaphorical identification that precedes and sets up the metonymy of desire.

Unlike Irigaray who rejects the logic of metaphor because she accepts the traditional notion of metaphor as substitution, Kristeva reinvents metaphor as a dynamic transference that is never complete. Kristeva defines metaphor as "a heterogeneous displacement shattering the isotopy of organic needs" (*TL* 31), "an indefinite jamming of semantic features one into the other, a meaning being acted out; and , . . . the drifting of heterogeneity within a heterogeneous psychic apparatus, going from drives and sensations to signifier and conversely" (*TL* 37). As Kristeva describes it, metaphor is the process through which the nonobject becomes object and Lacan's bodily "stuff" that has no specular image becomes visible (*TL* 30). Drives are transferred into signification through the logic of metaphor, which "bends the drive toward the symbolic of an other" (*TL* 31). In so doing, metaphor negotiates between need and demand, but not as desire—the gap between them. Rather, metaphor transports bodily needs or drives into demands and thereby begins to fill the gap. The metaphoric transference supports needs as they break into demand through a fantasy of completion, wholeness, *jouissance*, rather than lack. As Kristeva describes it, the primary identification is not an identification with an object; rather it is a transference to the place of a loving other who metaphorically represents wholeness and completion.

Kristeva proposes a metaphoric transference that is a non-object-oriented identification which allows drives to enter subjectivity, desire, and language. It is this non-object-oriented identification that makes treatment possible because the non-object-oriented drives can make their way into the analytic session through the transference identification, or what Kristeva calls transference love. In *Tales of Love* she says, "Metonymic object of desire. Metaphorical object of love" (*TL* 30). Desire must be founded on love. For Kristeva the infant's primary identification is with a loving other, and on the basis of this loving support the infant leaves the maternal container and enters the social. The mother's love enables the infant to wean itself from its dependence on her body; but she can love only because she is a speaking subject ("love is always spoken"). And it is through love that the infant identifies with the speech of the other, which, like the mother's body, is not an object and yet provides a joyful relationship with an other (*TL* 26).[5]

Kristeva criticizes Lacan's notion of desire as founded on a lack and therefore ultimately unfulfillable (*RPL* 131–32). In *Revolution in Poetic Language*, she claims that the exemplary subject of Lacan's desire is the masochistic neurotic engaging in autocastration and bodily mutilation, or the completely catatonic body of the clinical schizophrenic (RPL 132). If the object of desire is receding, metonymical, it is because it does not correspond to the primary identification with a *loving* other (*TL* 36). This primary identification with a loving other precedes Lacan's inaccessible

Other of desire and "is neither an object of need nor one of desire" (*TL* 35-36). In *Tales of Love* Kristeva claims that behind Lacan's metonymy of desire is a metaphor of love. And primary identification is set up through this metaphor of love.

This primary identification is with what Kristeva calls "the imaginary father," who is really "a coagulation of the mother and her desire" (TL 41).[6] The imaginary father is a loving father that Kristeva opposes to Lacan's stern father of the Law. In *Tales of Love* she says that the advent of this imaginary father "takes place thanks to the assistance of the so-called pre-Oedipal mother," because she is a desiring mother and her relation to the child is through a third party; her relationship is through discourse (*TL* 40). Kristeva suggests that without a desiring mother we have a clinging devouring mother. Like Irigaray, she suggests that the identification with the mother is threatening only if we forget that the mother is a desiring speaking subject herself. On the other hand, if the mother is recognized as desiring—that is social, then and only then can she be a loving mother. In *Tales of Love* Kristeva says:

> The loving mother, different from the caring and clinging mother, is someone who has an object of desire; beyond that she has an Other with relation to whom the child will serve as the go-between. She will love her child with respect to that Other, and it is through a discourse aimed at that Third Party that the child will be set up as "loved" for the mother . . . . Against this verbal backdrop or in the silence that presupposes it the bodily exchange of maternal fondness may take on the imaginary burden of representing love in its most characteristic form. Nevertheless, without the maternal "diversion" toward a Third Party, the bodily exchange is abjection or devouring (34)

Kristeva calls for a new notion of the social based on a reconceived maternity that is seen as the knot between nature and culture. She maintains that maternity cannot be reduced to either nature or culture but problematizes that very distinction by straddling the two; "a woman as mother would be, instead, a strange fold that changes culture into nature, the speaking into biology" (*TL* 259, see also 234). For Kristeva the maternal body is the most obvious example of alterity within the body. Everybody is full of alterity. The social relation with an other is already operating on a material, and therefore psychic, level within everyone; the social relation is interior to the psyche. The social relation is a relation to difference, which includes but is not limited to sexual difference. The social relation should be modeled on an embrace of the return of the repressed other within ourselves, within our psyches, within our culture.

Ethics, then, is based on the love of the other within that cannot be reduced to the selfsame; only when you learn to love the other within can you learn to love others. And by reconceiving of maternity we can see that the other is within and yet never reducible to the same. Unlike Lacan, Kristeva suggests that the child's relation to the maternal body prefigures, rather than threatens, the social relation.

By juxtaposing Irigaray's and Kristeva's criticisms of Lacan's paternal metaphor I am attempting to destabilize the opposition between metaphor and metonymy. Like need, demand, and desire in both Irigaray's and Kristeva's revolutionary reformulations of Lacanian theory, metaphor and metonymy are interdependent. And it is their interdependence that makes language fluid and dynamic. Without the logic of metaphor metonymy's associations cannot make sense. For example, Irigaray's use of feminine lips as a model of the metonymic dynamic at work in feminine sexuality relies on a metaphor between lips and metonymy—the lips represent a metonymic association between two different parts constantly touching each other.[7] On the other hand, metaphor is dynamic, possibly revolutionary, because its substitutions rely on metonymic displacements. As Kristeva points out, the power in metaphoric transference is that the metaphoric "is" always necessarily wears its "is not" on the surface and thereby shows the disruption of semiotic drive force into language. It shows that language is heterogeneous and dynamic. For example, Kristeva quotes Romeo's metaphor "Juliet is the sun." This metaphor is powerful precisely because Juliet is *not* the sun and is in fact quite different from the sun. But through metonymic associations Romeo is able to create a metaphor that equates Juliet and the sun: "Juliet *is* the sun."

The constant conjunction of the ontological "is" and "is not" of metaphor opens the possibility of movement within language and shows us that language is always a fluid exchange motivated by the wonder-full excess and pleasure that is the "bodily" difference between two parts of a metaphor. Making associations between these differences is what delights us about speaking. We don't have to speak as/out of loss or lack to console ourselves. Rather, by using both metaphor and metonymy we can speak as/out of excess to engage in what Drucilla Cornell, following Domna Stanton, calls "metaforeplay":

> We need both writing "strategies," and . . . not in the least because there
> can be no pure divide between metaphor and metonymy. Indeed,
> metonymy is always contaminated by the metaphors which allow
> continuity to be comprehensible. But more importantly, it is the "excessive,

tumescent metaforeplay" that allows for the "mimetic" practice of feminine writing to be other than mere repetition of the pregiven stereotypes. As Kristeva herself has remarked, metaphor creates a "surplus of meaning" which manages to open the surface of signs toward the unrepresentable. (*BA* 168, see also 203–204)[8]

This surplus of meaning or "metaforeplay" is what Irigaray calls speaking from the "the feminine side" (*TS* 78). And it opens up an alternative to the patriarchal economy of scarcity that makes women-mothers either a lack within the social or an excess outside the social. The intercourse between metaphor and metonymy makes it possible to do things with words. Through imagination, the metaphoric "is not" (yet) can become the metaphoric "is" and give us hope that we can redeploy and reinvent the condensations and displacements in the representations which have traditionally been used to oppress women, particularly representations of maternity which reduce the mother to nature. We can redeploy metaphors and metonymies, in order to remodel our conception of maternity, which in turn suggests a new model for intersubjective relations and ultimately a new model for ethical relations.

Against the traditional psychoanalytic account of the mother as the child's first object or partial object and never as a social subject, I have extracted the call for this social mother from both Kristeva's and Irigaray's writings. By using new metaphors and metonymies we can construct this new image of the social mother by articulating the mother as desiring. Irigaray attempts to revive the mother from patriarchal matricide by describing a desiring maternal body. She describes a mother that is not and never was a phallic mother because if she is desiring, social, in a relationship with a third, she is not all-powerful or threatening: "This third term can show up within the container as the latter's relationship with his or her own limits: a relationship with the divine, death, the social or cosmic order. If such a third term does not exist within and for the container, the latter may become *all-powerful*. Therefore, if one deprives women, who are one of the poles of sexual difference, of a third term, then this makes them dangerously all-powerful in relation to men" (*IR* 170–171). The desiring mother is not the threatening phallic mother who must be annihilated in order to secure patriarchal culture. In this account the male child no longer has to fear either a castrated or castrating mother. Only the phallic mother is castrating or can be castrated.

The articulation of the mother's desire not only is important for men but is also especially crucial for women, who within patriarchal culture are forced to identify with the remains of a dead maternal body after that body has been sacrificed to the social. In *Black Sun* Kristeva diagnoses feminine sexuality within Western patriarchal culture as a melancholy sexuality: "in order to separate from their mothers' bodies, females must separate from themselves as women; and in order to maintain some identification with their mothers as the bodies of women, females carry around the "corpse" of their mothers' bodies locked in the crypt of their psyches" (*BS* 28–29). Because feminine sexuality is primarily a homosexual sexuality—the girl's first love is her mother—in a heterosexist culture, "normal" feminine sexuality remains repressed and we lack ways of describing loving relations between women, homosexual or otherwise.

Rather than experience her relationship with the mother as a nostalgia for reunion with the maternal body as a mother-earth, a body that she carries with her in her own, for Irigaray a woman experiences this relationship as a longing for reciprocal exchange, intersubjective language: "Woman, born from the same as herself, knows much less and more artificially the nostalgia for regression in the mother" (*Jat* 212, see also 213). Unlike the man's, hers is not a desire to reunite with nature in the place of the maternal body motivated by Thanatos; rather hers is a desire to *communicate* with the mother-woman motivated by Eros. While the man's nostalgic desire is to return to the maternal womb, to mother earth, the woman remembers her mother as a desiring subject. She wants to maintain her relationship and dialogue with her mother. But the paternal genealogy of Western culture obscures the mother-daughter relationship, which must be articulated if we are to recuperate the mother from nature. Irigaray suggests that we women need to refigure our relationships with our mothers so that we can refigure all of our relationships with both men and women: "As for us, the daughters, if our relationship with our mothers is a relationship with need, with no possible identity, and if we enter into desire by becoming objects of/for the father, what do we know about our identity and our desires? Nothing. That manifests itself in somatic pain, in screams and demands, and they are quite justified. . . . But if mothers could be women, there would be a whole mode of relationship of desire in speech between daughter and mother, son and mother, and it would, I think completely rework the language that is now spoken" (*IR* 52). If mothers were seen as desiring women, speaking subjects, and not merely as objects, partial objects, or containers, then our primary relationship would be reconstituted as would all subsequent relationships. The primary relationship would be a model for subsequent relationships rather than sacrificed so that they might be.

In *J'aime à toi* Irigaray says that love and desire cannot be separated in woman (211). In her both exist without prohibitions. She appeals to the myth of Aphrodite as the first figure of embodied love, "nonchaotic love, without measure, without tempo or temporality, simply cosmic, purely incestuous" (*Jat* 211). Before and after Aphrodite, however, Western tradition has insisted on the power of the man-father who takes his identity through differentiating himself from the mother by putting her on a level of "nature without consciousness" (*Jat* 211). He makes himself who he wants to be by making her everything that he is not. Irigaray says that "in this perspective, the relation between the genders is determined by the necessity of man and without consideration for the identity of woman, who rather admits the desire for and with an other" (*Jat* 212). For Irigaray, man abjects woman so that he might be himself; he excludes her desire so that his can become necessity.

Although, like Irigaray, Kristeva maintains that the maternal body is a desiring body, she emphasizes love over desire. This love is the between, her desiring angel. Unlike Irigaray's desire, however, it is not erotically charged. Kristeva imagines lesbian loves which "comprise the delightful arena of neutralized, filtered libido, devoid of the erotic cutting edge of masculine sexuality" (*TL* 81). And this is what is at stake in reconceiving the mother and remodeling ethics: women's relationships to each other and to themselves. Kristeva seems willing to accept traditional psychoanalysis's insistence that the mother's body is not erotic and that it is necessary to abject the bodily relationship with the mother in order to enter the social. Kristeva tries to recuperate the maternal through a love that can be achieved only by a desiring, speaking subject yet precedes desire. But isn't this nonerotic mother love patriarchy's image of "mother love?"

Irigaray, on the other hand, will not accept the insistence on abjecting or separating from the mother's body. She refigures that body so that an identification with it is not a threat to the infant's psychic development. It is necessary that women identify with their mothers as women so that women can love each other. Whereas Kristeva recognizes this need, she always stops just short of articulating an erotic love between women. Yet if there is hope for desire and erotic love between people, then we need a discourse that allows maternal *jouissance*, unfiltered, with its rough edges. If our primary identification is a model for all subsequent identifications then it should be an erotic loving relationship. If our primary relationship is a relation with a dynamic exchange between need, desire, and demand, then we don't have to mourn a tragic loss in order to become social.

Mother Nature

I have shown that once we examine the traditional psychoanalytic (and philosophical) conceptions of the maternal it becomes clear that the associations between the mother and nature or needs are in conflict with the notion that the child's relationship with the mother is the model for all subsequent relations. In our culture the relation between man and nature has traditionally been described as a struggle. And the relationships between men in the state of nature are essentially and fundamentally hostile and antagonistic. How is it, then, that we could ever imagine that culture and social relations are grounded in this hostile antisocial nature? The result, of course, is the violent Hegelian model of the onset of subjectivity and intersubjectivity, the lordship-bondage relation in which the social relation is fundamentally hostile and antagonistic, or Sartre's "hell is other people." Once we recognize that we are by "nature" social beings, then we have to rethink the relationship between nature and culture or the social. After all, human infants are unique among animals in that they simply cannot survive without several years of care. Human beings are born into the social. We are not born into, or out of, nature or some prediscursive realm of needs against which we struggle to make demands and become social.

Because women are reduced to maternity and maternity is in turn reduced to a body that is a desireless container of needs, women-mothers are seen as a threat to the social. Therefore relations, especially identifications, with women-mothers are seen as a threat. The identification with the mother is a threat, however, only because this identification is seen as an identification with nature. And needs are said to operate at the level of nature, which precedes the onset of culture and desire. Only if the mother operates merely as the container of needs and not at the level of desire (in the Lacanian sense) is she anti- or presocial. If and only if the mother's body the intersection of need and desire can an identification with that body be the beginning of a social relation—a renewed social relation—rather than a threat to the social.

The social relation is already set into place through, rather than against, an identification with the maternal body insofar as that body is a site of a fluid exchange that cannot be catalogued or cut up into needs versus desire or demands, or the logic of metaphor versus the logic of metonymy. With the maternal body there can be no clear cut between codes—within which metaphors transfer meanings—and contexts—within which metonymy associates; one requires the other, irreducible yet engaged in constant exchange. The mother's body is a site of the intersection of need, desire and demand, of nature and culture. We *need* desire and demand just as we need food and warmth. Desire and demand, or language, cannot be separated from need. We are by "nature" social beings.

The relationship, or separation, of need, demand, and desire can be reformulated as the problem of the relation between drives and language or culture. The question "How does need become demand or desire?" is an analog to the question "How do drives make their way into language?" The question of the relation between drives and language is the central question of Kristeva's *Revolution in Poetic Language*. The project of *Revolution* is to bring the body back into theories of language. Kristeva attempts to do this in two ways. First, she maintains that semiotic drive force makes its way into language through the tones, rhythms, and affects of language. Second, she suggests that the structure or logic of language is already operating within the material of the body. Most of Kristeva's critics have overlooked this second thesis, which is central to reconceiving the relation between drives and language, between needs and desire, between nature and culture. I will not only elaborate her thesis but also go beyond it here.

As I proposed in *Reading Kristeva: Unraveling the Double-Bind*, Kristeva suggests at least two ways in which the logic of signification is already set up within the material of the body, particularly the maternal body. She identifies a maternal law that regulates the exchange between the maternal body and the infant's body which is in operation before the Law of the Father. Within the maternal body there is a regulated exchange between the maternal body and the fetus. After the child is born the mother regulates what goes in and comes out of the child's body. This maternal regulation prefigures and sets up the paternal regulation that has traditionally been associated with culture. So within "nature" the laws of social exchange are already operating on a material level.

In addition, Kristeva argues that within the body there is a process of separation that prefigures the process of separation from the maternal body that supposedly marks the entrance into culture. She talks about anality as an example of bodily separation or privation that is pleasurable. Separation or privation does not have to be experienced as a painful lack. The incorporations and separations of the body, taking in and expelling food, are pleasurable and set up the possibility of pleasurable incorporations and separations on a "properly" social level. Just as the separation of waste products from the body prefigures the infant's separation from the mother, the incorporation of food into the body prefigures the incorporation of language by the child.[9] In a sense, the patterns of both incorporation/identification and separation/differentiation that make language use possible are already operating in the body. One implication of this analysis is that we cannot set the body against language or language against the body. We cannot turn this relationship between body and language into a dualistic opposition. Rather, in Kristeva's account, body and language operate according to the same logic on different levels. The logic of both demand and desire is already operating within, and set up by, need.

Recall Judith Butler's analysis of the relation between the material body and language. Butler maintains that material and language are never entirely distinct. Language always "takes place" in some material, and material, including the body, is always what it is by virtue of language. The metaphors and metonymies with which we describe our bodies serve to shape and define those bodies. Even when we talk about the body as it is in itself outside of language, we necessarily do so in language. If the body and language cannot be so easily opposed to one another, and the body is traditionally associated with nature while language is associated with culture, then perhaps nature and culture cannot be so easily opposed to one another.

I want to continue to challenge the opposition between nature and culture in order to set up the possibility of reconceiving the associations between the maternal body and nature. I want to reiterate that traditional conceptions of the maternal body cannot provide adequate models for subsequent social relations because that body has been identified with a prelinguistic, antisocial conception of nature. In order to continue to challenge the traditional model of the child's relation to the maternal body and sketch out an alternative model, I will return to the problem of the relation between drives and language. Certainly my reading of Kristeva's theory of drives goes some distance to challenge theories that oppose drives to language. But perhaps we need a new conception of the drives themselves. In *The Interpretation of the Flesh: Freud and Femininity* Teresa Brennan develops what I call an "intersubjective" theory of drives that is useful in reconceiving the child's relation to the maternal body and all of its subsequent relations.

In *The Interpretation of the Flesh: Freud and Femininity* Teresa Brennan suggests not only that the ego is formed through its relations with others, as Freud maintains, but also that it is neither self-generating nor self-contained in those relations. She takes Lacan's metaphor that "the unconscious is the desire of the other" literally and proposes a revolutionary intersubjective theory of the drives. Brennan argues that her theory of the drives splits the superego and repression in such a way that many of the contradictions in Freud's theory of femininity can be resolved. In addition, she uses her intersubjective theory of drives to explain how, in general, women experience psychic repression in relation to their socioeconomic oppression.

Brennan develops Freud's theory of drives using his account of excitations from *Project for a Scientific Psychology* and *The Interpretation of Dreams*. She emphasizes Freud's theory of excitations, which is modeled on physics, rather than his theory of drives which is modeled on biology. Following one Freud and not the other, Brennan provides descriptions of ego formation, the superego, repression, psychosis, Oedipal resolution, and masculinity and femininity based on a physics that circumscribes energy exchange within a spatiotemporal field constructed through that exchange. As she explains the physics of psychic energy, originally the fetus in utero is literally one with its mother's body, and it is the distance and delay that result from birth that give rise to a sense of space and time. Both space and time arise from the exchange between mother and infant that revolves around the infant's needs: "*In utero*, there is no or less delay between the sense of a need and its fulfillment. It is only after birth that the sense of time is born of the sense of delay. Of course this hypothesis, especially where it concerns the origins of delay, relies on the idea of a non-reductionist materialism. It supposes some fleshy memory of a state in which the delay between need and fulfillment did not exist or was less, and where subject and other were not differentiated. But it is precisely this fleshy memory that the unconscious construction of spatio-temporal bearings will conceal" (*IF* 33). The gap between the need and its fulfillment creates a sense of space and time, which in turn conceals the "fleshy memory" of an original psychophysical connection with the mother's body. Insofar as there is an intimate connection between psychic and physical processes evidenced by the ways in which emotions, traumas, and repression cause physical "symptoms," then we can suppose that the fetus is affected by its mother's psychophysical states, since it is part of her body.

What is striking in Brennan's analysis is her claim that this type of in utero psychophysical connection operates ex utero, only at a "slower pace" (*IF* 34). Human beings exchange energy via these psychophysical connections. Emotions and affects migrate between human beings; we can hand off emotions to each other or trade affects. In fact, for Brennan, it is the exchange of affect in the form of directed energy, or attention, that gives the ego its coherence and identity. She concludes that the ego is neither self-contained nor self-generating but rather the effect of an interplay of intersubjective psychic forces.

These psychic forces can be either active or passive. The infant's original identification is a passive identification with the mother's active capacities; it is both passive and active. The infant very literally identifies with its mother's activities and takes them for its own. It passively turns her action inward. But the direction of this energy must be reversed so that the infant itself can act in the world. The infant's passive ego must become active. For Brennan it is the Oedipal complex that divides the passive and active forces which coexist in the infant prior to the Oedipal situation. Also, it is in the Oedipal situation that the active forces are "cemented" to the masculine and the passive forces are cemented to the feminine.

Insofar as Brennan rejects Freud's biological hypotheses and insists on the physical interpretation of the drives, she is careful to avoid any sort of biologism in her analysis of masculinity and femininity. In her account there is a dialectic of sorts between the socioeconomic oppression of women and the association of the feminine position with passivity. The ways in which little girls are given (conscious and unconscious) attention determines whether or not they will take up the feminine position; there is no inherent link between femininity and females. In fact, Brennan brings into focus that for Freud the mystery in the riddle of femininity is how to explain the appearance of femininity in men; even for Freud femininity is not restricted to females nor is masculinity restricted to males.

In the masculine Oedipal complex, the mother's active executive capacities, which have been turned inward to form the ego ideal or superego, are taken over by the masculine position and redirected outward, while in the feminine Oedipal complex, the direction of energy remains inward:

> If it is accepted that the superego predates the Oedipus complex, the ideal resolution of the masculine Oedipus complex can be read as a forging, a union of capacities that were thitherto identified with the mother and original superego, but come to belong to the masculine ego. In this process, the early superego changes its character. Before the Oedipus complex, the active and passive experience of these executive or subjective capacities was a fluid one; the subject was still finding its sexual bearings. The Oedipus complex cements the active deployment of these capacities to the masculine position. But in the feminine case, the capacities for attempting to and acting on reality are reversed back to their original passive state. Femininity constitutes a passive overlay on an originally passive experience, and this passive overlay is not restricted to the female sex. (*IF* 32)

The difference between femininity and masculinity is the *direction* of energy. The masculine directs energy outward and is thereby able to act in the world. The feminine, on the other hand, directs energy inward and is thereby unable to act in the world. Brennan maintains that the direction that the drives take in the Oedipal situation is dependent on the attention that the infant is given. Attention, directed energy, from an external source is necessary for redirecting energy outward and for constructing and sustaining a self-image. Brennan describes this external attention as a kind of support for the ego and its actions. Without this support the ego must try to produce its own support through daydreams and hallucinations that ultimately expend more energy than they produce and thereby render the subject unable to act in the world; energy turned inward in these kinds of self-sustaining endeavors at its limit becomes self-destructive.

Brennan argues that the feminine ego gives "living attention" that supports an active self-image to the masculine ego. Other feminist theorists have pointed out many of the ways in which women—mothers, wives, and lovers—have traditionally performed most of the emotional labor that supports men in their careers and public lives. Brennan's argument is more radical. She maintains that the feminine ego becomes a kind of receptacle for disabling affects projected out of the masculine ego. In an aggressive but unconscious act, the masculine ego dumps his hostility and disabling emotions onto the other and then forgets that he has done so. In this way the feminine other contains masculine anxiety so that he can be productive. The masculine drives "immobilize, hold back and hold still, [and] make the other an anchor by depositing unwanted affects in her, and thereby secure a surplus of living attention" (*IF* 234).

Brennan suggests that in order for a woman to "overcome femininity," she needs to reconnect "words to affects in a way that preserves her identity while it facilitates acting on reality" (*IF* 177). This is extremely difficult given that the woman who has the feminine ego has an inward-turned image of herself and, more than this, she is constantly confronted with this image of herself in patriarchal culture. Insofar as she takes on the desire of the other she cannot overcome femininity on her own. Brennan ends *The Interpretation of the Flesh* with a call to action, but she does not provide any specific account of how we can overcome femininity and become productive. Her theory, however, provides a model for reconceiving the fundamental relationship between self and other in such a way that we can at least imagine the transformation of the asymmetrical relation between masculine and feminine egos into a reciprocal exchange between two human beings who are both active and passive (in

Brennan's sense). Although Brennan does not discuss the ethical implications of what I am calling her intersubjective theory of drives, her theory
of drives can contribute to my theory of the ontological foundations of
ethics and help provide an alternative conception of the subject-object
relationship which renegotiates the exchange between the two so that one
party does not "win" at the other's expense.

Brennan's claim that the superego originates with the mother's executive capacities suggests that the mother not only provides the satisfaction of physical needs but also provides a precursor to the Law of the
Father. Brennan's suggestion is similar to Kristeva's notion of the law
before the law in *Tales of Love*.[10] Brennan presents a similar argument
when she concludes that it is the in utero communication code used
between maternal body and fetus, and the infant's fleshy memory of this
code, that sets up the possibility of language. In addition to bringing the
maternal function into the center of psychoanalytic theory, this argument
provides a new way to conceive of the primary relation between subject
and object.

Brennan, like Kristeva and Lacan, believes that a third party is necessary in order to propel the subject into language. Something needs to
break up the infant's dyadic dependence on the mother. If the mother possesses this executive function as the law before the Law, then I maintain
that the third term is already operating within the dyad; the dyad is
already/also a triad. This is significant because now we can take the relationship between the maternal body and the fetus/infant as a model for a
social relationship. Unlike the Hegelian-Lacanian model of the onset of
intersubjectivity as a fight to the death, this model allows us to imagine a
relationship where identity does not require the death or repression of the
other. Unlike Lacan, or even Kristeva, on this model we can see the
mother-fetus/infant relation as exhibiting the logic of a social relation.
The move into the social no longer needs to be an essentially violent rejection of the mother or the maternal body. Rather, the mother-infant dyad
sets up the social relation, which always risks violence but is not reduced
to violence.

The "Nature" of Ethics

I began this chapter by pointing out that many feminists are suspicious of
any return to the maternal body as a model for ethics. Feminists, however,
are not the only ones suspicious of the maternal body. Men (both feminists and nonfeminists) often ask if a model of ethics grounded in the

maternal body applies only to women since men cannot be mothers. How can a model grounded in the maternal body set up the possibility of conceiving of ethical relations in general, between men and women or men and men or women and women? This particular concern points to a problem that many people have with psychoanalysis in general. These people ask how a newly born infant can have such complex notions of its relation to its mother and father. The psychoanalytic talk about an infant's desires may seem simply absurd. How could a baby only a few months old conceive of its mother as phallic, see itself as her phallus, or envision its imaginary father?

What is important to remember is that in clinical psychoanalysis all of these strange theories should attempt to describe the ways in which the analysand imagines his or her infantile relationship with a mother or father. Psychoanalysis addresses the fantasies with which we form conceptions of ourselves and our relations to others, and the development of both. Psychoanalysis, especially as it is conceived by Irigaray and Kristeva, works on the level of the imaginary in order to diagnose *how* it is that we take ourselves to be *who* we take ourselves to be. The analysand in the psychoanalytic session is the adult imagining him or herself as the child. When psychoanalytic theories describe maternal and paternal functions, they do so in relation to the child. The child is the center of the psychoanalytic universe.

My ethical ontology, based on a description of the maternal body or the mother's relation to the child, therefore, does not purport to describe the mother's phenomenological experience of maternity, childbirth, or child care. This model is not developed on the basis of some supposition about how a mother feels or how it feels to be a mother. It is not a so-called ethics of care. Rather, the power of this theory comes from the fact that we all have mothers, dead or alive, known or unknown. So far, all human beings have been born of women's bodies. Moreover, like any model, it describes the pattern, logic, or structure of a relationship that is not necessarily inherent in only this particular model. The model is meant to vividly indicate how intersubjective relationships operate.

Traditionally, philosophers have employed models and metaphors in order to describe the "nature" of subjectivity and intersubjective relationships: recall Plato's metaphorical model of the soul as a chariot, Kant's metaphorical model of rational subjects as members of the Kingdom of Ends, Descartes's metaphorical ground for intellectual intuition as the Light of Nature, and Hegel's metaphorical model of subjectivity/intersubjectivity as the master-slave relationship. Certainly Hegel cannot be suggesting that we all must literally become slaves in order to become self-conscious. He is presenting the master-slave relationship as a model whose pattern, logic, and structure hold for the onset of self-consciousness and mutual self-recognition in all self-conscious persons. With the model of the maternal body, I am attempting to provide an alternate account of the pattern, logic, and structure of intersubjective relations. I am not suggesting that we need to become mothers in order to achieve this intersubjectivity. It will suffice that we all were born from the body of a mother.

If, following Kristeva, the logic and structure of bodily drives is the same as the logic and structure of language, then the primary relation between the bodies of mother and child does not have to be antisocial or threatening. And if, following Brennan, bodily drives are not contained within the boundaries of one body or subject but are intersubjective, then bodily drives are always a matter of social exchange. There is no autonomous individual or unified subject on this model. Rather all subjectivity is inherently and fundamentally intersubjectivity, constituted through communication and exchange. As Kristeva maintains, all subjects are always subjects in process. The intersubjective theory of drives radicalizes the notion of a subject in process in that it can no longer be identified with one process or any determinate being. In other words, the constant exchange that makes up the process is no longer taking place within one human life, but between human lives. The subject in process becomes subjects in processes; the subject in process becomes intersubjective. The monologue of Kristeva's extra-terrestrial becomes a constitutive dialogue that can never be broken down into the possessions of two autonomous interlocutors. This dialogue begins in utero and continues on different levels throughout human life.

Within the maternal body, the placenta plays the mediating role in a proto-social exchange. In an interview with Luce Irigaray in *Je, Tu, Nous*, biologist Hélène Rouch discusses the role of the placenta as a medium of communication within the maternal body:

> It plays a mediating role on two levels. On the one hand, it's the mediating space between mother and fetus, which means that there's never a fusion of maternal and embryonic tissues. On the other hand, it constitutes a system regulating exchanges between the two organisms, not merely quantitatively regulating the exchanges (nutritious substances from mother to fetus, waste matter in the other direction), but also modifying the maternal metabolism: transforming, storing, and redistributing maternal substances for both her own and the fetus' benefit. It thus establishes a relationship

between mother and fetus, enabling the latter to grow without exhausting the mother in the process, and yet not simply being a means for obtaining nutritious substances. (Irigaray, *JTN* 39)

As Rouch describes it, the placenta plays the kind of mediating role that Brennan identifies as the fleshy code that sets up the possibility of language. The placenta is the medium of communication between the maternal body and the fetus. Yet at the same time these two are neither autonomous nor identical. Within the maternal body our traditional notion of identity is problematic to the point that it must be reconceived. Within the maternal body we have a relationship that is neither an identity nor an absolute separation. This relationship is one of exchange that cannot be reduced to a Hegelian fight to the death. The placenta is a medium of exchange that protects the fetus from the maternal body's defense mechanisms; it communicates to the maternal body that the fetus is not an alien other. Ex utero, language and drive-affect are mediums of exchange that should mutually feed both subjects in process.

Insofar as the model of the maternal body and its relation to the fetus does not involve two autonomous subjects, it should not be taken to fortify the rhetoric of so-called right to life arguments. It is in fact traditional views about the mother's body as a natural container and the associations between the mother and nature that make possible the rhetoric of the "right to life" movement. If the mother is seen as a speaking, desiring subject, then her body cannot be reduced to a container for the fetus/child. More than this, if the relationship between the maternal body and fetus is not taken as a relationship between two autonomous subjects, then the debate cannot be formulated in terms of conflicting rights. The rights talk presupposes some form of an autonomous subject or potential autonomous subject. In my discussion it becomes impossible to identify such an autonomous subject and the whole framework of rights would have to be reconceived. In addition, the relationship between the maternal body and the fetus has to be rethought.

When I invoke the "biological" model of the maternal body and the fetal relationship to it through the placenta in this framework, it should not be seen as some type of naturalism or biologism. On the contrary, the model is invoked in order to call into question the opposition between the natural and the biological on the one hand, and the cultural and the sociological, on the other. I use this model to demonstrate that there is no nature in itself, no biology in itself. Rather the biological and the social are mutually constitutive. On the other hand, my insistence that the social relation is prefigured in the body should not be read as some type of nominalism or crude constructivism. Once again, this model reduces the maternal body neither to nature/biology nor to culture/sociology. To say that there is a dialectical relation between the two provinces captures perhaps their mutual interdependence but does not capture their mutual constitution. To employ the metaphor of a conversation, I would say that it is not that nature and culture are two interlocutors in a dialogue that makes up human experience; rather nature and culture *are* by virtue of the dialogue. In other words, it is not that nature and culture both contribute something whose combination results in human experience; rather both "nature" and "culture" are psychophysical or socio-bio or linguistic-material.

When the relation between self and other becomes ambiguous, when identity is an exchange between self and other, only then can we begin to talk about ethics. Ethics requires a relationship between two that are neither identical nor autonomous. For if they are identical, there is no relationship and therefore no ethics. And if they are completely autonomous then there is only external law to bind two individuals together and ground obligations to the other; and in light of the horrors of the recent past (Fascism and Stalinism) and of the present ("ethnic cleansing" in the former Yugoslavia), we know that law can just as easily lead to totalitarianism and annihilation of the other as it can lead to recognition of the other.[11] An ethical relationship takes place between two, by virtue of their difference, who are not self-possessed. On this model, we are not the autonomous agents of Kantian ethics. Rather we are fundamentally and intrinsically dependent on each other for the generation and maintenance of our identities. We are not dependent on each other just on a conscious level but on an unconscious level as well. Brennan's intersubjective theory of drives challenges any notion of autonomy on an ontological level. This is why, as Kristeva or Irigaray might say, we have to work on the level of the imaginary in order to change our very image of relationships. The inter-subjective theory of the drives provides us with a new image of relationship, a more fluid and potentially reciprocal relationship, a relationship that engenders a new conception of ethics.

Kristeva calls for a new conception of ethics based in the maternal body and the child's relation to it. "Herethics," as she calls it in "Stabat Mater," would be an ethics that takes seriously the experience of maternity and a discourse of maternity that can account for relations between mothers and daughters as well as relations between men and women. Although Kristeva says very little about this "herethics" and mentions it only in the last few paragraphs of "Stabat Mater," it is clear that herethics is a heretical ethics, because it would be founded on a reconceived image of maternity that is not restricted to what Kristeva takes to be one of the most powerful images of maternity in Western culture, the Virgin Mary.

Both Kristeva and Irigaray tell new tales of the Virgin Mary, Mother of God. In "Stabat Mater" Kristeva traces the history of the cult of the Virgin in Catholic church doctrine. She points out that it is through Mary that Christ is human; yet because Christ is also God, Mary's humanity falls under question. How can Christ be without sin if he is born of a sinner? So Mary is also presumed to be born without sin, hers is the immaculate conception. And because she is born without sin, unlike Christ the god-man, she will not die. She is the Mother of God, the Queen of Heaven, Our Lady. She has the purity of God, the eternal life of God, and the power of a queen. As Kristeva points out, in different periods of church doctrine Mary becomes daughter and wife as well as mother to Christ (*TL* 243). While this feminine divinity provides an image of feminine power as mother, daughter and wife, she seems heavenly rather than earthly. Her humanity has evaporated until with Francis of Assisi she becomes the "Madonna of humility," poor and modest, a peasant rather than a queen (*TL* 246). She becomes an ordinary woman, without the sin. She becomes a model of motherhood, both suffering and pure.

Kristeva criticizes this Catholic model of motherhood, which does not account for the mother's relations with men or other women, especially with a daughter (*TL* 261). The Virgin is alone of her sex and stands above both men and women (*TL* 258). She has relations only with God and her son. This story has been taken over by psychoanalysis. Freud emphasizes the relationship between women and their sons, their penis-substitutes, while Lacan emphasizes the relationship between women and God, their phallus substitutes. If the child's relationship to the mother is going to continue to serve as the prototypical relation that sets up the possibility of all subsequent relations—as it still does in psychoanalytic theory—then we need a model of the mother-child relationship that does not exclude (erotic) relations between women and men.

Irigaray imagines Mary as such a model. She imagines a divine made flesh that engenders a loving relationship with the other that is not violent and destructive like the divine figures of Dionysus, Apollo, and Christ. In Mary the union of divine and human leads neither to the Dionysian passionate dismemberment of the body nor to the Apollonian dispassionate denial of the body.[12] With the figure of Mary we have the word made flesh and the advent of a nonviolent erotic divinity (*ML* 181).

In the body of Mary we have the fertile marriage of logos and cosmos, spirit and body (*ML* 190). Mary's maternal body is the incarnation through otherness: "With the penetration of the word into a body still recalling and summoning the entry of that body into a word. Exit from the tombs. Access to a beyond here now. Passage from body-corpses to a saying that transfigures them—pulls them out of the walls of their death. Crossing their own frontiers in a meeting with the flesh of the other. Living, if she speaks. She too incarnating the divine" (*ML* 169).

She is neither merely the body-object since she is the incarnation of the divine spirit, nor merely the spirit, since the god-child must be born from a body. Rather, for Irigaray, Mary represents the in-between, what she calls elsewhere "the sensible transcendental," through whom we might imagine another economy of exchange that does not require sacrifice, a divine that does not require a dead god. In response to Nietzsche's "God is dead," Irigaray asks, "if for men their God is dead, where can the divine be spoken without preaching death?" (*ML* 20). And in turn she asks "and the unceasing movement of two springs feeding each other could be the pledge of eternal happiness, could it not?" (*ML* 37). Perhaps the divine is produced in the exchange between two living springs nourishing each other. For Irigaray, the divine is necessarily incarnate and the result of two different sexes giving (themselves) to each other through the wonder at their difference.

For Irigaray ethics is the ethics of this sexual difference. This is why, although in her interview with biologist Hélène Rouch, Irigaray remarks on "the almost ethical character" of the fetal relation, she does not propose taking the maternal body as a model for ethics (*JTN* 41). She may even object to an ethics modeled on the maternal body, because it is not necessarily an ethics based on an exchange across sexual difference. I maintain, however, that only when the mother is seen as a speaking, loving, desiring human being will ethics be possible. An ethics of sexual difference requires a rearticulation of maternity which resuscitates the mother from the patriarchal association with nature/death. If our first relationship is with the maternal body, then we need to reconceive that relationship as an ethical relationship before we can conceive the relationship between two sexes as an ethical relationship. While Kristeva's theories of the drives, the semiotic, the subject in process, and the maternal function provide useful conceptual tools for formulating such an ethical model, Kristeva never uses them in order to build her "herethics." She claims that we need a herethical ethics, but she does not provide one. She develops neither an ethical theory nor the implications of her notions of subjectivity for an ontology of ethics.[13]

The intersubjective theory of drives combined with my analysis of the maternal body, however, gives us the language with which to talk about Irigaray's vision of reciprocal exchange between two different sexes and embrace Kristeva's other within. Although Kristeva and Irigaray propose very different accounts of alterity—Kristeva suggests an alterity within and Irigaray suggests a radical alterity outside—I can use both notions in developing my model for a mutually constitutive relation between self and other.[14] Alterity is neither within nor outside once the opposition between inside and outside is called into question. If subjectivity is constituted as and through intersubjectivity, then interiority and our notions of our interior mental life or interior sense of ourselves never exist in opposition to what is outside. As Levinas says, the interior and the exterior are constituted through the same gesture, a gesture of hospitality not reducible to hostility.[15]

On my model the primary relationship is not one in which the subject has identity only by annihilating difference or the other. Rather, the subject's very identity is *sustained* by virtue of an ongoing exchange with the other. When the maternal body is taken as the model of this relationship then the exchange can be seen as cooperative rather than threatening. As Brennan demonstrates, within contemporary patriarchal culture the psychophysical exchange of energy works to women's detriment, but if we can reconceive the primary relation with the mother, then we can also reconceive the psychophysical exchange of energy as reciprocal and mutually supportive of active self-images for women and men.

Within the maternal body the codes of communication and the very foundation of the social relations are already operating, so the maternal body functions as a limit to the nature/culture distinction. In fact, the biological is itself called into question. If the logic or structure of language is operating within the material of the body, then how can we separate the biological from the sociological, the body from language? The maternal body points to the mutually constitutive relation between the bio and the socio, between nature and culture. This is one of the reasons why the model of the maternal body is so powerful. The maternal body can be neither substituted for nor merely associated with nature. Both metaphorical substitutions between mother and nature and metonymical associations between mother and nature must be re-examined.

Although the model that I have proposed is based on exchange and communication, this theory is not a form of Habermasian communitarianism or discourse theory. In my model there is no Kantian autonomous rational agent who engages with another such agent in order to reach a consensus. Rather the model of the maternal body calls into question this Kantian agent who makes conscious agreements that lead to consensus. The Habermasian model lacks any account of the unconscious. More than this, it lacks any account of the intersubjective nature of subjectivity. It is not merely the case that our ideas about our world, who we are, and the truth are products that result from our communal relations; rather, the very possibility of having such ideas is constituted intersubjectively. The intersubjective notion of subjectivity operates not only on an epistemological level but also on an ontological level. And if being is constituted through intersubjective relations, then, following Levinas, we could say that ethics is first philosophy and philosophy is ethics first.[16] Philosophy itself becomes what it is through its articulation of the relation between self and other and in its dialogue with its other, an other that is never its own because philosophy as thought can never be self-possessed. Philosophy is always a subject in process.

CONCLUSION

The Ethics of Intersubjectivity: Acknowledging the (m)Other

*You have navigated with raging soul far from the paternal home,
passing beyond the seas' double rocks and now you inhabit a
foreign land.* —Medea

Responsibilities of Affect

My account of the intersubjective ontology of the ethical relationship has
profound implications for the way in which we talk about rights and responsibilities. For example, if we begin to think of an ethics that has its basis in a
conception of the ethical agent as an intersubjective agent whose subjectivity
is always intersubjectivity, then discussions of altruism and self concern have
to be reformulated. One's responsibilities to oneself cannot be easily separated, conceptually or practically, from one's responsibilities to others.
Within feminist ethics, for example, Carol Gilligan's distinction between an
altruistic ethics of care and the self concerned ethics of justice would begin to
dissolve when we think through the ontology of subjectivity presupposed in
her distinction. As Gilligan describes it in *In a Different Voice*, the type of
subjectivity that is associated with the ethics of care is an interconnected sense
of the self as a network; the type of subjectivity associated with the ethics of
justice, on the other hand, is a separated sense of the self as autonomous. Yet,
as my discussion indicates connection and separation cannot themselves be
so easily separated. Issues of separation and connection always work
together. Moreover, even within the logic of Gilligan's theory of the interconnected and separated selves, the distinction between altruism and self concern collapses when we realize that the subject who is operating with the
interconnected network conception of him/herself is acting in his/her own self
interest by helping those others who constitute his/her sense of self. The
altruism of the ethics of care turns out to be just as self interested as the self
concern of the ethics of justice. What is at stake, then, is not altruism or self
interest. Rather, what is at stake is the ontology of the ethical agent.

Before we can address questions of rights and responsibilities to others or ourselves, we must address the prior question of the relationship between the self and the other. Before we can discuss our obligations to others, we have to begin to think through our relationship to others on an ontological level. My analysis of an intersubjective notion of subjectivity that does not reduce our primary relationship to violence and hostility opens up a new realm of ethical rights and responsibilities that must be secured in new ways. In order to draw out some of the implications of my intersubjective ontology of ethics it will be useful to return to one of the most influential models of the onset of subjectivity as intersubjectivity, the Hegelian lordship/bondage model, and delineate how my model is different from the Hegelian model.

In *Phenomenology of Spirit*, Hegel presents us with an intersubjective model of subjectivity. The onset of self-consciousness or subjectivity comes through the violent struggle with another self-consciousness in the lordship/bondage stage of the *Phenomenology*. Although this stage is merely one early stage in the dialectic of self–consciousness, and it is subsequently superseded by various more sociable stages of development, this initial fight to the death is necessary for the experience of self–consciousness. For Hegel, self–consciousness begins from the desire to consume the other. While I agree that the onset of self-consciousness and subjectivity is necessarily intersubjective and motivated by desire, I do not figure that desire as a necessarily hostile desire to annihilate the other. Rather, I figure that desire as a desire for exchange that benefits both parties.

On the model of the maternal body, exchange is primarily cooperative, which is not to say that it excludes violence or the possibility of violence. On the contrary, the processes of the maternal body and birth contain their own forms of violence. In fact, violence may be a necessary constituent of the maternal body and birth. But, these processes are not reducible to violence. What makes birth birth is not violence. Although violence is possible, perhaps constitutive, it is neither what motivates the relationship or the onset of self-consciousness, nor does it define the intersubjective relationship. If the model of the maternal body involves violence, this violence is constitutive of cooperation and not a violence directed towards the other motivated by the desire to annihilate that other. In birth, for example, the maternal body—for its own sake and the sake of the infant—violently expels the infant from the womb; yet, this "violence" or force is neither directed against the infant nor does it define giving birth. While there is much more to be said about the constitutive role of violence in the processes of the maternal body, let these comments suffice to suggest that although the maternal model of the ontology of intersubjectivity is not motivated by violence, it can contain a certain constitutive violence or force.

Nietzsche identifies the necessity of constitutive violence or force in any act of creation, which does not mean that creation can be reduced to violence. Recall that Derrida, following Nietzsche, uses the notion of force to distinguish between constitutive and excessive violence. As I have indicated throughout this book, my problem with Nietzsche is that too often in his writings there is also the violence of the lordship/bondage sort that is aimed toward annihilating the other, specifically the feminine maternal. While my model cannot prevent the possibility of annihilating the other, it does not begin with the necessary attempt at that annihilation. Rather, it begins with cooperation which can break down if, as Derrida points out, it does not *risk* violence by continuing to attempt an exchange across difference. We have to be willing to take the chance of misunderstandings or assimilations in order to cooperate.

In addition, with the intersubjective theory of the drives and affects, it becomes necessary to talk about a new type of violence and a corresponding new type of responsibility. If ego boundaries are permeable and we are all in a constant process of exchanging psychic energies and affects, then don't we have some responsibility for our effects/affects on another person? If there is always more going on in any conversation than the exchange of words, if interpersonal interaction is always operating on a psycho–physical level, then don't we have to reformulate our traditional conceptions of the cultural and the natural, the social and the physical? The body, "nature," is returned to culture and vice versa. The social extends into the psycho-physical and therefore so do our ethical obligations.

Recall what I have called Brennan's theory of intersubjective drives. Recall that on her theory affective energy transfers take place in all interpersonal interactions. The idea that we can transfer affects through contact and conversation resonates with most people who have had the experience of a conversation with a loved one in which s/he is upset during the conversation and after the conversation s/he feels much better but now the other party to the conversation is upset. This kind of situation suggests a transfer of affect. Even our language in such interpersonal situations suggests an exchange of affect: "I won't take it any more." "Don't give me that."

If, as Brennan argues, women are oppressed by the ways in which affective exchange takes place within our culture, then don't we have a responsibility to change these exchanges? Sandra Bartky's work in

Feminism and Domination also indicates ways in which women have traditionally been subject to an inequitable division of emotional labor. If groups of people can be oppressed by systematic asymmetries in affective energy exchange, then don't we have social responsibilities to overcome oppression on this affective level? In addition to this question of social and political responsibility, doesn't the intersubjective theory of drives and affects raise the question of an ethical responsibility on the level of affect? How do we attend to our affective responsibilities to others? What kinds of affective rights do we have?

In this book I can do no more than make suggestions about the implications of my intersubjective ontology of ethical agents for discussions of rights and responsibilities. Yet, one thing should be clear: Feminist ethical theories that rely on notions of connectedness or network theories of the self are not immune from a new possibility of violence or hurting others. Although, as Gilligan maintains, the prime directive of the ethics of care is not to hurt others, the very notion of an interconnected sense of self—a notion that Gilligan's theory does not think through—makes it possible to recognize violence on another level, the level of affect. We have to start to think of this new set of ethical rights and responsibilities; we have to begin to formulate an ethics of interpersonal relations. In order to avoid violence towards the other, in order to acknowledge our violence towards the other, we must imagine a new beginning for subjectivity in an intersubjective exchange that is not fundamentally the hostile and violent annihilation of the other.

Philosophy Otherwise . . .

> *I call myself the last philosopher, because I am the last man. No one speaks with me but myself, and my voice comes to me like the voice of a dying man!*
> —Friedrich Nietzsche, *Notebooks of the early 1870's*

> *If you were to break your "no" instead of breaking yourself? And to recast your kingdom of exile instead of reigning in sovereignty there as a master of the end of the world. In the emanation of dreams cradled in the illusion that the lack created is source and sign of higher fortune. These are the last priests—the scientists who preach famine. Degenerate men who still barely survive on the smoke from the sacrifice of others. And who take pride in being more than men, since they have climbed to such heights. And gaze on the desert as proof of their power.*
> —Luce Irigaray, *Marine Lover of Friedrich Nietzsche*

Perhaps we can learn from Nietzsche's last philosopher, the last man, who hears only his own dying voice returning to himself because he listens to no other. Nietzsche's last man dies of loneliness and lack of love. The last voice he hears is his own as he deludes himself into thinking that he is talking to an other. Without the other he dies and with him philosophy dies. Like the last man, philosophy dies from the lack of dialogue with an other.

The names Nietzsche and Derrida have, along with Freud, perhaps more than any others, become associated with philosophy's attempt to break out of Enlightenment notions of reason and subjectivity in order to open onto something other. They are associated with a new kind of philosophy. When it comes to the specifically feminine other, however, none of these theorists move beyond the Hegelian model of intersubjectivity, which requires that the relationship to the other always is hostile; it requires a violence at the onset of self–consciousness which demands the enslavement of another (feminine) self–consciousness. Both life and philosophy have become a hostile struggle for dominance between masculine and feminine elements in which one always wins at the expense of the other. Yet, even within the Hegelian model, the murder of the other is equivalent to suicide. Each self–consciousness needs the other.

What I have attempted to do in *Womanizing Nietzsche* is open up a critical discourse, through which philosophy can be called to account for its violence to the feminine and the maternal. I have specifically chosen to focus on the texts of Nietzsche and Derrida, which, in the history of philosophy, have become associated with an opening onto the feminine or philosophy's "becoming female." Following Derrida's prescription in "Force of Law"— that we must think, know, represent for ourselves, formalize, judge the possible complicity between all these discourses and the worst"—I have tried to diagnose the worst places for woman in these non-traditional discourses (FL 63).

I will conclude by returning to the question with which I began, Heidegger's question, "What does it mean that philosophy is in its final stage?" What happens to *philosophy* if it is seen as a response to the invitation of the other? In this case, what could the end, or death, of philosophy mean? If philosophy is a discourse and all discourse is a response to a call or invitation from something other, then philosophy dies/ends only with the death, or end, of the other. In "Of an Apocalyptic Tone" Derrida insists that this call, this "come," from the other cannot be determinate; it is not a call from a determinate sex, male or female, masculine or feminine (ATP 66). Yet, it is the indeterminacy of the call from this abstract Other that makes the call apocalyptic: "No longer is one very sure who loans its voice and its tone to the other in the Apocalypses; no longer is one very sure who addresses what to whom. But by a cata-strophic reversal here more necessary than ever, one can just as well think: as soon as one no longer knows who speaks or who writes, the text becomes apocalyptic" (ATP 57). The indeterminacy of the call from the other is apocalyptic because it ensures the impossibility of a determinate answer to the call. Derrida concludes that the "come" from the other is the apocalypse of apocalypse, the end of ends, a (new) beginning.

For a new beginning, the possibility of that other in all of its deter-minations, and not just as an abstract Other, must be kept open. The "come" or call of/from the other that engenders discourse, and prevents its end, is not the "last apocalypse"—or more accurately the impossibil-ity of the "last apocalypse"—*because*, as Derrida suggests, it is abstract or indeterminate. Rather, this abstract, formal "come" or call finds its power in the always available possibility that it can or will become, if always only provisionally, determinate. In other words, I would say that it is through the determinate and concrete engagements with others that we sense the awe of this abstract invitation, "come."

In my engagement with another person through language, broadly conceived, I sense something beyond either of us that makes the end of discourse impossible even as it makes discourse possible. We need to speak; we need to communicate. As Kristeva might say, meaning itself is the Other. Meaning is what is beyond us. In my engagement with language itself, in the experience of writing for example, the interaction between us, me and you—neither of us determinate for the other—I sense some-thing beyond myself. The "come" or the call is in itself indeterminate, but it constitutes, and is constituted by, determinate relations between people.

To close off discourse to some particular determinate other is to close off the ear to the invitation or call of the Other that makes it possible to speak and to live as a human being. To silence the "come" or the call is to live in silence, and to live in silence is to die. This silence is what Derrida identifies as the realm of absolute violence; it is violence to the Other which makes possible a violence to a particular other, which in turn pre-vents absolute violence or absolute death. With the recent talk of the death of philosophy, it seems important to diagnose this apocalyptic tone in philosophy. I agree with Derrida when he points out that within the his-tory of philosophy (specifically for Kant) it is the threat from the other that rings the death knell for philosophy (ATP 33, 48–49). At our moment in the history of philosophy, it is the feminine other that threatens to make its presence known to philosophy; feminist philosophers in particular are threatening to lift the veil of Isis. Many philosophers, feminists and oth-ers, ask, "Can philosophy address this other, even represent this other, and still remain philosophy?" The related question "Is feminist philosophy, philosophy?" comes from both proponents and opponents of feminism.

To ask these questions, however, is to *presuppose* that philosophy is masculine. To ask these questions is to presuppose that if philosophy becomes anything other than what it has been, then it is no longer philosophy. This view not only presupposes that philosophy has one and only one essence but also that the essence of philosophy is masculine. To maintain this position requires that once the feminine enters the scene, philosophy must exit. Philosophy runs away from the feminine. And some philosophers would rather talk about the death, or end, of philosophy than admit the excluded feminine other. To view the feminine other as a threat to philosophy is more than an acknowledgment that the history of philosophy has been masculine. It is an insistence that philosophy continue to be masculine or not at all.

In spite of their attempts to open discourse onto the other, the writings of both Nietzsche and Derrida exhibit this tendency to privilege what has been excluded in the name of the death, limit, or closure of philosophy. Although Derrida claims that he pushes philosophy to its limit and not to its death, and he acknowledges the Heideggerian–Levinasian "come" or call from the other, there are places in his texts that echo the death knell for philosophy (*P* 6; see WM 271). As Irigaray suggests, some philosophers would rather break themselves than break their no to the other, a specifically feminine other, a specifically feminine mother (*ML* 63). They revel in their mastery over the barren field of philosophy rather than admit the feminine other who might bring her immemorial waters to the desert.

If, however, philosophy can engage in a dialogue with its feminine other, perhaps we can imagine doing philosophy otherwise. We can conceive of philosophy as a dialogue of human experiences, masculine and feminine, that—even while risking violence—does not require either murder or suicide. We can imagine a dialogue with multiple voices, even multiply sexed voices. We can imagine a reading and a writing that is life-affirming without being reduced to violence, a philosophy that continually calls itself to account for its violence. Philosophy becomes a subject in process; it becomes ethical; "*it becomes female.*" As Heidegger says, it listens to, and speaks, that which demands to be admitted, that which has been excluded. Feminist philosophy can listen to, and speak, the excluded feminine(s) and recall the importance of the feminine maternal.

Within the imaginary of Western culture, the first call or invitation from an other comes from the mother. Her call is an invitation to speak, to respond. Her body opens an invitation to both sexes without discrimination. It provides the first model of discourse as a call that cannot be reduced to either biology or culture. It provides a model for an economy of exchange that is not defined by a violent struggle to the death. By acknowledging the importance of the maternal body to our culture and to our philosophy, philosophy becomes a subject in process; it becomes ethical; "*it becomes maternal.*"

NOTES

PART ONE

1. The most representative sample of philosophical discussions of the death or end of philosophy, from various traditions in philosophy, is the sizable collection of essays edited by K. Baynes, J. Bohman, and T. McCarthy entitled *After Philosophy: End or Transformation?*, (Cambridge MA: MIT Press, 1987). Philosophers from Michel Foucault, Jean-François Lyotard, and Jürgen Habermas to Richard Rorty, Alasdair MacIntyre, and Hilary Putnam discuss the death/ends of man and the death/ends of philosophy.

2. For demonstrations that the history of philosophy denies or excludes the feminine see, for example, Geneviève Lloyd, *Man of Reason: "Male" and "Female" in Western Philosophy* (University of Minnesota Press, 1984); L. Clark and L. Lange (ed.s), *The Sexism of Social and Political Theory* (University of Toronto Press, 1979); R. Baker and F. Elliston (ed.s), *Philosophy and Sex* (Prometheus Books, 1975); S. Harding and M. Hintikka (ed.s), *Discovering Reality: Feminist Perspectives on Epistemology, Metaphysics, Methodology, and the Philosophy of Science* (Reidel Press, 1983); A. Garry and M. Pearsall (ed.s), *Women, Knowledge, and Reality: Explorations in Feminist Philosophy* (Unwin Hyman, 1989); L. Alcoff and E. Potter (ed.s), *Feminist Epistemologies* (Routledge, 1993). M. Whitford and M. Griffiths (ed.s), *Feminist Perspectives in Philosophy* (Indiana University Press, 1988); S. Bordo and A. Jaggar (ed.s), *Gender/Body/Knowledge* (Rutgers University Press, 1989); Luce Irigaray, *Speculum of the Other Woman*, trans. Gillian Gill (Cornell University Press, 1985); Bat-ami Bar On (ed.), *Modern Engendering* (SUNY Press, 1994.)

3. In "The Ends of Man," in *Margins of Philosophy*, Derrida uses "ends" to mean the telos, both the limit and the purpose.

4. See Hélène Cixous's "The Laugh of the Medusa," *Signs* 1. p 875–99; reprinted in *New French Feminisms*, E. Marks and I. Courtivron (eds.) (New York: Schocken Books, 1980), 245–64; Irigaray's *Speculum of the Other Woman*; Jane Gallop's *The Daughter's Seduction* (Ithaca: Cornell University Press, 1982).

5. Both Elizabeth Grosz and Sarah Kofman argue in different ways that Freud's theory presupposes castration in order to set up castration in the girl. See *Jacques Lacan: a feminist introduction* (New York: Routledge, 1990)

6. I would like to thank Daniel Conway and Alan Schrift for generous comments on an early version of this section. I would also like to thank Kathleen Higgins, Elissa Marder, and Johanna Seibt for their invaluable help and suggestions. A version of "A Dagger through the Heart" was previously published in *International Studies in Philosophy*, Summer 1993.

7. Friedrich Nietzsche, *On the Genealogy of Morals*, Trans. Walter Kaufmann and R. J. Hollingdale, (New York: Random House, 1967); referred to as *OGM* in the text from now on followed by the page number and then the section number.

8. Alan Schrift, *Nietzsche and the Question of Interpretation* (New York: Routledge, 1991).

9. For an impressive account of the difference between active and reactive forces and their relation to the master and slave moralities, see Gilles Deleuze, *Nietzsche and Philosophy*, Trans. Hugh Tomlinson (New York: Columbia University Press, 1983).

10 Nietzsche is a bad reader insofar as he denies sexual difference.

11. Gallop is quoting Shoshana Felman's "To Open the Question," *Yale French Studies* 55–56 (1977): 5–10. Gallop is applying Shoshana Felman's distinction between two aspects of psychoanalysis—interpretation and transference reading. Gallop suggests that an analysis of the text that recognizes the operations of transference in reading—investing the text with the authority of meaning—can open up the process of reading beyond mere interpretation. In this context, Gallop means something more specific by interpretation than my use of "interpretation" in this essay. She uses "interpretation" in a way akin to my use of reactive or simple reading which I oppose to interpretation. I use interpretation to designate something like what she calls a reading that includes the recognition of transference; that is, a reading that diagnoses the symptoms of investing the text with the authority to mean . See Jane Gallop, *Reading Lacan* (Ithaca: Cornell University Press, 1985).

12. John Walchak suggests that my distinction between active and reactive reading is similar to Roland Barthes's distinction between writerly reading, through which the reader creates a new text, and readerly reading, through which the reader closes off possibilities for further investigation in the text. See Roland Barthes, *Writing Degree Zero*; Noëlle McAfee suggests that my description of active reading is similar to Simon Critchley's description of deconstructive reading. See Simon Critchley *The Ethics of Deconstruction* (Blackwell, 1992). I will make the connection between Nietzsche's style and Derrida's style in chapter 2.

13. This question is echoed in Freud's lecture on femininity. There Freud asks "*Was will das Weib?*" in order to read sexual difference, and ultimately the very possibility of difference itself. Nietzsche's lesson in reading is a lesson in reading difference. It is the ascetic ideal that insists on one reading and excludes the very possibility of difference.

14. Michael Newman makes this argument in his thought-provoking, if problematic, essay "Reading the Future of Genealogy: Kant, Nietzsche, Plato," in Keith Ansell-Pearson (ed.), *Nietzsche and Modern German Thought*, 264.

15. For an insightful discussion of Nietzsche's writing styles, see Gary Shapiro, *Nietzschean Narratives* (Bloomington: Indiana University Press, 1989). For a discussion of Nietzsche's bodily metaphors see Eric Blondel, *Nietzsche: The Body and Culture*, Trans. Seán Hand (Standford: Stanford University Press, 1991).

16. Luce Irigaray, *Marine Lover of Friedrich Nietzsche*, Trans. Gillian Gill (New York: Columbia University Press, 1991).

17. In *Gynesis*, Alice Jardine presents a very nice summary of Derrida's positions on woman and the feminine in some of his essays. Although she raises many questions for feminists, she neither answers these questions nor criticizes or deconstructs Derrida's texts from a feminist perspective.

18. I will analyze the centrality of the question of belonging in *Spurs* in chapter 3 below.

19. Gayatri Chakravorty Spivak, "Displacement and the Discourse of Woman," in Mark Krupnick (ed.), *Displacement: Derrida and After* (Indiana University Press: Bloomington). 171.

20. Gayatri Chakravorty Spivak, "Feminism and Deconstruction, Again: Negotiating with unacknowledged Masculinism," in Teresa Brennan (ed.), *Between Feminism and Psychoanalysis* (London: Routledge, 1989) 215.

21. Sally Robinson, "Misappropriations of the 'Feminine,' " in *SubStance 59* (1989).

22. Sally Robinson argues that Derrida's appropriations of the feminine and "woman" operate within a masculine desire to avoid castration and protect the phallus. See "Misappropriations of the 'Feminine.' " Given Freud's analysis of fetishism, we must remember that it is not just any woman but the mother who is fetishized. I suggest that this is because the male child was once part of his mother's body (a castrated body) and therefore he must deny her castration in order to deny his own.

23. This passage from Nietzsche is quoted in Sarah Kofman's "Baubô: Theological Perversion and Fetishism," in Gillespie and Strong (eds). *Nietzsche's New Seas* (Chicago: University of Chicago Press, 1988), 193. The quotation is from Nietzsche's *Le Livre du philosophe*.

24. Kaufmann's translation reads "not easy to penetrate." I have altered his translation.

25. Arthur Danto, "Some Remarks on *The Genealogy of Morals*," in K. Higgins and R. Solomon (eds.) *Reading Nietzsche*, (Oxford: Oxford University Press, 1988),

26. Daniel Conway, "Comedians of the Ascetic Ideal: The Performance of Genealogy," in *The Politics of Irony: Essays in Self-Betrayal* D.W. Conway and J.E. Serry, eds. (St Martin's Press, 1992), 80.

27. Friedrich Nietzsche, *Thus Spake Zarathustra*, Trans. by Walter Kaufmann in *The Portable Nietzsche* (New York: Viking Press, 1969); referred to from now on as Z in the text followed by page numbers and then part numbers and section titles.

28. German texts are quoted from Karl Schlechta's *Friedrich Nietzsche Werke in Drei Bänden* (Munich: Carl Hanser Verlag, 1966); referred from now on as KS followed by the volume number and then the page number.

29. With David Krell's *Postponements* Nietzsche's uninhibited hand becomes the dismembered hand of woman when Krell claims that Nietzsche writes with the hand of woman—but I must postpone my discussion of Krell's hand.

30. Alexander Nehamas emphasizes that the warrior in Zarathrustra's aphorism is a writer and is not concerned with "armed warfare" (114).

31. Michael Newman suggests that the intended effect of Nietzsche's own genealogy is self-parody (271). Daniel Conway makes a more substantial case for reading Nietzsche's genealogy as self-irony. Conway argues that Nietzsche's "performance" of genealogy is his "sole means of challenging" the ascetic ideal. He also defines comedy as "the species of Nietzschean irony peculiar to genealogy," which makes Nietzsche a comedian of the ascetic ideal (73–95).

32. Friedrich Nietzsche, *The Antichrist*, Trans. by R. J. Hollingdale (New York: Penguin, 1968); referred to from now on as AC followed by the section number.

33. See *BGE* §9: "what formerly happened with the Stoics still happens today, too, as soon as philosophy begins to believe in itself. It always creates the world in its own image; it cannot do otherwise."

34. Daniel Conway very persuasively argues that the only thing that *possibly* separates Nietzsche from the ascetic priest is comedy, particularly his self-irony. Conway points out that Nietzsche employs an ascetic logic in his genealogy: Like the ascetic priest, Nietzsche alters the direction of resentment; rather than continue to direct our *ressentiment* inward we direct it at the priest. Like the priest, Nietzsche provides a singular interpretation of guilt and bad conscience. (At this point I have some questions about Conway's reading.) Like the ascetic priest, Nietzsche promises redemption even though he knows that he cannot deliver. Because Nietzsche's genealogy is self-referential, however, Conway argues that he is distinguished from an ascetic priest as a comedian of the ascetic ideal. Yet even this move to self-irony follows the ascetic logic by directing violence inward.

35. Friedrich Nietzsche, *Ecce Homo*, Trans. Walter Kaufmann (New York: Random House, 1969). I have suggested that the *Übermensch* is the "counterideal" to which Nietzsche alludes in both *Genealogy* and *Ecce Homo*. Although the *Übermensch*, as Nietzsche draws her, may store values to the earth and live outside the confines of the ascetic ideal, his postulation of the *Übermensch* as a redeemer or goal of modern man makes his vision of the *Übermensch* one more ascetic delusion.

36. Kaufmann intensifies Nietzsche's masculine metaphors by translating "*des vertieften Blicks*" as "penetration." Thanks to Peter Heckman for pointing this out to me.

37. In *Spurs* Derrida describes Nietzsche's style as a type of spur or oblong probe that rips through resistant tissues. Derrida reads and compounds the masculine metaphor of erection and penetration (for example see *S* 41).

38. "Assorted Opinions and Maxims" §137, quoted in Schrift, *Nietzsche and the Question of Interpretation,* 164.

39. Although there are many recent attempts to bring deconstruction and politics and ethics together, I especially appreciate the attempts of Drucilla Cornell, *Beyond Accommodation* and *The Philosophy of the Limit,* and Simon Critchley, *The Ethics of Deconstruction.*

40. I have altered Barbara Harlow's translation to render what I take to be a more exact translation.

41. For an analysis of Derrida's three types of women, castrated, castrating and affirmative, with whom Nietzsche is identified see my "Woman as Truth in Nietzsche's Writings," *Social Theory and Practice* 10, no. 2 (Summer 1984):185–99.

PART TWO

1. This and all other translations of *J'aime à toi* are my own. In Irigaray's latest work love becomes political. She is not arguing against equal rights for women; rather, she insists that men and women should have "rights that correspond to the reality of their respective needs" (Jat 205). These different needs can only be recognized by the civil code once sexual difference is inscribed in that code. Citizens must be men and women who meet each other and respect each other through love.

2. Alan Schrift provides a very nice reading of Derrida's *Spurs* in which he identifies the three main questions as "the question of the text, the question of *propre,* and the question of style" (Schrift, *NQ* 97). My discussion of belonging is a discussion of the question of *propre.*

3. Alan Schrift provides an excellent analysis of Derrida's deconstruction of Heidegger's notion of the proper, an analysis that goes beyond my comments here (See *NQ* 95-119).

4. Rosi Braidotti argues that Derrida accepts and promotes Heidegger's neutrality of Dasein (*PD* 104–6). She overlooks Derrida's explicit criticism of this thesis and his attempt to deconstruct the opposition between ontological and sexual difference. Of course, I do not believe that Derrida succeeds.

5. My thoughts on dissemination are the result of conversations with Roberta Weston, to whom I am grateful. In *Reading Kristeva,* I suggest the notion of an abject father as an analog to Kristera's notion of the abject mother. My notion of an abject father might be useful to analyze Derrida's morbid fascination with the Russian Roulette played by sperm in conception.

6. Further on I will argue that Derrida's economy of the undecidable still operates within the logic of castration and thereby favors the masculine.

7. Some critics suggest that Derrida's reading does violence to Heidegger's texts. For example, in a conversation Greg Reihman suggested that in Heidegger's terms we could say that reading, particularly Derrida's reading of Heidegger in *Spurs*, takes the text as ready-to-hand and uses it for its own purposes rather than listening to the text. For criticisms of Derrida's reading of Heidegger, see David Couzens Hoy, "Forgetting the Text: Derrida's Critique of Heidegger," *Boundary 2*, 8, no.1. (Fall 1979) and John Caputo, "'Supposing Truth to be a Woman . . . ': Heidegger, Nietzsche, Derrida," *Tulane Studies in Philosophy* 32, 15–21. (1984): For an insightful criticism of Heidegger's reading of Nietzsche see Gary Shapiro's *Alcyone* (Albany: SUNY Press, 1991), 39-49. For a judicious discussion of the relationship between Derrida's reading of Nietzsche and Heidegger's reading of Nietzsche, see Alan Schrift, *NQ* 113-119.

8. I heard Louis Mackey present this metaphor in a seminar on textuality that he taught at the University of Texas, Austin in the Spring of 1993.

9. For discussions of Derrida's criticisms of Lacan , see Braidotti, *PD* 100–102 and Cornell, *BA* 79–118.

10. Parts of this chapter were previously published as "The Plaint of Ariadne: Luce Irigaray's *Amante Marine de Friedrich Nietzsche*," in (eds.) by Keith Ansell-Pearson and Howard Caygill, *The Fate of the New Neitzsche* (Aldershot England: Avebury Press, 1993).

11. Ellen Mortensen develops a reading of *Marine Lover* in her work on Irigaray, which is forthcoming from Scandinavian University Press, Oslo, entitled *Nihilism and the Feminine: Luce Irgaray with Nietzsche and Heidegger*.

12. Irigaray uses both productive and reproductive mimesis. I conjecture that her unnamed use of Derrida may reproduce the "regimen of property" by once again setting up speaking in opposition to, and against, that which is silenced. I do believe, however, from the effect of silencing the dominant position is different that the effect of continuing to silence the dominated position.

13. The objectification/subjectification of the penis is prevalent in Western culture. It has been given several different names, e.g., "Willy," "Johnson," "Dick," etc. And men often refer to their own penses as separate "agents," calling them "him," for example.

14. See Derrida's claim that "there is no such thing as a woman" [*Il n'y a pas une femme*] (*S* 100-101).

15. Kathleen Higgins has a provocative interpretation of Zarathustra's remarks to the old woman in "Nietzsche and Woman," an unpublished paper presented at the Modernism Institute at the University of Texas, Austin, April 1993.

16. For an analysis of Derrida's reading of Levinas, see Robert Bernasconi's "Skepticism in the Face of Philosophy," in S. Critchley and R. Bernasconi (ed.s) *Re-*

reading Levinas (Bloomington: Indiana University Press, 1991; R. Berncasoni, "Deconstruction and the Possibility of Ethics," in John Sallis (ed), *Deconstruction and Philosophy* (Chicago: University of Chicago Press, 1987); Simon Critchley, *The Ethics of Deconstruction* (London: Blackwell, 1992); S. Critchley, " 'Bois'— Derrida's Final Word on Levinas," in *Re-reading Levinas*.

17. These thoughts on violence are the result of a conversation with Elissa Marder, to whom I am grateful. She probably will disagree with some, perhaps all, of what I am saying.

18. Compare Ellen Mortensen's argument that the feminine operates in Irigaray's metaphysics in the same way that Being operates in Heidegger's. "Woman's (Un)Truth and *Le Fèminin:* Reading Luce Irigaray with Friedrich Nietzsche and Martin Heidegger," a paper presented at the Nietzsche conference in London, 1992. A version of this talk is included in her forthcoming from *Nihilism and the Feminine.*

19. Alan Schrift's "On the Gynecology of Morals: Nietzsche and Cixous on the Logic of the Gift" in Peter Brugard (ed.), *Nietzsche and the Feminine* (University of Virginia Press, 1994). Since I am working with a preprinted version I will not cite page numbers.

20. For examples of Nietzsche's use of sun metaphors in *Zarathustra*, see, in particular, essay III, "Before Sunrise," and essay IV, "At Noon."

21. Freud's "Medusa's Head," *SE*, vol, 18, pp. 273–4.

22. Pautrat gives the citation of the Nietzsche fragment as follows: "See Nietzsche, quoted in the French edition of *Ainsi parlait Zarathustra, Oeuvres philosophiques complètes* (Paris: 1971), pp. 422–423, and *Edition de poche* (Paris: *Collection des Idées,* 1972), p. 477" (*NM* 171).

23. See Apollodorus III. 4. 3.

24. Euripides, *Bacchae*, Trans. William Arrowsmith (Chicago: University of Chicago Press, 1959), p. 156.

25. See the discussion of the worship of Ariadne in Plutrach, *Theseus*, XX.

26. For Irgaray's discussion of Persephone see *ML* 112-116.

27. See Apollodorus, I. 4. 1.

28. Aeschylus, *Oresteia*, "*The Eumenides,*" Trans. Richard Lattimore (Chicago: University of Chicago Press, 1953), 140, 141.

29. Irigaray claims that Athena's femininity covers over the death of the mother. Patriarchy can continue to forget the mother because it puts femininity in her place; feminity becomes the medium for relating to women so that men can forget about maternal procreation and any debt to the maternal (*ML* 97, see 94). I will return to Irigaray's analysis of femininity in my last chapter.

PART THREE

1. See my "Nietzsche's 'Woman': The Poststructuralist Attempt to Do Away with Women," *Radical Philosophy*; "Woman as Truth in Nietzsche's Writings," *Social Theory and Practice*; "Who Is Nietzsche's Woman?" in Bat Ami Bar-On (ed),. *Modern Engendering*, "Nietzsche's Abjection," in Peter Burgard (ed.) *Nietzsche and Feminism*. Much of my analysis in chapter 5 is taken from these essays.

2. Ellen Mortensen develops this analogy between Heidegger's notion of Being and Irigaray's notion of the feminine in her forthcoming, *Nihilism and the Feminine: Luce Irigaray with Nietzsche and Heidegger* (Oslo: Scandinavian University Press).

3. Kristeva argues that becoming abject is the body's defense against cannibalism. If it is disgusting, it won't be eaten (*PH* 39, 78–79).

4. David Farrell Krell, *Postponements* (Bloomington: Indiana University Press, 1986), 10; Ofelia Schutte, "Nietzsche on Gender Difference: A Critique," in *Newsletter on Feminism and Philosophy*, Nancy Tuana (ed.), (1990), 64. See also Ofelia Schutte, *Beyond Nihilism, Nietzsche without Masks*, (Chicago: University of Chicago Press, 1984), 176–185. For examples of the position that Nietzsche's writings are feminist or useful to feminism, see Erik Parens, "Traces of Derrida, 'woman', and Politics: A Reading of Spurs," in *Philosophy Today,* 33 (4) 291–301, winter 1989; Gayle Ormiston, "Traces of Derrida: Nietzsche's Image of Woman," *Philosophy Today* 28 (2/4) 178–188, Summer 1984; Rosalyn Diprose, "Nietzsche, Ethics, and Sexual Difference," *Radical Philosophy* 52, p. 27–32, Summer 1989; Imafedia Okhamafe, "Heidegger's Nietzsche and Nietzsche's Play: The questions of wo(man), Chritianity, Nihilism, and Humanism," *Soundings: An Interdisciplinary Journal* 71 (4) 533–553, Winter 1988; Shari Neller Starrett, "Nietzsche: Women and Relationships of Strength," *Southwest Philosophical Review* vol 6 (1), p. 73–79, Jan 1990; Keith Ansell-Pearson, "Who is the Übermensch? Time, Truth, and Woman in Nietzsche," *Journal of the History of Ideas,* p. 301–331, vol 53, no. 2, April June 1992; Lawrence Habib, "Nietzsche on Woman, "*Southern Journal of Philosophy,* 19(3), 333–346, Fall 1981; Robert John Ackerman, *Nietzsche: A Frenzied Look (*Amhers: University of Massachusetts Press, 1990), p. 122–137. Linda Singer's "Nietzschean Mythologies: The inversion of valve and the war against women," *Soundings: An Interdisciplanary Journal*, 66(3) p. 281–295, 1983 is an example of the opposite view.

5. I find Graybeal's argument that Nietzsche abjects his own mother Franziska problematic. Although psychoanalysis can provide an interesting and useful way to read texts, I am wary of extending that analysis to a diagnosis of the author's actual psychological problems.

6. For passages in which Nietzsche praises war and conquering, see KS 2:311–12; *HATH* §477; WTP, §53, 125, 975; KS 5: 120–21; *BGE* , §00. Also, *OGM* Nietzsche argues in favor of the master morality; for places where Nietzsche praises Napoleon and Caesar, see, for example, WTP §27, 41, 104, 128, 129, 380, 422, 544, 665, 740, 829, 877, 975, 1017, 1026, 380, 684, 751, 776; KS 5: 119-120,

140-142, 170–172, 184–186, 187-188, 201-204; *BGE* § 199, 209, 232, 244, 245, 256; *KS* 2: *154–156*; *HATH* §164.

7. Krell quotes an unpublished note in which Zarathustra tells the cat maidens: "weep no more Pallid Dudu! Be a man, Suleika!" §77; see also 24, 27, 58.

8 . Eric Blondel gives an interpretation of Nietzsche that emphasizes that man gives birth to himself because bad conscience is his mother, the mother of sublimation. See "Nietzsche: Life as Metaphor," in David Allison (ed.), *The New Nietzsche* (Cambridge, MA: MIT Press: 1988), p 153.

9. Nietzsche presents this saying in Italian: "from old Florentine novels; also—from life: '*Bouna femmina e mala femmina vuol bastone*' " (*BGE* "E&I" §147).

10. Freud suggests that the Oedipal complex is resolved by both identifying with the father and fearing the father. For Freud, it is castration by the father that the boy fears as punishment for his incestuous desire.

11. I am following Irigaray in my use of "mother-woman." This is not a lapse back into a conflation of the two, but rather an attempt to begin to reconceive of their relation. I will come back to this project and explain the strategy in chapter 6.

12. It is interesting, and perhaps telling, that here in *The Ear of the Other* and in "The Law of Genre" Derrida associates the law with the feminine and maternal, yet in "The Law of Genre" he also claims that "'I' . .. can give birth . . . to law" (LG 76; see LG 77, *EO* 21).

13. Although in this passage Derrida seems to be complicating the relation between the mother and nature, he continually reasserts a mother who is outside of culture.

14. Lisa Walsh argues that the mother operates as a blind spot in Derrida's in *Of Grammatology* (Master's Thesis, University of Texas, Austin, 1993). She maintains that in spite of Derrida's insistence that the mother is always already a trace and therefore never original, this trace is always a trace of Nature that stands outside of culture (see Derrida *OG* 156).

15. See, for example, Geneviève Lloyd, *Man of Reason: "Male" and "Female" in Western Philosophy* (Minneapolis: University of Minnesota Press, 1984); L. Clark and L. Lange (ed.s), *The Sexism of Social and Political Theory (*Toronto: University of Toronto Press, 1979); R. Baker and F. Elliston (ed.s), *Philosophy and Sex* (Buffalo: Prometheus Books, 1975); S. Harding and M. Hintikka (ed.s), *Discovering Reality: Feminist Perspectives on Epistemology, Metaphysics, Methodology and the Philosophy of Science* (Boston: Reidel Press, 1983) A. Garry and M. Pearsall (ed.s), *Women, Knowledge and Reality: Explorations in Feminist Philosophy* (Boston: Unwin Hyman, 1989); L. Alcoff and E. Potter (ed.s), *Feminist Epistemologies* (New York: Routledge 1993). M. Whitford and M. Griffiths (ed.s), *Feminist Perspectives in Philosophy* (Bloomington: Indiana University Press, 1988); S. Bordo and A. Jaggar (ed.s), *Gender/Body/Knowledge* (New Brunswick: Rutgers University Press, 1989); Luce Irigaray, *Speculum of the Other Woman*, trans. Gillian Gill (Ithaca: Cornell University Press, 1985); Bat-Ami Bar On (ed.), *Critical Feminist Essays in the History of Western Philosophy* (Albany: SUNY Press, 1993).

16. Margaret Whitford explains this distinction very clearly in *Luce Irigaray: Philosophy in the Feminine* (London: Routledge, 1991).

17. On my reading, Lacan's description of desire seems in keeping with what Irigaray describes as the mechanics of fluids. In addition, if Irigaray is suggesting that Lacan's metonymy of desire poses as metaphor, I think that Lacan would agree. Lacan maintains that desire is an endless series of substitutions which pretend to operate according to a logic of metaphor, equal exchange, but really operate according to a logic of metonymy, never equal. While Lacan emphasizes that this never equal is experienced as a lack, Irigaray interprets it as excess. My reading of Kristeva in *Reading Kristeva* brings her closer to Irigaray in this regard.

18. For a discussion of Irigaray's use of morphology and its relation to anatomy, see Elizabeth Grosz, *Sexual Subversions* (Sydney: Allen Unwin, 1989), especially 111–12.

19. For a developed account of this reading of Kristeva, see my *Reading Kristeva: Unraveling the Double-Bind* (Bloomington: Indiana University Press, 1993).

20. I have argued elsewhere that the imaginary father can be read as a screen for the mother's love. See "Julia Kristeva's Imaginary Father and the Crisis in the Paternal Function," *diacritics*, summer 1992 and *Reading Kristeva*.

21. Diana Fuss also makes this argument in *Essentially Speaking* (New York: Routledge, 1989). Although she begins her chapter on Irigaray with the claim that "what I propose to argue here is that, for Irigaray, the relation between language and the body is neither literal nor metaphoric but *metonymic*," she concludes that "the figure of the 'two lips' never stops functioning metaphorically" (62, 66). Drucilla Cornell makes a similar point when she mistakenly criticizes Fuss for her "reliance on the 'two lips' as a metonymic figure, as against a metaphorical figure," which she says "is too neat, since the refiguration is inescapably metaphorical" (*BA* 184).

22. Cornell is referring to a passage from Stanton's "Difference on Trial: A Critique of the Maternal Metaphor in Cixous, Irigaray and Kristeva," Nancy K. Miller (ed.), *The Poetics of Gender* (New York: Columbia University Press, 1986): "For metonymic deferral, postponement or putting off ironically represents the traditional feminine posture whenever a question of inter(dis)course arises. Nevertheless, in the present imperfect, that putting off, however off-putting it may seem, is the more desirable course for diverse female explorations than excessive, tumescent metaforeplay" (Quoted in Cornell *BA* 167–68).

23. For a more developed account of this argument, see my "Nourishing the Speaking Subject," in D. Curtin and L. Heldke eds. *Cooking, Eating, Thinking* (Bloomington: Indiana University Press, 1992).

24. In *Tales of Love* Kristeva describes the law that operates within the mother's body and her regulation of the infant's body. Recall from earlier in this chapter that this maternal law before the law sets up the Law of the Father and the infant's

entrance into language. Also recall that this maternal law is a material law and that the logic of language operates within the body.

25. Recall John Stuart Mill's criticism of Kant's ethics in *On Utilitarianism*. Mill argues that reason alone can be used to justify all sorts of atrocities and torture. Horkheimer and Adorno make a similar kind of argument about instrumental reason in *Dialectic of Enlightenment*, Trans. John Cumming (New York: Continuum Press, 1993).

26. For a discussion of Dionysus and Apollo, see "The Birth of Gods" in chapter 4, "The Plaint of Ariadne."

27. I have developed some of the ethical implications of Kristeva's theories in my introduction to *Ethics, Politics, and Difference in Julia Kristeva's Writing* (New York: Routledge, 1993).

28. I am not suggesting here that the difference between Kristeva and Irigaray should be read in terms of a difference between an emphasis on the interior and the exterior, but in their discussions of alterity such emphases sometimes seem to predominate. I do not think, however, that either Kristeva or Irigaray are attempting to propose such one-sided theories. For both theorists there are complex relations between the interior and exterior, between subjectivity and intersubjectivity. I have tried to analyze some of these complexities earlier in this chapter.

29. In the conclusion to *Totality and Infinity* Levinas says: "To posit being as Desire and goodness is not to first isolate an I which would then tend toward a beyond. It is to affirm that to apprehend oneself from within—to produce oneself as I—is to apprehend oneself with the same gesture that already turn toward the exterior to extra-vert and to manifest—to respond for what it apprehends—to express; it is to affirm that the becoming-conscious is already language, that the essence of language is goodness, or again, that the essence of language is friendship and hospitality. The other is not the negation of the same, as Hegel would like to say" (*TI* 305).

30. See, for example, Levinas, *Totality and Infinity,* 304.

BIBLIOGRAPHY

Ackermann, Robert. *Nietzsche: A Frenzied Look*. Amherst: University of Massachussetts Press, 1990.

Aeschylus. *Oresteia*. "The Eumenides," Trans. Richard Lattimore, Chicago: University of Chicago Press, 1953; cited as E.

Allison, David (ed.). *The New Nietzsche*. Cambridge MA: MIT Press, 1988.

Ansell-Pearson, Keith, and Howard Caygill (eds.). *The Fate of the New Nietzsche*. Aldershot: Avebury Press, 1993.

Bataille, Georges. *On Nietzsche*. Trans. Bruce Boone. New York: Paragon House, 1992.

Bartky, Sandra. *Femininity and Domination*. New York: Routledge, 1990.

Beauvoir, Simone de. *The Second Sex*. Trans. H. M. Parshley. New York: Random House, 1989; cited as *SS*.

———— *The Ethics of Ambiguity*. Trans. B. Frechtman, Secaucus New Jeresy: Citadel Press, 1980; cited as *EA*.

Benjamin, Jessica. *The Bonds of Love*. New York: Pantheon, 1988.

Bennington, Geoffrey. *Jacques Derrida*. Chicago: University of Chicago Press, 1993.

Bernasconi, Robert, and David Wood (eds.). *Derrida and Différance*. Evanston, IL: Northwestern University Press, 1988.

Blondel, Eric. *Nietzsche: The Body and Culture*. Trans. Seán Hand. Stanford: Stanford University Press, 1991.

Braidotti, Rosi. *Patterns of Dissonance: A Study of Women in Contemporary Philosophy*. New York: Routledge, 1991; cited as *PD*.

Brennan, Teresa. *The Interpretation of the Flesh: Freud and Femininity*. New York: Routledge, 1993; cited as *IF*.

Butler, Judith. *Subjects of Desire*. New York: Columbia University Press, 1987.

———— *Gender Trouble*. New York: Routledge, 1990; cited as *GT*.

———— *Bodies That Matter*. New York: Routledge, 1993; cited as *BM*.

Butler, Judith, and Joan Scott (eds.). *Feminists Theorize the Political*. New York: Routledge, 1992.

Cixous, Hélène, and Catherine Clement. *The Newly Born Woman.* Trans. B. Wing. Minneapolis: University of Minnesota Press, 1986; cited as *NBW*.

Cornell, Drucilla. *The Philosophy of the Limit.* New York: Routledge, 1992; cited as *PL*.

────── *Beyond Accommodation.* New York: Routledge, 1991; cited as *BA*.

────── *Transformations.* New York: Routledge, 1993; cited as *T*.

Critchley, Simon. *The Ethics of Deconstruction: Derrida and Levinas.* London: Blackwell, 1992; cited as *ED*.

Danto, Arthur. "Some Remarks on The Genealogy of Morals," in K. Higgins and B. Solomon (eds.). *Reading Nietzsche.* New York: Oxford University Press, 1988, p. 13-28.

Deleuze, Gilles. *Nietzsche and Philosophy.* Trans. Hugh Tomlinson. New York: Columbia University Press, 1983; cited as *NP*.

Derrida, Jacques. "The Law of Genre." Trans. Avital Ronell. *Critical Inquiry.* 17, no. 1 (Autumn 1980): 55-81; cited as LG.

────── interview with Richard Kearney, Richard Kearney (ed.). in *Dailogues with Contemporary Continental Thinkers.* Manchester: Manchester University Press, 1984; cited as *RK*.

────── "*Geschlecht*: Sexual Difference. Ontological Difference." Trans. Peggy Kamuf. *A Derrida Reader: Between the Blinds.* New York: Columbia Univeristy Press, 1991; cited as G(I).

────── "Of an Apocalyptic Tone Newly Adopted in Philosophy." Trans. John P. Leavey Jr. *Derrida and Negative Theology.* H. Coward, and T. Foshay (eds.). Albany: SUNY Press, 1992. pp. 25-72; cited as ATP.

────── "*Geschlecht* II: Heidegger's Hand." Trans. John P. Leavey Jr.. *Deconstruction and Philosophy: The Texts of Jacques Derrida.* John Sallis (ed.). Chicago: University of Chicago Press, 1987. 161-195; cited as G(II).

────── "Force of Law: The 'Mystical Foundation of Authority'." Trans. M. Quaintance. *Deconstruction and the Posibility of Justice.* Drucilla Cornell. et.al. (eds) New York: Routledge, 1992; cited as FL.

────── *The Post Card: From Socrates to Freud and Beyond.* Trans. Alan Bass. Chicago: University of Chicago Press, 1987.

────── "*Le facteur de la vérité*," in *The Post Card: From Socrates to Freud and Beyond.* pp. 411-96; cited as FV.

Positions. Trans.Alan Bass. Chicago: University of Chicago Press, 1981; cited as *P*.

────── *Given Time: I. Counterfeit Money.* Trans. Peggy Kamuf. Chicago: University of Chicago Press, 1992; cited as *GT*.

────── *Writing and Difference.* Trans. Alan Bass. Chicago: University of Chicago, 1978; cited as *WD*.

────── "Violence and Metaphysics: An Essay on the Thought of Emmanuel Levinas" in *Writing and Difference*; cited as *VM*.

Derrida, Jacques. *Of Grammatology*. Trans. Gayatri Spivak. Baltimore: Johns Hopkins University Press, 1976; cited as *OG*.

—— "The Laws of Reflection: Nelson Mandela. in Admiration." in *For Nelson Mandela*. ed. Derrida & Tlili. Trans. Mary Ann Caws & Isabelle Lorenz. New York: Seaver Books, 1987; cited as LR.

—— *Of Spirit*. Trans. G. Bennington and R. Bowlby. Chicago: University of Chicago Press, 1989; cited as *OS*.

—— *Dissemination*. Trans. Barbara Johnson. Chicago: University of Chicago Press, 1981; cited as *Diss*.

—— "The Double Session," in *Dissemination*. pp. 173-286; cited as *DS*.

—— *Margins of Philosophy*. Trans. Alan Bass. Chicago: University of Chicago Press, 1982; cited as *MP*.

—— "Tympan," in *Margins of Philosophy*; cited as T.

—— "Différance," in *Margins of Philosophy*; cited as D.

—— "The Ends of Man," in *Margins of Philosophy*; cited as *EM*.

—— "White Mythology: Metaphor in the Text of Philosophy," in *Margins of Philosophy*; cited as WM.

—— *Living On: Border Lines*. Trans. James Hulbert. *Deconstruction and Criticism*. Bloom et. al. New York: Continuum Press, 1990. 75-176; cited as *LO*.

—— *The Ear of the Other*. Trans. Peggy Kamuf & Avital Ronell. Christie McDonald & Claude Lévesque (ed.). Lincoln: University of Nebraska Press, 1985; cited as *EO*.

—— *L'oreille de l'autre*. Montréal: VLB Éditeur, 1982.

—— *Spurs: Nietzsche's Styles*. Trans. Barbara Harlow. Chicago: University of Chicago Press, 1979; cited as *S*.

—— *Glas*. Trans. John P. Leavey Jr. and Richard Rand. Lincoln: University of Nebraska Press, 1986; cited as *Glas*.

—— "At this very moment in this text here I am," in *Re-Reading Levinas*. (eds) Robert Bernasconi and Simon Critchley, Trans. Ruben Berezdivin, Bloomington: Indiana University Press, 1991, pp. 11-50; cited as *ATVM*.

—— "Psyche: Inventions of the Other," in *Reading DeMan Reading*. Trans. Catherine Porter, (eds.) L. Waters and W. Godzich, Minneapolis: University of Minnesota Press, 1989, pp. 25-65; cited as Psy.

—— "The Politics of Friendship," Trans. Gabriel Motzkin, *The Journal of Philosophy*. vol. LXXXV, no. 11, Nov. 1988, pp.632-45; cited as PF.

—— *Nietzsche aujourd'hui?* Paris: Union Générale D'Éditions, 1973, vols. 1-2.

—— "Circumfession," in *Jacques Derrida*. Trans. Geoffrey Bennington, Chicago: University of Chicago Press, 1993; cited as C.

Freud, Sigmund. *The Interpretation of Dreams*. Trans. James Strachey. New York: Avon Books, 1965.

—— "Femininity," in *The Standard Edition of the Complete Psychological*

Works of Sigmund Freud (*SE*) ed. and Trans. James Strachey, in collaboration with Anna Freud, vol. 22, 1933; cited as F.

———— "Female Sexuality," *SE*, vol. 21, 1931, pp. 225-43; cited as FS.

———— "On Sexual Theories of Children," *SE*, vol. 9, 1908, pp. 209-26; cited as OSTC.

———— "Three Essays on Sexuality," *SE*, vol. 7, 1905; cited as TES.

———— "Jokes and their Relation to the Unconscious," *SE*, vol. 8, 1905; cited as JRU.

———— "Project for Scientific Psychology," *SE*, vol. 1, 1950.

Gillespie. Michael and Tracy Strong. (ed.)*Nietzsche's New Seas*. Chcago: University of Chicago Press, 1988.

Gilligan, Carol. *In a Different Voice*. Cambridge, MA: Harvard University Press, 1982.

Graybeal, Jean. *Language and "The Feminine" in Nietzsche and Heidegger*. Bloomington: Indiana University Press, 1990; cited as *LF*.

Handelman, Susan. *The Slayer of Moses*. Albany: SUNY Press, 1982.

Hegel, G.W.F. *Phenomenology of Spirit*. Trans. A. V. Miller, Oxford UK: Oxford University Press, 1977.

Heidegger, Martin. *On Time and Being*. Trans. Joan Stambaugh. New York: Harper and Row, 1972; cited as *TB*.

———— "The End of Philosophy and the Task of Thinking" in *On Time and Being*. cited as *EP*.

———— *Nietzsche*. volumes 1-4. Trans. David Farrell Krell. New York: Harper and Row, 1982.

hooks, bell. *Ain't I a Woman?: Black Women and Feminism*. Boston: South End Press, 1981.

Irigaray, Luce. *Marine Lover of Friedrich Nietzsche*. Trans. Gillian Gill. New York: Columbia University Press, 1991; cited as *ML*.

———— *Amante Marine de Friedrich Nietzsche*. Paris: Les Éditions de Minuit, 1980; cited as *AM*.

———— *This Sex Which is Not One*. Trans. Catherine Porter. Ithaca: Cornell University Press, 1985; cited as *TS*.

———— *Speculum of the Other Woman*. Trans. Gillian Gill. Ithaca: Cornell University Press, 1985; cited as *SOW*.

———— *Sexes and Genealogies*. Trans. Gillian Gill. New York: Columbia University Press, 1993; cited as *SG*.

———— *je, tu, nous: Toward a Culture of Difference*. Trans. Alison Martin. New York: Routledge, 1993; cited as *JTN*.

———— *Elemental Passions*. Trans. Joanne Collie and Judith Still. New York: Routledge, 1992; cited as *EP*

——— *J'aime à toi*. Paris: Grasset, 1992; cited as *Jat*.

——— *The Irigaray Reader*. (ed.) Margaret Whitford, Cambridge MA: Basil Blackwell, 1991; cited as *IR*.

Irigaray, Luce. *L'Oubli de L'Air*. Paris: Les Éditions de Minuit, 1983.

——— *An Ethics of Sexual Difference*. Trans. Carolyn Burke and Gillian Gill. Ithaca: Cornell University Press, 1993; cited as *ESD*.

Jardine, Alice.*Gynesis*. Ithaca, NY: Cornell University Press, 1985.

Kofman, Sarah. *Nietzsche et la Métaphore*. Paris: éditions galilée, 1983.

——— *Nietzsche et la scène philosophique*. Paris: éditions galilée, 1986; cited as NSP.

——— *The Enigma of Woman*. Trans.Catherine Porter. Ithaca: Cornell University Press, 1985.

——— "Baubô: Theological Perversion and Fetishism," in *Nietzsche's New Seas*. (eds) M. A. Gillespie and T. B. Strong, Chicago: University of Chicago Press, 1988, pp. 175-202; cited as B.

——— "Nietzsche and the Obscurity of Heraclitus," *Diacritcs*. Fall 1987, pp. 39-55.

——— "Metaphor, Symbol, Metamorphosis," in *The New Nietzsche*. David B. Allison, (ed.) Cambridge, MA: MIT Press, pp. 201-14.

Krell, David Farrell. *Postponements: Woman. Sensuality. and Death in Nietzsche*. Bloomington: Indiana University Press, 1986; cited as *P*.

Krell, David, and David Wood. (ed.)*Exceedlying Nietzsche*. London: Routledge, 1988.

Kristeva, Julia. *Revolution in poetic language*. Trans. Margaret Waller. New York: Columbia University Press, 1984; cited as *RL*.

——— Leon Roudiez edited. *Desire in Language*. New York: Columbia University Press, 1980; cited as *DL*

——— *Power of Horrors*. Trans. Leon Roudiez. New York: Columbia University Press, 1982; cited as *PH*.

———*Tales of Love*. Trans. Leon Roudiez. New York: Columbia University Press, 1987; cited as *TL*.

———"Stabat Mater," in *Tales of Love*; cited as SM.

——— *Black Sun*. Trans. Leon S. Roudiez, New York: Columbia University Press, 1989; cited as *BS*.

Lacan, Jacques. *Écrits. A Selection*. Trans. Alan Sheridan. New York: Norton, 1977.

Levinas, Emmanuel. *Totality and Infinity*. Trans. Alphonso Lingis, Pittsburgh: Duquesne University Press, 1969; cited as TI.

Magnus, Bernd. et.al.. *Nietzsche's Case: Philosophy as/and Literature*. New York: Routledge, 1993.

Martin, Biddy. *Woman and Modernity*. Ithaca: Cornell University Press, 1991.

Mohanty, Chandra. "Under Western Eyes" *Boundary 2*. vol. 12, 1984.

Mortensen, Ellen. *"Le féminin" and Nihilism: Reading Irigaray with Nietzsche and Heidegger*. Doctoral Dissertation. University of Wisconsin-Madison, 1989. Forthcoming from Oslo: Scandinavia University Press.

———— "Irigaray and Nietzsche: Echo and Narcissus Revisited?" in *The Fate of the New Nietzsche*, (eds) K. Ansell-Pearson and H. Caygill, Aldershot UK: Avebury Press, pp. 229-50; cited as IN.

Nehamas, Alexander. *Nietzsche. Life as Literature*. Cambridge: Harvard University Press, 1985.

Newman, Michael. "Reading the future of genealogy: Kant, Nietzsche, Plato," in Keith Ansell-Pearson (ed.), *Nietzsche and Modern German Thought*. New York: Routledge, 1991.

Nietzsche, Friedrich. *On the Genealogy of Morals*. Trans. W. Kaufmann. New York: Random House, 1966; cited as *OGM*.

———— *Thus Spake Zarathustra*. Trans. W. Kaufmann. New York: Viking Press, 1965; cited as *Z*.

———— *Beyond Good and Evil*. Trans. W. Kaufmann. New York: Random House, 1968; cited as *BGE*.

———— *Gay Science*. Trans. W. Kaufmann. New York: Random House, 1966; cited as *GS*.

———— *Daybreak*. Trans. R.J. Hollingdale, Cambridge UK: Cambridge University Press, 1982; cited as *D*.

———— *The Case of Wagner*, Trans. Walter Kaufmann, New York: Vintage Books, 1967; cited as *CW*.

———— *Nietzsche Contra Wagner*, in *The Portable Nietzsche*. Trans. W. Kaufmann. New York: Viking Press, 1965; *NCW*.

———— *The Will to Power*, Trans. Walter Kaufmann and R.J. Hollingdale, New York: Vintage Books, 1968; cited as *WTP*.

———— *Ecce Homo*, Trans. Walter Kaufmann and R.J. Hollingdale, New York: Vintage Books, 1969; *EH*.

———— *Twilight of the Idols*. Trans. R. J. Hollingdale, New York: Penguin, 1968; cited as *TI*.

———— *Birth of Tragedy*. Trans. Walter Kaufmann, New York: Vintage Books, 1967; cited as *BT*.

———— *The Antichrist*. Trans. R. J. Hollingdale, New York: Penguin, 1968; cited as *AC*.

———— *Human all too Human*. Trans. Marion Faber, Lincoln: University of Nebraska Press, 1984; cited as *HATH*.

———— *Philosophy and Truth, Selections from Nietzsche's Notebooks of the early 1870's*. Trans. Daniel Breazeale, New Jersey: Humanities Press, 1979; cited as *Nietzsche's Notebooks of the early 1870's*.

———— *Friedrich Nietzsche Werke*. (ed.) Karl Schlechta, München: Carl Hanser Verlag, 1969; cited as *KS*.

Oliver, Kelly. *Reading Kristeva: Unraveling the Double-bind*. Bloomington: Indiana University Press, 1993.

Oliver, Kelly. "Recalling the Flesh: Using Brennan's Model of Intersubjectivity for Ethics." *Radical Philosophy*. vol. 65. Autumn 1993. p. 30-33.

———— "Julia Kristeva's Imaginary Father and the Crisis in Paternity." *Diacritics*. Summer 1991. p. 43-63.

———— "Revolutionary Horror: Nietzsche and Kristeva on the Politics of Poetry." *Social Theory and Practice*. vol. 16. no. 1, 1990. p. 305-320.

———— "Nietzsche's 'Woman': The Poststructuralist Attempt to do Away with Women." *Radical Philosophy*. issue 48. Spring 1988. p. 25-29.

———— "Woman as Truth in Nietzsche's Writings." *Social Theory and Practice*. vol. 10. no. 2. Summer 1984. p. 185-199.

———— "Nietzsche's Abjection." in *Nietzsche and Feminism*. ed. Peter Burgard. University Press of Virginia. 1994. p. 53-67.

———— "Who is Nietzsche's Woman?" in *Critical Feminist Essays in the History of Western Philosophy*. ed. Bat-Ami Bar On. SUNY Press, 1993.

———— "The Plaint of Ariadne: Luce Irigaray's Marine Lover." in *The Fate of the New Nietzsche*. ed. Caygill & Ansell-Pearson. Avebury Press, 1993. p. 211-228.

———— "The Ethics of Reading Nietzsche's *On The Genealogy of Morals*". *International Studies in Philosophy*. Summer 1993. XXV/2. p. 13-28.

Pautrat, Bernard. "Nietzsche Medused," in *Looking After Nietzsche*. (ed.) L. Richels. Albany: SUNY: Press, 1990, pp. 159-174; cited as NM.

Sallis, John. ed. *Deconstruction and Philosophy*. Chicago: University of Chicago Press, 1987.

Salomé, Lou. *Nietzsche*. Trans. Siegfried Mandel. Redding Ridge CT: Black Swan Press, 1988; cited as *N*.

Schrift, Alan. *Nietzsche and The Question of Interpretation*. New York: Routledge, 1990; cited as *NQ*.

———— "On the Gynecology of Morals: Nietzsche and Cixous on the Logic of the Gift." Peter Burgard ed. *Nietzsche and the Feminine*. University of Virginia Press; cited as OGM.

Schutte, Ofelia. *Beyond Nihilism: Nietzsche Without Masks*. Chicago: University of Chicago Press, 1984; cited as *BN*.

Sedgwick, Eve Kosofsky. *Epistemology of the Closet*. Berkeley: University of California Press, 1990; cited as *EC*.

Shapiro, Gary. *Nietzschean Narratives*. Bloomington: Indiana University Press, 1989; cited as *NN*.

———— *Alcyone. Nietzsche on Gifts, Noise, and Women*, Albany New York: SUNY Press, 1991; cited as *A*.

Spivak, Gayatri Chakravorty. "Feminism and deconstruction, again: negotiating with unacknowledged masculinism," in *Between Feminism and Psychoanalysis*, (ed.) Teresa Brennan, New York: Routledge, 1989, pp. 206-22; cited as FD.

—— "Displacement and the Discourse of Woman," in *Displacement Derrida and After*, (ed.) Mark Krupnick, Bloomington: Indiana University Press, 1983, pp. 169-95; cited as DDW

Staten, Henry. *Nietzsche's Voice*. Ithaca: Cornell University Press, 1990; cited as *NV*.

Walsh, Lisa. "The Figure of the Mother in Contemporary French Fiction." Masters Thesis. University of Texas at Austin, 1993.

Weston, Roberta. "Free Gift or Forced Figure? Derrida's Usage of Hymen in *The Double Session*." forthcoming in Oliver (ed.) *Feminism. Philosophy and Language*. Bloomington: Indiana University Press.

Whitford, Margaret. *Luce Irigaray: Philosophy in the Feminine*. London: Routledge, 1991; cited as *LI*.

Wood, David. "Nietzsche's Transvaluation of Time," in *Exceedingly Nietzsch* (eds.) David Farrell Krell and David Wood, New York: Routledge, 1988, pp. 31-62; cited as NTT.

Index